GLENCOE

PRE-GED READING SKILLS
FOR LIFE AND LITERATURE
REVISED

GLENCOE
Macmillan/McGraw–Hill

New York, New York   Columbus, Ohio   Mission Hills, California   Peoria, Illinois

GED • GED • GED • GED • GED

ILLUSTRATION ACKNOWLEDGMENTS

Unless otherwise indicated, all photographs are the property of Glencoe Publishing Co. **46** PEANUTS® cartoon by Charles M. Schulz. August 16, 1987. Copyright © 1987 by Universal Press Syndicate. Reprinted by permission of UFS, Inc. **62** CATHY® cartoon by Cathy Guisewite. Copyright ©1988 by Universal Press Syndicate. **78** MARMADUKE® by Brad Anderson. Copyright © 1980 by Universal Press Syndicate. Reprinted by permission of UFS, Inc. **84** Robert Tolchin. **97** "A Negro Wedding Scene" by Clementine Hunter, Collection of Anglo-American Art Museum, Louisiana State University, Baton Rouge. Gift of Mr. and Mrs. Lewis A. Bannon. **129** Thomas England. **145** UPI/Bettmann Newsphotos. **152** Camerique/H. Armstrong Roberts. **158** Comstock. **167** DENNIS THE MENACE®, used by permission of Hank Ketcham and © by North American Syndicate.

TEXT ACKNOWLEDGMENTS

9 Excerpt from HELEN KELLER by Carolyn Sloan. Copyright © 1984 by Carolyn Sloan. Reprinted by permission of Hamish Hamilton Ltd. **21** Carol A. Emmens, STUNT WORK AND STUNT PEOPLE. New York: Franklin Watts, 1982, p. 20. **48** From "Meet Jay J. Armes, Private Eye," in THEY TRIUMPHED OVER THEIR HANDICAPS by Joan Harries. Copyright © 1981 by Joan Harries Katsarakis. Reprinted by permission of Franklin Watts. **79** Excerpt from BILL COSBY: MAKING AMERICA LAUGH AND LEARN by Harold and Geraldine Woods. Copyright © 1983 by Dillon Press, Inc. Reprinted by permission. **81** From "Ray Charles Brings Back the 'Good Old Days,'" from THEY TRIUMPHED OVER THEIR HANDICAPS by Joan Harries. Coyright © 1981 by Joan Harries Katsarakis. Reprinted by permission of Franklin Watts. **87** From "Jean-Claude Killy, Downhill Skier," from THE WINTER OLYMPICS by Caroline Arnold. Copyright © 1983 by Caroline Arnold. Reprinted by permission of Franklin Watts. **88** From "Two Time Winner," from GREAT MOMENTS IN THE INDY 500 by Edward F. Dolan, Jr. Copyright © 1982 by Edward F. Dolan, Jr. Reprinted by permission of Franklin Watts. **92** Adapted from ROUGH AND READY by Richard L. Allington et al., Copyright © 1985 Scott, Foresman and Company. **95** Arnold Hano, MUHAMMAD ALI: THE CHAMPION. New York: G. P. Putnam's Sons, 1977, p. 11. **111** Excerpt from "Sequoyah," from CLAIMING A RIGHT by Muriel Ringstad. Copyright © 1972 by New Readers Press. Reprinted by permission. **124** "The Ghosts of Eastern Airlines," reprinted by permission of The Putnam & Grosset Group, from GREAT MYSTERIES OF THE AIR by Edward F. Dolan, Jr., copyright © 1983 by Edward F. Dolan, Jr. **138** Dan Rather with Mickey Herskowitz, THE CAMERA NEVER BLINKS: ADVENTURES OF A TV JOURNALIST. New York: William Morrow and Company, 1977, pp. 102, 103. **139** Bernard Malamud, THE NATURAL. New York: Farrar, Straus and Giroux, Inc., 1952, pp. 62, 63. **140** "When I Heard the Learn'd Astronomer," from LEAVES OF GRASS by Walt Whitman, 1865. **142** Jim Hargrove, ENCYCLOPEDIA OF PRESIDENTS: THOMAS JEFFERSON, THIRD PRESIDENT OF THE UNITED STATES. Chicago: Childrens Press, 1986, p. 33. **143** Excerpt from "A Child's Garden of Manners," from HOW I GOT TO BE PERFECT by Jean Kerr. Copyright © 1978 by Collins Productions, Inc. Reprinted by permission of Doubleday, a division of Bantam, Doubleday, Dell Publishing Group, Inc. **144** Excerpt from A SENSE OF WHERE YOU ARE by John McPhee. Copyright © 1965 by John McPhee. Originally appeared in THE NEW YORKER. Reprinted by permission of Farrar, Straus and Giroux, Inc. **144** Sam Levenson, IN ONE ERA AND OUT THE OTHER. New York: Simon and Schuster, 1973, p. 30. **146** From THE WORLD BOOK ENCYCLOPEDIA. © 1988 World Book, Inc. **147** John Steinbeck, TRAVELS WITH CHARLEY: IN SEARCH OF AMERICA. New York: The Viking Press, 1962, pp. 31, 32. **148** From GIFT FROM THE SEA by Anne Morrow Lindbergh. Copyright © 1955 by Anne Morrow Lindbergh.

Copyright © 1994 by the Glencoe Division of Macmillan/McGraw-Hill School Publishing Company. All rights reserved. Copyright © 1989 Rena Moran. Pages 142–168, 177–202, 236–240. Copyright © 1989 Scott, Foresman and Company. All other material. All rights reserved. Printed in the United States of America. Except as permitted under the United States Copyright Act of 1976, no part of this publication may be reproduced or distributed in any form or by any means, or stored in a database or retrieval system, without prior written permission of the publisher.

Send all inquiries to
GLENCOE DIVISION
Macmillan/McGraw-Hill
936 Eastwind Drive
Westerville, OH 43081

ISBN 0-02-802067-7

Reprinted by permission of Pantheon Books, a Division of Random House, Inc. **152** Excerpt from "Letter Writing," in AND MORE BY ANDY ROONEY by Andrew A. Rooney. Copyright © 1979, 1980, 1981, 1982 by Essay Productions, Inc. Reprinted by permission of Atheneum Publishers, an imprint of Macmillan Publishing Company. **154** SCENIC WONDERS OF AMERICA, copyright © 1973 The Reader's Digest Association, Inc. Reprinted by permission. **155** Adapted from CULTURES, edited by Violet M. Malone. Copyright © 1982 by Scott, Foresman and Company. Reprinted by permission of the Glencoe division of Macmillan/McGraw-Hill School Publishing Company. **155** William Manchester, THE GLORY AND THE DREAM: A NARRATIVE HISTORY OF AMERICA 1932–1972. Boston: Little, Brown, and Company, 1974, p. 1157. **156** Excerpt from THE LAND I LOST by Huynh Quang Nhuong. Text copyright © 1982 by Huynh Quang Nhuong. Reprinted by permission of Harper & Row, Publishers, Inc. **162** From THE WORLD BOOK ENCYCLOPEDIA. © 1988 World Book, Inc. **163** From A PRECOCIOUS AUTOBIOGRAPHY by Yevgeny Yevtushenko. Copyright © 1963 by E. P. Dutton & Co., Inc. Reprinted by permission of the publisher, E. P. Dutton, a division of NAL Penguin Inc. **170** Excerpt from "Georgia O'Keeffe" by Susan Riemer. Used by permission of HIGHLIGHTS FOR CHILDREN, Columbus, Ohio. Copyright © 1988. **172** Hunter Davies, THE BEATLES: THE AUTHORIZED BIOGRAPHY. New York: McGraw-Hill Book Company, 1968, pp. 19, 20. **177** Willa Cather, MY ANTONIA. Boston: Houghton Mifflin Company, 1949, pp. 135, 136. **179** Bernard Malamud, THE ASSISTANT. New York: Farrar, Straus and Giroux, 1957, p. 18. **180** Excerpt from "Key Item," from BUY JUPITER by Isaac Asimov. Copyright © 1968 by Mercury Press. Reprinted by permission of Doubleday, a division of Bantam, Doubleday, Dell Publishing Group, Inc. **181** Excerpt from "Confrontation" by Elizabeth Neal Wells, from YANKEE, April 1975. Reprinted by permission of YANKEE. **182** Excerpt from "Gentleman of Río en Medio" by Juan A. A. Sedillo, from THE NEW MEXICO QUARTERLY, August 1939. **188** Excerpt from "Fetch!" by Robb White, from BOY'S LIFE, January 1975. Reprinted by permission of the author. **194** Adapted from "Search for Freedom," from SIGHTS AND SOUNDS by Richard L. Allington et al. Copyright © 1985 by Scott, Foresman and Company. **196** Adapted from "Search for Freedom," from SIGHTS AND SOUNDS by Richard L. Allington et al. Copyright © 1985 by Scott, Foresman and Company. **196** Excerpt from p. 10 in THE ASSISTANT by Bernard Malamud. Copyright © 1957 by Bernard Malamud. Reprinted by permission of Farrar, Straus and Giroux, Inc. **197** Excerpt from "A Man Who Had No Eyes" by MacKinlay Kantor. Copyright 1931 by LIBERTY MAGAZINE. Reprinted by permission of Tim Kantor and Layne Kantor Schroder, children of deceased author. **202** Natalie Babbitt, TUCK EVERLASTING. New York: Farrar, Straus and Giroux, 1975, pp. 23, 24. **204** Excerpt from "The Man Who Came to Dinner" by George S. Kaufman and Moss Hart. Copyright 1939 by George S. Kaufman and Moss Hart. Reprinted by permission of Grove Press. **205** Excerpt from "Mister Roberts" by Thomas Heggen and Joshua Logan. Copyright 1948 by Thomas Heggen and Joshua Logan. Reprinted by permission of Random House, Inc. **206** From "The Little Foxes" by Lillian Hellman. Copyright 1939 and renewed 1967 by Lillian Hellman. Reprinted by permission of Random House, Inc. **212** "Water Picture" (first stanza) by May Swenson is used by permission of the author. Copyright © 1956, Renewed © 1984 by May Swenson. First printed in THE NEW YORKER magazine. **212** "Soup," from SMOKE AND STEEL by Carl Sandburg. Copyright 1920 by Harcourt Brace Jovanovich, Inc. Renewed 1948 by Carl Sandburg. Reprinted by permission of the publisher. **212** "Seagulls," reprinted from ROBERT FRANCIS: COLLECTED POEMS, 1936–1976 (Amherst: University of Massachusetts Press, 1976). Copyright © 1976 by Robert Francis. **213** "A Time to Talk," from THE POETRY OF ROBERT FROST, 1916. **214** "African Dance" by Langston Hughes. Copyright 1926 by Alfred A. Knopf, Inc., and renewed 1954 by Langston Hughes. Reprinted from THE DREAM KEEPER AND OTHER POEMS by Langston Hughes, by permission of Alfred A. Knopf, Inc. **214** "The Fly," from VERSES FROM 1929 ON by Ogden Nash. Copyright 1942 by Ogden Nash. First appeared in THE SATURDAY EVENING POST. By permission of Little, Brown and Company. **214** "Waking from a Nap on the Beach" by May Swenson is used by permission of the author. Copyright © 1966 by May Swenson. **214** "Broken Sky," from GOOD MORNING, AMERICA. Copyright 1928, 1956 by Carl Sandburg, reprinted by permission of Harcourt Brace Jovanovich, Inc. **215** "Home Thoughts," from SMOKE AND STEEL by Carl Sandburg. Copyright 1920 by Harcourt Brace Jovanovich, Inc. Renewed 1948 by Carl Sandburg. Reprinted by permission of the publisher. **217** "Funny the Way Different Cars Start" by Dorothy W. Baruch. Reprinted by permission. **217** "Snowy Morning," from I THOUGHT I HEARD THE CITY by Lilian Moore. Copyright © 1969 by Lilian Moore. Reprinted by permission of Marian Reiner for the author. **218** Reprinted by permission of OUTSIDE MAGAZINE, Mariah Publishing Corporation. Copyright © 1988. **219** Toni Morrison, BELOVED. New York: Alfred A. Knopf, 1987, pp. 248, 249. **222** "You Can't Take It With You" by George S. Kaufman and Moss Hart. Copyright 1936, 1937, renewed 1963, 1964. Reprinted by permission of Grove Press. **223** "Wires" by Philip Larkin, from THE LESS DECEIVED, © copyright by The Marvell Press 1955, 1971, reprinted by permission of The Marvell Press.

Cover Photo: Charles Campbell/Westlight

Consultants to the Program

Jeff Bishop
New Brunswick Adult Learning Center
New Brunswick, NJ

Kathryn Boesel-Dunn
Columbus Public Schools
Columbus, Ohio

Toby G. Cannon
Cohn Adult Learning Center
Nashville, Tennessee

Charmaine M. Carney
Hawkeye Institute of Technology
Waterloo, Iowa

Mary S. Charuhas
College of Lake County
Grayslake, Illinois

Lee Chic
Sequoia Adult School
Redwood City, California

James R. Fryxell
College of Lake County
Grayslake, Illinois

Marcia Harrington
D.C. Public Library
Washington, D.C.

Cynthia A. Green
Lincoln Instructional Center
Dallas, Texas

Esther Gross
Petit Jean Technical College
Morrilton, Arkansas

Theodore M. Harig
Ellsworth Correctional Center
Union Grove, Wisconsin

Chuck Herring
GED Institute
Seattle, Washington

Linda L. Kindy
Little Rock Adult Education Center
Little Rock, Arkansas

Claudia V. McClain
South Suburban College
South Holland, Illinois

Ed A. Mayfield
Fayette County Adult Education Center
Lexington, Kentucky

Valerie Meyer
Southern Illinois University
Edwardsville, Illinois

Pat Mitchell
Dallas Independent School District
Dallas, Texas

Laura Morris
Center for Community Education
Tallahassee, Florida

Evelyn H. Nunes
Virginia Commonwealth University
Richmond, Virginia

Ann Kuykendall Parker
Cohn Adult Learning Center
Nashville, Tennessee

Jill Plaza
Reading and Educational Consultants
Palatine, Illinois

John H. Redd
Dallas Independent School District
Dallas, Texas

Gail Rice
Adult Basic Education Program
Palos Heights, Illinois

Karen Samson
Chicago State University
Chicago, Illinois

Yvonne E. Siats-Fiskum
Gateway Technical College
Elkhorn, Wisconsin

Sheldon Silver
Truman College
Chicago, Illinois

Robert T. Sutton
Central Piedmont Community College
Charlotte, North Carolina

Dee Swanson
Minnesota Correctional Facility
Stillwater, Minnesota

Contents

Acknowledgments / ii
How to Use this Book / ix

Part A
Reading Skills for Life / 1

Measuring What You Know / 2

Lesson 1
Giving Care / 6

Skill   Main Idea / 6
Reading   "Helen and Annie" / 9
The Active Reader   Taking Stock / 12

Lesson 2
Take Care! / 14

Skill   Unstated Main Idea / 14
Reading   "Relax!" / 16
The Active Reader   Thinking Ahead / 20

Lesson 3
Caring About Others / 22

Skill   Supporting Details / 22
Reading   "A Better Hut" / 24
The Active Reader   Energy-Saving Eye Movements / 28

Lesson 4
Love and Marriage / 30

Skill   Author's Purpose / 30
Reading   "The Single Life" and "Three Brides" / 33
The Active Reader   Using What You Know / 36

Lesson 5
Learning About Your Roots / 38

Skill   Listing / 38
Reading   "Finding Family Roots" / 40
The Active Reader   Setting a Purpose / 44

Lesson 6
An Exciting Job / 46

Skill   Time Order / 46
Reading   "Jay J. Armes, Private Eye" / 48
The Active Reader   Controlling Your Reading Rate / 52

Lesson 7
Step-by-step Learning / 54

Skill   Steps in a Process / 54
Reading   "How to Change a Tire" / 57
The Active Reader   Visualizing / 60

Lesson 8
On the Job / 62

Skill   Classifying / 62
Reading   "Finding a Good Job" / 65
The Active Reader   Restating / 68

Lesson 9
Learning for Living / 70
Skill Comparing and Contrasting / 70
Reading "What You Should Know About Credit Cards" / 72
The Active Reader Summarizing / 76

Lesson 10
The Entertainers / 78
Skill Inferring Ideas / 78
Reading "Soul Is a Way of Life" / 81
The Active Reader Self-Questioning / 84

Lesson 11
The Winners / 86
Skill Drawing Conclusions / 86
Reading "Two-Time Winner" / 88
The Active Reader Self-Checking and Self-Correcting / 92

Lesson 12
A Zest for Life / 94
Skill Cause-and-Effect Relationships / 94
Reading "The Story of Clementine Hunter" / 96
The Active Reader Word Maps / 100

Lesson 13
Keeping Healthy / 102
Skill Applying What You Read / 102
Reading "How to Care for Your Hair" / 104
The Active Reader Reading Directions / 108

Lesson 14
Working for What You Believe / 109
Skill Facts and Opinions / 109
Reading "Sequoyah's Talking Pages" / 111
The Active Reader Taking Notes / 115

Lesson 15
Words That Persuade / 117
Skill Noting Bias / 117
Reading "Up in Smoke, Down to Ashes" / 120
The Active Reader Reading a Newspaper / 123

Lesson 16
Just for Fun / 124
Reading "The Ghosts of Eastern Airlines" / 124
The Active Reader Using a Library / 129

Measuring What You've Learned / 131

Part B
Reading Skills for Literature / 137

Measuring What You Know / 138

Lesson 1
Reading Nonfiction / 142

Lesson 2
Living Simply / 145
Skill Main Idea and Supporting Details / 145

Reading "Beach Living" / 148

The Active Reader Setting Your Own Purpose / 151

Lesson 3
Staying Young / 153

Skill Seeing Patterns / 153

Reading "Young at Heart" / 156

The Active Reader Varying Your Reading Rate / 160

Lesson 4
Conquering Fear / 161

Skill Cause and Effect / 161

Reading "Poetry and Jujitsu" / 163

The Active Reader Summarizing / 167

Lesson 5
Reading Commentary / 169

Skill The Author's Tone / 169

Reading "The Birth of the Beatles" / 172

The Active Reader Judging the Author's Qualifications / 175

Lesson 6
Reading Fiction / 177

Lesson 7
A Man of Honor / 180

Skill Character and Setting / 180

Reading "Gentleman of Río en Medio" / 182

The Active Reader Visualizing / 186

Lesson 8
Courage / 187

Skill Plot and Conflict / 187

Reading "Fetch!" / 188

The Active Reader Predicting Outcomes / 193

Lesson 9
Making the Most of What You Have / 195

Skill The Author's Craft / 195

Reading "A Man Who Had No Eyes" / 197

The Active Reader Self-Checking / 202

Lesson 10
Reading Drama / 203

Skill Speech and Stage Directions / 203

Reading "The Little Foxes" / 206

The Active Reader Using the Powers of Your Imagination / 210

Lesson 11
Reading Poetry / 211

Skill Understanding Poetry / 211

Reading "A Time to Talk," "African Dance!" "The Fly," "Waking from a Nap on the Beach," "Broken Sky," "Home Thoughts" / 213

The Active Reader Reading Aloud / 217

Measuring What You've Learned / 218

Answers / 225

Especially for You / 244

Index / 246

How to Use This Book

Reading is important in life. You've probably found that out. Reading literature is important on the GED Test. That's why this book is divided into two sections. In the first section, you'll learn skills to help you your entire life. In the second section, you'll practice skills for the GED Test.

Measuring What You Know

Each section starts with a survey of what you know. Use this survey to guide you. Your answers will help you plan your study time.

The Lessons

Here, you'll find interesting articles to read. You'll also build your reading skills. Each lesson follows the same order:

In this lesson you will: It's always good to know where you're going. This list will tell you that. It tells you what you will do in the lesson.

Skills for Reading: This section tells you how to get the most meaning from what you read. It starts by showing you how a skill works, often with a picture. Then you're given an example of how to use the skill as you read. Finally, you get a chance to practice the skill.

Writing to Improve Your Reading: This section gives you great tips on how to help yourself. Underlining, taking notes, outlining—they're all here. Using these tips will help your reading. It will also help your writing.

Reading On Your Own: Here's your chance to read a longer article. The articles and stories were chosen with adult interests in mind. You can use the tips you've learned as you read something interesting.

Thinking About What You've Read: After you read an article, you need to check yourself. The questions in this section help you do that. You'll apply the lesson skill to the long article you just read. You'll also review other skills.

GED Warm-up: You can "warm up" for the GED test here with a multiple-choice question. Sometimes A Test-Taking Tip comes before the GED Warm-up.

Working with Words: Good readers know many words. They also know how to read words they *don't* know. You'll learn to do that too in this section. You'll build your word power with words from the long article.

Looking Back: This review helps you "look back" to see what you've learned.

The Active Reader
After each lesson comes a one- or two-page tip. Here you'll learn to *do* something as you read. You'll learn to *work with* the information you read.

Answer Explanations
All the answers in the book are explained in this section. It helps you know *why* you answered wrong. It also helps to know why you answered right!

Measuring What You've Learned
Each section ends with a test. The test shows how much you've learned. It also helps you see what you need to review.

Goals are important to learning. This book can help you reach two goals: (1) to enjoy reading more and (2) to improve your skills. With these goals reached, you'll be ready to study for the GED Test.

Part A
Reading Skills for Life

In **Part A,** you will build skills in general reading. This is the kind of reading you come across every day. You will read selections like those you might find in magazines or newspapers. You will read practical advice and tips for living. Often you'll read about real people.

The lessons are grouped around life themes: loving and caring for others, working and learning, playing and creating, and making things better.

You probably will enjoy this reading. Quite likely, you will learn something useful. Certainly you will become a better reader. The skills you develop will help you go on to GED-level books. They will also help you in the rest of your life—at your job, with your family and friends, and in your free time. Reading well is a skill you can use for life.

Measuring What You Know

You can test your reading skills with this short survey. There are 3 reading selections and 12 questions. The survey is here to help you. It will show you what you already know. It will also tell you what you need to study.

Read each selection carefully. Then answer the questions about it. Take your time. When you're finished, check your answers on page 243. The table on page 5 will help you plan your study time.

Read the article about computers. Then answer the questions that follow.

Computers affect us in so many ways that we can say we live in the computer age. Nearly everything we do today is touched by a computer. More than a million computers are at work just in Canada and the United States.

Computers have changed the way we work. Each time we make a phone call or mail a letter, we use a computer. Many machines in our workplaces are run by computers. Often, our paychecks are printed by a computer.

Computers have changed the way we have fun. They keep time in team sports. We play games on computers. Many books and magazines are printed with the help of computers.

Computers affect our lives and health. They keep our doctors' records. They help scientists learn about illnesses. Computers play a large part in the way our country is run. They help keep track of the taxes we owe. And they help keep track of how our taxes are spent.

1. In your own words, tell the main idea of the article.
   _____
   _____

2. According to the article, what is one way in which computers affect our health?
   _____

3. The author's purpose is to (Circle one.)

       entertain   inform

4. Write a few words to tell what the word *track* means in the last paragraph.
   _____

Read this article about bicycles. Then answer the questions that follow.

In the late 1800s, bicycling became a popular sport. Many people rode a type of bicycle called the High-wheeler. If you were to put a High-wheeler next to a bicycle of today, you would see many differences.

The front wheel of the old bicycle was about five feet high. This means that the bicycle was as tall as some riders! The seat was on top of the high front wheel. To get up to the seat, the rider had to put a foot on a footrest and jump up on the high wheel. The back wheel was much smaller.

Today's bicycle, in contrast, has two wheels of equal size. A rider can get on the bike by standing next to it and putting one leg over the frame.

The bicycle of yesterday had some safety problems. Riders sat so high that they could tip over easily. The tires were made of thin, hard rubber. A small bump in the road could jar a rider or make a rider fall.

Today's bicycles, on the other hand, are safer to ride. The wheels are easier to keep on the road. Tires filled with air make the ride softer and smoother.

The old High-wheeler may have been exciting. But most people would probably prefer to ride today's safer, faster bikes.

5. The author tells how the old bicycles and today's bicycles are (Circle one.)

   alike   different

6. What are two ways in which today's bikes are safer than the old High-wheelers?

   _____
   _____

7. The word *jar* in the fourth paragraph means

   _____

8. Read these two summaries of the article about bicycles. Decide which is the better summary.

   A. Bicycles of the late 1800s were different from today's bikes. The old bikes had high front wheels, small back wheels, and hard, thin tires. Today's bikes have two wheels of the same size. The tires are filled with air for a softer ride.

   B. The high front wheel of the old bikes made it hard for a rider. It was hard to get up on the bike. The bike could easily be tipped over. Today's bikes are easier to ride.

   Which of the two is the better summary? _____
   Why?

   _____
   _____

Read the article about basketball. Then answer the questions that follow.

The year was 1891. The place was Springfield, Massachusetts. It was a cold, snowy winter. At the YMCA Training School, the young men wished they knew a team sport they could play indoors. Their teacher, James C. Naismith, made up one for them.

He told the school janitor to nail a box to each side of the balcony. The janitor could not find boxes, so he used half-bushel baskets instead.

Naismith split the 18 players in his class into two teams. Each team had 9 players. He told the players that they should try to throw a soccer ball into the other team's basket.

The players loved the game. They quickly learned to pass the ball to the player who was near the other team's basket. They tried to get the ball into a bushel basket. But, as hard as they tried, only one goal was made in the first game. That probably was a good thing since they had to climb up a ladder to get the ball out of the basket.

Even with its problems, the game was a hit. Soon other schools tried it too. Some changes were made. Rules were rewritten. The baskets were made with a hole so the ball could drop through. A new, larger ball was made out of leather with a rubber liner. Today, basketball is one of our most popular team sports.

9. Which of these inferences can be drawn from the article? (Circle one.)
   A. At first, nobody wanted to play basketball.
   B. Other schools in areas where it snowed shared the need for an indoor team sport.

10. Why did the young men want to play an indoor team sport?
    _____
    _____
    _____

11. What change was made in the game so the players no longer needed a ladder?
    _____
    _____

12. You can conclude that Naismith decided to have nine players on each team because (Circle one.)
    A. The game could not possibly be played with a team of any other size.
    B. His class had 18 students, so he just divided the players into two equal teams.

Using the Results

This table shows you the *main* skill tested by each question in Measuring What You Know. Did you have problems with some questions? If you did, find those questions on the table. You'll see which skills you need to practice. You'll also find which lessons teach those skills.

Did you find the lessons that teach the skills you need to practice? You can study those lessons carefully. You will want to work through every lesson in the book, of course. That will strengthen skills you already have. The reading practice will help you build your word power and read more smoothly.

When you have finished all the lessons in this book, you'll take another test. The results of that test will show you how much you have improved on each reading skill.

Question	Skill	Lesson
1	Main Idea	1–2
2	Supporting Details	3
3	Author's Purpose	4
4	Word Meanings	6
5, 6	Seeing Patterns	5–9
7	Understanding Homographs	14
8	Summarizing	9–10
9	Inference	10
10, 11	Causes and Effects	12
12	Drawing Conclusions	11

Part A
Lesson 1

Giving Care

In this lesson you will
- read how a teacher helped blind and deaf Helen Keller learn to "speak," "hear," and "read"
- learn how to find the main idea as you read
- put ideas you have read into your own words
- learn to find meanings for new words

Skills for Reading: Main Idea

Picture It

What is this picture about?

The picture is about football players. Football players are the topic of the picture. What does the picture show *about* the players? Two players are taking care of one who has been hurt. That is the **main idea** of the picture.

Understanding the main idea of the picture is important. It helps you see how the people and things in the picture fit together. When you read, you also need to know the main idea. The main idea helps you see how all the ideas in a piece of writing fit together.

Suppose you're reading an article about buying a used car. You need to find the main idea so you'll know how to choose the right car. Finding the main idea helps you tie together all the pieces of advice in the article.

How do you find the main idea? Ask yourself these two questions.

1. What is the topic? You can state the topic in one or two words.
2. What is the author telling you about the topic?

As you read, look for a sentence that answers the second question. It is the main idea.

Here's an Example

A paragraph is a group of sentences with one main idea about one topic. Read the following paragraph. The topic is Sandra and Mary's day-care problems. As you read, note the underlined sentence. It tells you the main idea of the paragraph.

■ <u>Sandra and Mary have found a good way to solve their day-care problems.</u> Sandra's mother is ill and needs special care. Mary is a single mother with two small children. Both women love their families. But both need some time for themselves. So for two afternoons a week, Mary takes care of her own children and Sandra's mother. For another two afternoons, Sandra takes care of the combined family. Everyone is happy with the plan.

See how the underlined sentence answers the two questions.

1. What is the topic? Sandra and Mary's day-care problems.
2. What is the main point the author is making about Sandra and Mary's problem? They have found a good way to solve it.

Note how the other sentences in the paragraph give details, or pieces of information, about the main idea. The main idea describes all the information, not just one or two pieces.

In that paragraph, the main idea was given in the first sentence. This drawing helps you picture a paragraph with the main idea first.

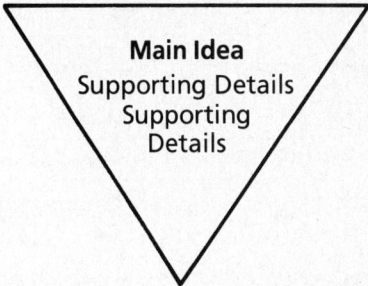

In some paragraphs, the main idea comes in the middle, like this.

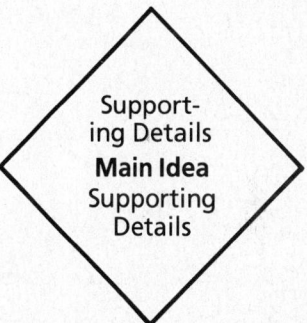

In other paragraphs, the main idea comes at the end, like this.

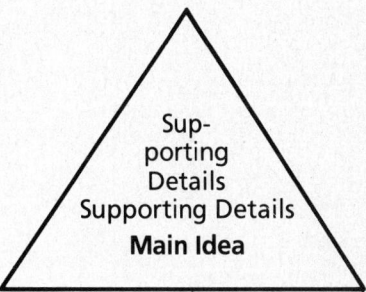

Working It Out

As you read the paragraph below, look for a sentence that answers these questions.

1. What is the topic?
2. What is the most important point the author is making about the topic?

■ Tom and his son Andrew were walking along the beach when they saw something strange. It looked like a lump of moving tar. Up close, Tom and Andrew saw it was a bird covered with dark, sticky oil. Tom wrapped his jacket around the bird. He told his son to rub the oil off its beak with his scarf. Several people on the beach saw what they were doing and came to help. One person brought clean towels to rub oil off the feathers. Another brought corn meal. Soon the bird was well enough to eat some of the meal. Tom and Andrew knew that they had helped save the bird's life.

Look back through the paragraph to find answers to these questions.

1. What two people are the topic of the paragraph?

   _____

2. Which sentence below tells the main idea of the paragraph? (Circle A or B.)
   A. Tom wrapped the bird in his jacket.
   B. Tom and Andrew's care helped save the bird.

3. Where in the paragraph does the author tell the main idea?
   (Circle A, B, or C.)
   A. in the first sentence
   B. in the middle
   C. in the last sentence

Writing to Improve Your Reading

If you read an idea and repeat the words you've read, you're showing you have memorized the idea. But if you can restate the idea in your *own* words, you know you have understood it. This cartoon shows how a man restates his son's message.

Restating ideas helps you check how well you understand what you read. To restate, work with one or two sentences at a time. Think how you would explain the same information to a friend. Write down your restated idea and then go on to the next sentence.

As you read **Helen and Annie**, choose at least three sentences. Restate them. If this book is yours, you can write your sentences next to the story. The example shows you how. If you're not using your own book, write on a sheet of paper. Save your sentences. They may help you answer questions about what you read.

Reading on Your Own

Helen Keller was born in 1880. When she was a baby, she was very sick. The sickness left her deaf and blind. Since she couldn't hear words, she did not learn to talk. She also did not know how to act with others. She seemed almost like a wild animal. Then a woman named Anne Sullivan was hired to give special care to Helen. Read to find out how Annie cared for Helen. As you read, watch for the main idea.

Helen and Annie

At breakfast, Helen ate with her fingers. She grabbed food from other people's plates. When Annie stopped her, she kicked and screamed. She bit and punched. Annie slapped her soundly. The dining room became a battlefield. Annie won, but they both ended up in tears. The same scenes started when Annie wanted Helen to comb her hair, or button her boots. Helen screamed and fought. Annie insisted firmly. Mrs. Keller wept.

Annie's task seemed doomed to failure—to everyone except Annie. She had found a little garden house in the grounds. She said that she and Helen would go and live there alone. It was the only way Annie could hope to make progress.

Helen fought Annie when Annie stopped her from acting wildly.

Helen was taken a roundabout way to the house. The furniture was moved about so that she didn't know where she was.

In two weeks, Annie and Helen were becoming the friends they would be for life. Helen could still be wild, but with Annie it was more fun to be good. They spent most of their time outdoors. They walked in the woods or romped in the grass. Annie was always showing her things—flowers, puddles, insects that buzzed in her hand. She taught Helen to sew and crochet. They did exercises each morning. And all the time Annie spelled words into Helen's hand.

Helen found her way around by touching furniture. Annie had the furniture moved so Helen would think she was in a new place.

It was a game to Helen. She spelled them back to Annie. But she did not know that they meant anything. One day, Annie was trying to explain to Helen that the word M-U-G meant the mug, and that W-A-T-E-R was the wet stuff inside it. But still Helen couldn't see the difference.

Annie used hand signals to spell out words in Helen's hand. Annie moved her fingers in a different way for each letter.

They went for a walk near the well house. Somebody was pumping water. Annie took Helen's hand. She held it under the spout. She took the other hand and spelled W-A-T-E-R into it. She spelled slowly at first and then faster and faster. A miracle happened. Helen's face lit up with excitement. The mystery of language was suddenly solved. She knew that the water flowing over her hand had a name, W-A-T-E-R.

Helen rushed about touching things and asking Annie what they were called. A whole new life had suddenly opened up for her.

Thinking About What You've Read

You find the main idea of a long piece of writing in the same way you find it in a short paragraph. Look for the sentence that tells two things: (1) the topic of the *whole* article and (2) the point the author is making in the *whole* article.

1. What two people are the topic of the article?

_____

2. Which of the following sentences restates the main idea of the article?
   A. Annie helped Helen understand words by working hard and patiently.
   B. When Helen ate, she didn't use a knife or fork.

Answer each of the following questions with a few words.

3. How did Annie try to teach words to Helen?

_____

4. What was the first word Helen learned from Annie?

_____

5. Do you think Annie was right to separate Helen from her parents? Explain why you think so.

_____

_____

A Test-Taking Tip

A multiple-choice item asks a question and then gives you two or more possible answers. You need to choose the answer you think is best. You may decide that you like multiple-choice items because you know the best answer is already written for you. All you have to do is make a good choice.

When you take the GED Test, you will find that it is made up of multiple-choice items. Follow the directions for marking answers carefully. Read each multiple-choice question slowly to see exactly what it is asking.

GED Warm-up

Read the question below. Fill in the numbered circle to show the answer you think is best. Which of the following sentences best restates the main idea of the very first paragraph of *Helen and Annie*?

(1) Both Helen and Annie cried at mealtimes.
(2) The dining room seemed like a battlefield during mealtimes.

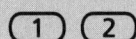

Working with Words

Look at these words from *Helen and Annie*.

battlefield   roundabout   outdoors

_____   _____   _____

_____   _____   _____

Each word is made up of two smaller words. Write the smaller words on the lines below each word or on your own paper.

A word made up of two smaller words is called a *compound*. If you read a compound you don't know, there is a simple way to find its meaning. Write the two smaller words separately. Write the meaning of each. If either of the small words is new to you, find its meaning in a dictionary. Then combine the meaning of the two small words to discover the meaning of the compound.

Which of the following compounds best completes each sentence below?

    anything   battlefield
    outdoors   roundabout

1. To avoid road repairs, I took a _____ way to work.

2. Our new patio carpet is made for use _____ .

3. The old _____ was marked with gravestones of soldiers.

4. Is there _____ you need from the hardware store?

▲ Looking Back

The article you read in this lesson described how Annie Sullivan patiently taught Helen Keller how to "speak" with hand signals. The lesson showed you how to find the main idea of a paragraph or an article. You practiced restating sentences. You also learned a method for finding the meaning of new compounds.

As you continue to read, practice looking for the main idea.

The Active Reader

Taking Stock

Picture It
What equipment is this carpenter using?

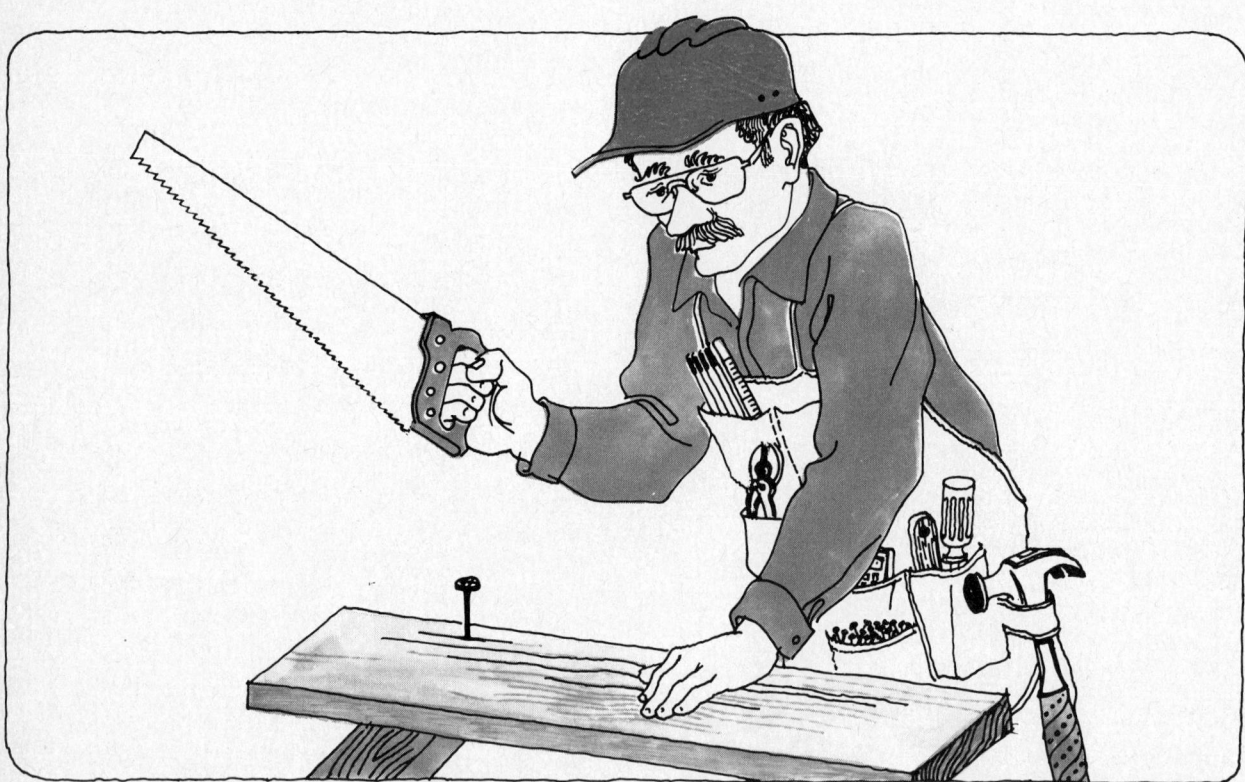

This carpenter is using the wrong tool. He's going to have a hard time doing his job.

Reading is like working. It calls for action. Your body and mind work together to help you do your best. But if you don't have the right tools, you cannot do your best. You have to "take stock" of your tools before you begin to read.

Here's an Example
Here's a checklist to help you decide how well prepared you are for reading right now. Answer each question *yes* or *no* in the blank before the number. Or write your answer on your own paper.

____ 1. Do you have a good light? (You need either a good overhead light or a study lamp.)

____ 2. Do you have a comfortable work space? (You need either a table or a desk to write notes.)

____ 3. Is the room free of distractions such as loud music?

____ 4. Have you planned enough time so you can finish your reading in one sitting?

____ 5. Do you have a clear idea of what work you are supposed to do?

____ 6. Is a dictionary handy?

____ 7. Do you have paper and pen to make notes?

If you answered *yes* to all but one or two questions, you're ready to become an active reader. If you answered *no* to more than two, make changes so that you can be more comfortable, better equipped, and ready for action.

Working It Out

Your feelings about reading are as important as equipment. Here are some comments that people make about reading. Do any of these comments sound like feelings you have about reading? Circle the numbers of comments that describe your feelings.

1. I wish I could concentrate better on what I read.

2. I want to remember more of what I read.

3. I want to learn to apply what I already know to new ideas that I read.

4. I need to learn how to use a dictionary to find the meanings of new words.

5. English is my second language. I need to learn more English words so I can read smoothly.

6. I would like to read longer stories and articles than I do now.

7. I would like to enjoy reading—to *want* to read.

After you've worked on improving your reading, turn back to this page. See if your feelings about reading are beginning to change. Many of the lessons in this book are meant to help you learn to concentrate, to remember what you've read, and to discover the meanings of new words. Take stock again at the end of your course, and see how your answers change!

Part A Lesson 2

Take Care!

In this lesson you will
- read about one important way to take care of yourself
- learn how to find the main idea when it is not given in a sentence
- make margin notes to help you concentrate on your reading
- study some different forms of words

Skills for Reading: Unstated Main Idea

Picture It

What is missing from this picture?

Did you figure out the patient was missing from the picture? Clues in the picture help you see what is missing.

The same skills that helped you understand the picture are important when you read. In some paragraphs the author does not come right out and tell you the main idea in one of the sentences. But don't make the mistake of thinking there isn't a main idea! Instead, you need to figure out the main idea yourself.

Do you remember the questions you use to find the main idea?

1. What is the topic?
2. What is the most important point the author makes about the topic?

When the writer doesn't write the main idea in a sentence, you need to find the answers for those two questions yourself. Then you put them together to form your own sentence with the main idea.

Here's an Example

The paragraph below has a main idea. But there is no sentence to tell what it is.

■ What can ruin a picnic more surely than rain? Ask someone who has had food poisoning. It's no picnic! What can you do to stay safe from food poisoning? First, always wash your hands before you touch food. Pack food in clean containers, or use fresh foil, waxed paper, or plastic wrap. Keep meat, fish, and dairy products in a cooler with ice. Be sure the lid is closed tightly. If you plan to cook out, make sure your meat is completely cooked. Last, plan to have your meal early so that the food will not have time to spoil.

You can see that all the sentences are about picnic food. Picnic food is the topic. Nearly all the sentences tell a way to avoid food poisoning when you're on a picnic. That is the most important point the writer is telling you about the topic. So the main idea is this: You can take steps to avoid food poisoning at a picnic.

Go back and read the paragraph again. See how each sentence helps you understand the main idea.

Working It Out

Read the following paragraph. It tells about some ways to take care of belongings. The questions that follow will help you find the main idea.

■ While Don was gone, a burglar broke into his apartment. After that, Don decided he needed to make some changes. He put a dead-bolt lock on his door. He borrowed an engraver from the police and put his name on things that might be stolen. Finally, Don got together with his neighbors. They all decided to work together to watch one another's apartments when someone was gone.

Write a few words to answer each question.

1. Who is the paragraph about?
   _____

2. What happened to Don?
   _____

3. Write a sentence that tells all the things Don decided to do.
   _____
   _____

4. The paragraph does not tell the main idea. It is up to you to put the main idea in your own words. Write the main idea.
   _____
   _____

Writing to Improve Your Reading

The space around the sides, top, and bottom of a page is called the margin. The margins in this book are especially wide. This is so you can use them as work space. If you own the book you are using, you can write notes in the margins. If the book is not your own, tuck a piece of paper under this page. Use it to make margin notes.

What type of information can you write in the margin? Here are some suggestions.

- comments or questions about what you've read
- meanings of new words
- sentences you've restated
- your feelings about a story
- markers to point out information you may need later
- ideas you have about reading

Writing margin notes helps you pay attention to what you're reading. Look at the article in Reading on Your Own. See how some notes have been made in the margin. As you read the article, keep a pen or pencil in hand. Write some notes of your own. See how the job of writing notes keeps your mind from wandering.

Reading on Your Own

A hard day. Too much pressure. Problems at work. Everyone must live with such things now and then. Afterward, you need to give extra care to an important person—yourself. You need to relax. Read to find some ways you can use to relax. As you read, decide what the main idea of the article is.

Relax!

"Relax!" It sounds easy. But how do you do it?

When people relax, they are healthier. Blood pressure is low. Breathing is slow. They're calm. But it can be hard to relax when things go wrong. You may need to work at it.

Exercise is one of the best ways to relax. Suppose you are tense about your job. You might try jogging for fifteen minutes when you get home from work.

As you jog, avoid thinking about problems. Tell yourself that you work hard. Soon your hard work will show results. Keep your mind on that idea. Push doubts and fears out of your mind. For this short time, think only positive thoughts.

Notes

It's hard to find time

Meditation is another way to relax.

Find a quiet spot where you can be alone for fifteen minutes. You might sit in a comfortable chair. Or you could sit cross-legged on the floor. You could even lie on the floor. It is better not to lie on your bed because you might fall asleep. Your mind should stay alert.

Close your eyes. Let your mind go blank. Clear away every worry. Breathe deeply. Let your mind think only about your breathing. As your mind clears, your body will relax.

Then think of something pleasant. Picture a park on a sunny day. Recall your favorite memory. The positive images will ease tension. Your body will feel better. Your mental state will be better, too.

Notes

It sounds strange, but one way to relax is to **tense your body.** The trick is to tense and relax one muscle at a time. For example, you can start with your toes. Hold them tense for a few seconds. Then relax them completely. Focus your mind on how good the relaxation feels. Next, tense the muscles in your feet. Relax them in the same way. Move on up your whole body. Tense and relax each group of muscles. At the same time, clear your mind of worries. Think only about how good your body feels. This is a good way to fall asleep at night!

Try this to fall asleep

Lesson 2 Take Care / 17

Thinking About What You've Read

1. What is the topic of this article?
   _____

2. Which of the following sentences best tells the main idea of the article? (Circle A or B.)
   A. Everyone needs time to relax after a busy day.
   B. There are different ways to relax your body and mind.

3. After closing your eyes, what two things should you do to meditate?
   A. _____
   B. _____

4. In a few words, tell how to relax by tensing muscles.
   _____
   _____

5. What piece of information in the article did you find most helpful? Why?
   _____
   _____

A Test-Taking Tip

To check your understanding of the main idea, a multiple-choice question might ask you to choose the best title for a paragraph or an article. To answer a question like that, first read the *whole* selection. Figure out the main idea. Choose the title that comes closest to telling the main idea.

GED Warm-up

Which of the following choices would make the best title for the article on pages 16–17?

(1) A Hard Day
(2) How to Relax

① ②

Working with Words

Read these sentences from the article in Reading on Your Own.

- Blood pressure is **low**.
- Breathing rate is **slow**.

18 / Part A Reading Skills for Life

The bold word in each is a word that describes. Words that describe have different forms. Read the sentences below. Find different forms of the words in bold above.

- Blood pressure is **lower** when you're calm than when you're upset.
- Breathing rate is **slowest** when you sleep.

The endings *-er* and *-est* have been added to *low* and *slow*. You know words with *-er* compare two things and words with *-est* compare three or more. You speak such words all the time.

When you read a word such as *lower*, you need to see that a word you know (*low*) has just had an ending added to it (*low + er*). Sometimes the spelling of the main word changes a bit before the ending is added. A *y* may change to *i* (*funny, funnier*), an *e* may be dropped (*wide, wider*), or a letter may be doubled (*fat, fattest*). But you can always spot enough of the main word to understand the new word.

Here are words from some articles you've read. *-Er* or *-est* has been added to each. Match them with their meanings.

1. earlier
2. gentlest
3. deeper
4. happiest
5. hotter
6. tensest
7. healthier

a. the least relaxed
b. the most glad
c. sooner in time
d. having more heat
e. having more health
f. going down further
g. the most soft and mild

Add *-er* or *-est* to one of the words below to make the best word to complete each sentence. Write the new word in the blank.

Words		
busy	rich	heavy
fast	hard	healthy

8. She's always in a hurry; she drives _____ than anyone I know.

9. My new job is very difficult; it's the _____ job I've ever had.

10. A 5-lb. bag is _____ than a 1-lb. bag.

11. He has a lot to do, but his wife is even _____.

12. If you exercise, your body will be _____.

13. I want to make lots of money and become the _____ person in the world.

▲ Looking Back

In this lesson, you've read several articles about caring for yourself and others. You've practiced discovering the main idea when the author does not tell it in a sentence. You've written notes in the margin to help you understand what you read and concentrate better. You've also learned how to read different forms of words.

As you continue to read, practice writing notes in the margins of your own books. See how much better you remember what you read. And always look for the main idea when you read.

The Active Reader

Thinking Ahead

Picture It
What's happening in this picture?

Imagine that you're in this theater watching an exciting movie. The main character is suddenly in danger. How do you feel? Perhaps your body is tense. Your throat feels dry. You wonder, "What will happen next? Will he be OK?" Your attention is on the screen until your questions are answered.

At the moment you're wondering, "What next?" you are most alert. You're concentrating on the story. You're using your energy to find answers.

Active readers keep their minds alert in the same way. Before they read an article, they look at the title and any pictures. Then they make some predictions about what the article will tell them. Next, they read the first few lines or paragraphs to find out whether their predictions were correct.

As active readers continue reading, they form more predictions about what they will find. In other words, they think ahead to what is next. They predict what it will be about. Then they read to find out whether they are correct.

Active readers keep their minds busy. They keep thinking about what they are reading at all times.

Here's an Example
Following is the first part of a paragraph from a book called *Stunt Work and Stunt People*. The title gives a clue to what you can expect to find in the reading. The active reader would think, "Maybe the author will tell about famous stunt people." "Maybe the author will tell about the need to take care in stunt work."

■ For a fight the stunt doubles plan all the moves and practice over and over. They must make the fight look real, but they never really hit each other. Hubie Kerns said the way the camera is set up is important. He was the double for Adam West, who played Batman on TV. He often fought Batman's enemy Penguin and other "bad guys" so he knows all the secrets of TV fights.

Did you notice that the first prediction was proved true? The author *does* tell about a stunt double, Hubie Kerns. Kerns is a stunt man who took the place of actor Adam West to do stunts on TV's *Batman*.

Working It Out

The writer has mentioned above that Hubie Kern knows the secrets of TV fights.

1. What do you predict the rest of the paragraph will describe?

_____

_____

Read to see if your prediction is correct. Here's the rest of the paragraph.

■ He [Hubie] said, "I face you. The camera is behind you or behind me. I throw a punch across your face, not towards you, but just across it. My fist goes in front of your face and past the camera. When you snap your head back, I throw my fist straight past your head to your ear. If the camera is at the side of us, it is seen as a miss. From behind us, it looks like a hit. But it takes a lot of practice to do it."

Was your prediction correct? _____
If your prediction doesn't turn out to be right, don't feel you have made a mistake. Just *making* the prediction is important. Predicting is a way of helping you keep your attention on your reading.

2. Read the first sentence of the next paragraph in the book *Stunt Work and Stunt People*. Write a prediction of what it will be about. Then read to see if you were right.

■ John Forster made a mistake in a fight and ended up with a very sore mouth.

Prediction: _____

_____

■ "The only time I got hurt was in a fight scene in *Buffalo Bill and the Indians*," he said. "I leaned into a punch when I should have pulled back. I ended up with a broken jaw."

Was your prediction correct? _____
As long as your predictions are reasonable, don't worry if you were wrong. A reasonable prediction shows you were paying attention. It helps you focus on the meaning of what you read.

Part A Lesson 3

Caring About Others

In this lesson you will
- read about a group of people who care about the homeless in their city
- learn how authors use details to explain a main idea
- write a prediction about the topic of an article
- learn one way words are used to describe things

Skills for Reading: Supporting Details

Picture It

This picture shows how an author uses details, or small pieces of information, to support his or her main idea.

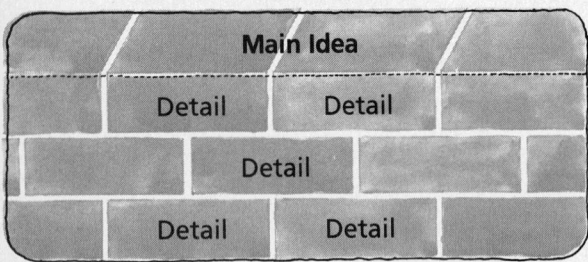

The drawing shows how important details are. The details that help you understand the main idea are called **supporting details.** They support, or give strength to, the main idea the way bricks give strength to a wall. They build it up by giving facts, examples, or other information that help support the main idea.

Not all details in a paragraph are supporting details. Some are just pieces of information that add interest. You can tell *supporting* details because they are the ones that help tell *who, how, where, when, what,* or *why* about the main idea.

Here are some types of information that supporting details might give.

- facts to show the main idea is true
- examples that help you picture the main idea
- explanations that show how the main idea might be useful to you

Here's an Example

The main idea of the following paragraph is underlined. The paragraph is about a group of men and women who care about younger people. You'll see that most of the other sentences give details to support the main idea.

■ Children from single-parent homes are not new. Many boys and girls grow up without fathers or mothers. <u>But today some of these children get help from a group called Big Brothers/Big Sisters.</u> The adults in Big Brothers/Big Sisters help children between the ages of six and sixteen. A case worker pairs women with girls and men with boys. The adult spends time with the child. He or she guides the child and becomes a needed friend. In effect, the adults become just like older brothers and sisters.

The main idea is this: Some children without fathers or mothers get help from Big Brothers/Big Sisters. (Notice that the main idea is a sentence, a *complete* thought. It is not just the phrase "Big Brothers/Big Sisters.")

Most of the sentences give details that help you understand *who* Big Brothers/Big Sisters help and *how* they help them. Here's how the details in the paragraph act like the bricks of a strong wall.

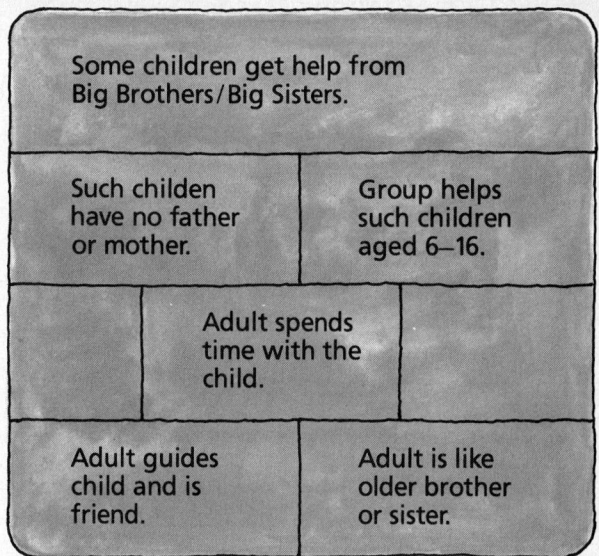

Two details in the paragraph are interesting, but they aren't really needed to explain *who* or *how*: (1) Children from single-parent homes are not new. (2) A case worker pairs women with girls and men with boys. Because those details don't help explain the main idea, they are not supporting details.

Working It Out

Read this paragraph about a health worker who cares about children. Try to see how the supporting details help you understand the main idea.

■ Gloria is learning how to test the hearing of babies and young children. First, she'll spend many hours watching babies and children with normal hearing. That will help her see how children with normal hearing act when they hear sounds. Next, Gloria will practice working with babies. She'll shake a rattle near each ear. She'll watch to see if the baby moves in response to the sound. Finally, she'll

Lesson 3 Caring About Others / 23

learn to use special machinery to test the hearing of children three to six weeks old. Someday, Gloria will work in a hospital.

Now answer these questions. You may look back at the article to find information.

1. What is the main idea? (Remember to write a complete sentence.)

   _____

2. Write one supporting detail from the article.

   _____

3. Which sentence does *not* help explain the main idea? Copy it here.

   _____
   _____

Writing to Improve Your Reading

Many good readers write down questions or ideas that come to them as they read. You might want to try this yourself. Writing can be a way to talk to yourself as you read.

One thing you can write down is a prediction. In Lesson 2, you learned how to predict what a reading passage will be about. For practice, try writing down a prediction next time you read something. Look over the article or story you plan to read. Decide what you think it is about. Write down your prediction. What you write doesn't have to be perfect. Your writing will be only for yourself.

Try writing a prediction about the reading passage that follows. Read the title and the first few sentences. What do you think this article will be about?

_____

When you finish reading the article, look back at your prediction. Were you right?

Reading on Your Own

In the following article you'll read about a group of people who are showing they care in a special way. They care enough to help the homeless people of their city. As you read, pay attention to details. Make margin notes if that helps. Your notes will help you write a summary of the article when you've finished.

A Better Hut

If you watch the news on TV, you've heard the story and seen the pictures: the growing number of people without homes is a sad fact. Some cities have shelters for the homeless. But such shelters can be dangerous. Many homeless people prefer to live in huts they make themselves. These huts are made from scrap metal and plastic sheets. Of course, such huts don't offer much protection.

Homeless persons in Atlanta have a third choice. It all began when a man named Mike Connor and a friend talked to some homeless people. They asked what kind of a hut the people would like. Mike and his friend used their answers to create a blueprint for a better hut.

The hut they designed is smaller than a bathroom. But a person can stand up in it and can put a mattress on the floor. The hut even has a window and shelves made out of two-by-fours. And it does what any good home does: it keeps out the wind and the rain.

Mike and a group of caring people now use the blueprint to build huts for the homeless. The group is called "the mad housers." Almost every other weekend, the mad housers get together. With donated money, they buy lumber, windows, and cinderblocks. The cinderblocks will be used to raise the huts above the ground. Then the mad housers drive to a spot where a "client" has been living in a lean-to or under a plastic sheet. On a good day, the mad housers take as little as twenty minutes to put up one of their huts. Some "clients" decorate their huts with paint or scrap pieces of carpet.

There is *one* problem for the mad housers. Because they build on public property and break zoning codes, they are breaking the law. Sometimes the city tears down their huts. But often police and other city officials look the other way. It seems many of them must care about the homeless too. And as one man who lives in a mad houser hut says, "You're not homeless when you got this."

A client, or customer, is a person who uses a business service.

Thinking About What You've Read

1. What is the main idea of the article? Try to write the main idea in a sentence of your own.

2. Which of these details supports the main idea?
    A. The mad housers take as little as twenty minutes to build a hut.
    B. If you watch the TV news, you know about the homeless.

3. Which of these details supports the main idea?
   A. The mad housers build huts that keep out the wind and rain.
   B. Sometimes the city lets the mad houser huts stand.

4. For what three items do the mad housers need money?
   _____
   _____

5. What do the homeless like about their new huts?
   _____
   _____

6. What suggestion does the writer offer to explain *why* the city officials sometimes allow the huts to stand?
   _____
   _____
   _____

7. Look back at the prediction you wrote on page 24. Was it right? _____ If not, you still might have had good reasons for predicting what you did. What led you to make your prediction?
   _____
   _____
   _____

A Test-Taking Tip

Sometimes a multiple-choice item doesn't actually ask a question. Instead, it gives you an incomplete sentence. One of the answer choices completes the sentence correctly.

When you read an item like this, try to finish the sentence yourself first. Then read the choices. Pick the one most like your own answer. This is where your skill at restating is useful. Because the answer on the test may not use the same words you do, you must be able to see when your answer says the same thing in different words.

GED Warm-up

Mike Connor and his friend talked to homeless people in order to
(1) teach them how to build a better hut
(2) learn what a good hut would be like
① ②

Working with Words

Look at these words from the article *A Better Hut.*

　　　growing　　donated　　caring

You might know those words as verbs— words that put action into sentences. In this case, the verbs have *-ed* or *-ing*

26 / Part A Reading Skills for Life

added to the end. But they aren't used as action words in the article. Instead, each is used to *describe* someone or something.

"the growing number" means "the number that is growing, or getting larger"

"caring people" means "people who care, or look out for others"

"with donated money" means "with money that has been donated, or given as charity"

Writers often use the *-ed* or *-ing* forms of verbs to describe other words. When you read such a word, don't be confused by its use in the sentence. Look at the main part of the word without its ending. Use its meaning *together* with the word it's describing. Restate the phrase if you need to, as the phrases above were restated.

Practice with these words now. Read each sentence below. Add *-ed* or *-ing* to the word that fits the sentence and write it on the line.

support   train   borrow   love

1. When you read, look for _____ details that explain the main idea.

2. Pay back _____ money quickly if you want to keep your friends.

3. Every child deserves _____ parents.

4. The factory is looking for _____ workers.

▲ Looking Back

In this lesson you read about a group who work to make life better for the homeless. The details helped you understand how they do this. The lesson showed you how supporting details in every article build up the main idea.

As you read, remember to write down questions or ideas that come to you. Try to write down your idea of what the article is about before you read it. This will help focus your attention on the details of the article.

The Active Reader

Energy-Saving Eye Movements

Picture It

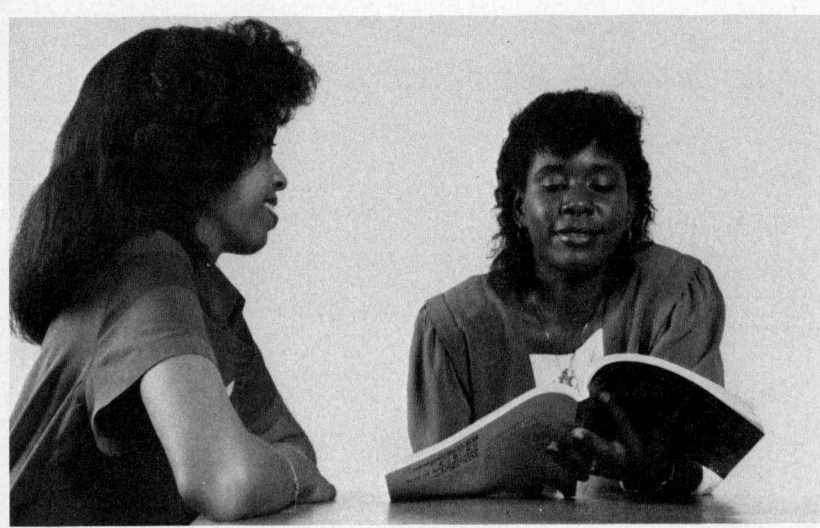

Here's an idea to try. Ask a friend to help. Have your friend watch while you read several lines from this page. Ask your friend to count how many times your eyes stop as you read each line.

Do your eyes stop and focus on each word in the line? If they do, you may be reading more slowly and using more energy than you need to. Good readers might stop two or three times per line. Their eyes stop after *groups* of words. Your eyes can too.

In the sentence below, look only at the *middle* word.

>   Pay your bill.

Although your eyes rest on the middle word, you can easily see the word before and after it. In other words, your eyes can take in more than just one word at a time. You can actually read a group of words all in one glance.

Reading words in groups is a big step in improving your reading. Reading groups of words instead of single words helps you to

- read faster
- pay attention to ideas
- use your energy for getting the meaning of whole sentences, not just single words.

Think about it. If you were listening to a speaker who paused after each word, you would have a hard time paying attention. Your mind would move faster than the speaker's words. You probably would lose interest. In reading, too, working with just one word at a time can bore you. It can keep you from understanding and enjoying what you read.

Here's an Example

The following two paragraphs are printed in groups of two to four words. The meanings of the words in each group fit together. The word groups on the page help you see how you can form words into groups as you read.

Start off with smaller groups (two to three words) and then use larger groups (four to five words). Try reading by moving your eyes from group to group, not word to word. Read the paragraph as many times as necessary to feel that your eyes are moving smoothly.

■ Every ten years   in the U.S.
a census   is taken.   The census
is a counting   of the people
who live here.   A census form
is sent   to each household.
The residents   are asked
to give information
about themselves.   They are to tell
their ages, education, and other facts.

■ The U.S. Department of Commerce
collects the information
and finds out   what new trends
are happening.
Information about individuals
is kept secret.   But information
about groups of people
is published.

Working It Out

Now read the next two paragraphs. You can practice grouping the words yourself as you read. As you practice over and over, can you tell how much better you are understanding the information?

■ Information from the census helps us plan for the future. It tells where we will need new roads and schools. It tells when we need hospitals and new homes. It points out where most people and industries are moving.

■ The census is required by the U.S. Constitution. It is needed to decide how many people will represent each state in the U.S. Congress. States that lose population or that grow slowly may lose places to fast-growing states.

For the next few weeks, practice this exercise often. In all your reading, make an effort to read in word groups, not word by word. Soon you'll find that you can read more with less effort and better understanding. You'll also begin to read a bit faster.

Part A Lesson 4

Love and Marriage

> *In this lesson you will*
> - read interesting facts and stories about weddings in America
> - learn about the author's purpose for writing
> - practice underlining important ideas as you read
> - learn about words that have the same meaning

Skills for Reading: Author's Purpose

Picture It

Which book on this shelf would probably help a person engaged to be married?

The titles of the books tell their topics. You probably guessed that *Plan a Perfect Wedding* would be helpful to someone getting married. Why? Because it must give information the person would like to know. Some of the other books are written to give information too: *The Dictionary of Musical Words*, *How to Cook Fish*, and *The Life of Ronald Reagan*. Which books are probably meant just for fun? You may guess that *Humorous Short Stories*, *1,001 Cartoons*, and *Modern Mysteries* are meant for fun reading.

Which books are probably meant to get you to do something? Most likely, *Quit Smoking Now* and *You Should Vote*.

An author usually writes an article or book for one of three reasons.

- to inform
- to entertain
- to persuade

Writing meant to inform contains ideas that can be proved. The author uses facts that are interesting or useful to the reader. Often the author studies the topic for months or even years before writing about it. Charts or drawings may be included to help you understand the facts. Notes may show where the facts came from so that you could check them.

Writing to entertain is meant just for fun. The author does not always check facts. The goal is to get your attention and amuse you. To do this, the author may include funny events or people, an exciting story, or a lot of wonderful imagination.

Writing to persuade tries to get you to believe or do something. Ads in newspapers and letters to the editor are examples of this type of writing. Writing that tries to persuade may have facts or the ideas of "experts." But you can't always be sure the facts are true or the ideas are good. When you feel an author is trying to persuade you, you need to ask yourself, "Does the author make sense to me? Has the author backed his persuasion with facts and ideas that *I* can check?"

When you want to decide what the author's purpose is, use this idea. Pretend that what you are reading is being read on a radio or TV program. Does the article sound as if it would be read by a news reporter? That is, does it sound serious? If so, it is probably meant to inform. Does it sound as if a comic or talk show host would read it? Then, most likely, it is meant to entertain. Does it sound like an ad? Then it's probably meant to persuade.

Sometimes an author will inform you in an interesting, lively, entertaining way. Sometimes an author will try to persuade you using facts and other information. In general, though, an author has *one main purpose* for writing.

Here's an Example

The author of this paragraph wants to persuade you that divorce laws should be changed.

■ Too many people get divorces these days. Some studies show that one in three marriages ends in divorce. Why? Because divorce is easy. In some states, a couple just has to file for divorce. No reason has to be given; no blame laid. So people are more willing to break up their marriages than work hard to save them. Any little problem sends them to divorce court. Laws should be changed to make divorce harder. Then more marriages would last.

The author used the fact that one in three marriages ends in divorce. That fact *does* inform you. But the author uses that fact to support a belief about divorce laws. The author mainly wants to persuade you to share this belief.

This next paragraph is meant mainly to entertain you. It's a story about a real wedding, but the author doesn't mean to give facts, or try to get you to do or believe anything.

■ Meg and Larry planned a perfect wedding. But the wedding did not follow the plan. In fact, it wasn't even *their* wedding because Meg changed her mind about Larry. She decided to marry Tim instead. On the day of Meg and Tim's wedding, the flowers were sent to Larry's church. After the wedding, Tim and Meg went to cut the cake. It wasn't there. At the last minute, the baker ran in with the cake. It was tall and beautiful and covered with roses made of sugar. A plastic love bird sat on top. And then the baker slipped. The cake sailed through the air. It landed upside down on the bird. At least Meg and Tim's marriage has been more successful than their wedding.

Working It Out

What do you think the author's main purpose is in this paragraph?

■ Wedding rings have been used since early times. As long as 1,000 years ago, Icelanders used a large ring of stone. Instead of wearing the ring, the couple joined hands inside the ring. In the past 500 years, wedding rings have become works of art. Most are made of gold or silver. Some have fancy patterns or jewels on them. The idea behind the rings is still the same, though. They are meant to join people in love.

Answer the following questions to help you decide the author's main purpose.

1. Are dates, place names, and other facts given?

2. Does the author try to get you to believe or do anything?

3. Does the author use humor, suspense, or imagination to get your attention?

4. What do you think the author's main purpose is?

Writing to Improve Your Reading

Underlining is a good way to call attention to important ideas. What sorts of things should you underline? A sentence that tells the main idea is good to underline. Other than that, there is no rule to tell you. Each reader must decide what is important to him or her.

Your reason for reading can help you choose what to underline. For example, if you're reading to answer a question, you'll pay attention only to the ideas about that question.

Here's a plan that can help you decide what to underline. As you read, watch especially for words or numbers that answer these questions:

Who? What? Where? When? How? Why?

The answers to these questions are probably things that you may want to remember or use later. Look at the example of underlining in the first note under Reading on Your Own on page 33. A reader has underlined the words that tell *who, what, when*, and *why*.

As you read the article ***The Single Life***, draw a line under ideas you may want to remember.

Reading On Your Own

Every ten years the U.S. government gathers facts about the way we live. The facts are used to help us plan for the future. A census was taken in 1970 and another in 1980. Many things had changed during the years between. Decide what the author's main purpose is as you read about changing patterns of marriage.

The Single Life

The florist, the baker, and the candle maker all know a change has taken place. There have been fewer weddings in recent years. Many young people are waiting to "tie the knot" until they are older. Some have decided never to marry. And many who have gotten divorces have decided not to marry again.

"To tie the knot" is an expression that means "to get married."

The facts show how things have changed. In 1970 only 36 percent of women between 20 and 24 had never been married. By 1982, over *half* the women in that age group had never married. Among older women, the difference was even greater. In 1970 only 11 percent of women between 25 and 29 had never been married. By 1982, that number had more than doubled. And the numbers of single women have increased since then.

These figures are reported by the U.S. government. The information is from census forms completed by U.S. citizens.

There are many reasons for the change. Many young men and women want to spend more years on their education. Others want to move ahead in their jobs before they begin a family. Some women have decided to continue their careers instead of becoming wives and mothers.

In the next article a dressmaker from a small town tells about some brides she has met. As you read, decide what purpose she has for sharing her stories.

Three Brides

I make dresses for a living. I like to sew, and wedding dresses are my favorites. I love the feeling of the rich cloth. I love making a dress that will be worn on a happy day. And I love the stories the women tell me as I work.

There is the story of Anna. She came to America to marry her

love. She had always lived on an island where the weather is hot. She had never needed a coat. Her new family wrote to tell her that she must wear a coat when she came to America. She would be cold without one. Anna wore a coat, but that is all she wore. She brought no dresses. I had to make a few everyday dresses for her before I could begin on her wedding dress.

There is the story of Catherine. She was crying when she came to get her wedding dress. Years before, she was ready to marry her love. On the day she went to get her dress, he was killed in an accident. Now she was reminded of that day and worried that something bad might happen again. But her wedding went beautifully.

When Jenny came to have a wedding dress made, her hair was gray. She was tall and beautiful and looked like a statue. I asked why she had waited so long to marry. She told me her father had died when she was young. She had worked to support her family. Now that her brothers and sisters were grown, she could marry. "He's a good man," she said about her love. I think Jenny will always make her own happiness.

Thinking About What You've Read

1. What was the author's main purpose for writing *The Single Life?*
   A. to persuade people to get married
   B. to inform you of changing facts about marriage

2. What was the author's main purpose for writing *Three Brides?*
   A. to entertain you with stories
   B. to persuade you to buy one of her wedding dresses

3. In *The Single Life,* what is one reason that fewer people are getting married?

   _____

4. In *Three Brides,* why do you think the brides told the dressmaker their stories?

   _____

A Test-Taking Tip

On a multiple-choice test like the GED Test, you may need to answer a question about the author's purpose. One mistake readers often make is to substitute *their own* ideas for the author's. They choose the answer that agrees with their own ideas.

If you must answer a multiple-choice question about the author's purpose, be sure you know what the author's point is or what sort of information he or she is giving. Then choose the answer that best tells the *author's* purpose, not your own ideas.

GED Warm-up

In *The Single Life,* why does the author mention that many people who are divorced decide not to marry again?

(1) to persuade you that divorce is wrong for some people
(2) to inform you of one reason there are fewer weddings

Working with Words

Synonyms are words that have the same or nearly the same meaning. For example, *merry* and *happy* are synonyms. Learning synonyms for common words will build up your vocabulary. The more words you can add to your own writing and speaking, the more words you'll be able to understand when you read.

You read the word *increased* in *The Single Life.* You probably know that word. *Increase* means "to make or become larger." Do you know the meaning of *augment*? If you know that *increase* is a synonym of *augment,* you can figure out the meaning of *augment.* It also means "to make larger."

You can practice using synonyms with the following exercise. The words in list A are from the readings in this lesson. List B gives a synonym for each word in list A, along with a definition. Draw a line from each word in list A to its synonym in list B.

A	B
1. statue	vocation = person's life-work
2. career	sculpture = piece of art carved from stone or wood
3. story	intricate = not simple; having many parts
4. continue	anecdote = tale about an event in a person's life
5. fancy	persist = keep doing the same thing

▲ Looking Back

In Lesson 4 you read some facts about changing marriage habits. You read interesting stories about three women who were getting married. You learned about the author's purpose for writing. You practiced underlining important ideas. And you learned how synonyms can make you a better reader.

As you continue to read, practice thinking about the author's purpose for writing. Continue to underline ideas that you think will be useful to you.

The Active Reader

Using What You Know

Picture It

Your mind is like a library of ideas and memories. Your past experiences have given you facts and ideas that you store in that "library." All that you've learned and remembered can help you learn new things. The "library" in your head offers a good base that you can build on each time you read.

When you read, your mind works with new ideas. Sometimes you add facts to what you knew before. At other times you compare or correct ideas from the past.

The more experiences you've had, the greater your "library" will be. Have you traveled to other states? Have you served in the military? Have you worked at different types of jobs? The words, skills, and ideas you learned each time will make your "library" richer.

Here's an Example

Suppose you decided to read *The Time Machine* by H. G. Wells. It's a famous book of science fiction. People have enjoyed it and talked about it for many years. It's about a man who builds a machine that can take him into the past or future. Of course, there is no such machine. But from real machines that you've seen and used in the past, you can put together your own idea of what a time machine might be like. What you already know could help you picture what you are reading about.

What if you can't easily recall what you know from the past? You can ask yourself questions that help jog your memory. Here are some examples.

1. What is the most important thing I know about the topic?
2. How many other things do I know about the topic? (Think of as many facts, memories, and ideas as you can.)

A further way to help yourself organize what you know about a topic is to make a list of all the facts you can think of. Then group those facts in smaller lists.

The example below shows how one person put his ideas into small lists. James was going to read a book about Colorado because he and his new wife were thinking of moving there. First, he "brainstormed"—he listed all the ideas about Colorado that popped into his head. Then he wrote those ideas in lists as you see them here.

Possible jobs	Cities to live in	Fun
mining—oil	Denver	skiing
selling ski supplies	Colorado Springs	hiking
farming	Pueblo	fishing

Think of the things you know about a topic before you start reading about it. Then as you read, ask yourself, "Did I already know this piece of information? Does it agree with what I do know?"

Working It Out

You can practice using the "library" in your mind. Choose a topic that could help you with your job or at home. Write down the topic and then answer the following questions.

1. What is the most important thing I know about this topic?
   _____

2. What else do I know about this topic?
   _____
   _____
   _____

3. How can I group the information I've remembered into smaller lists?
   _____
   _____
   _____

Get in the habit of letting your memory help you as you read.

Part A Lesson 5

Learning About Your Roots

In this lesson you will
- read how to learn about your family's past
- learn to look for lists as you read
- begin a journal of words and ideas
- use word endings called suffixes to build your word power

Skills for Reading: Listing

Picture It

What do these items have in common? They all show patterns.

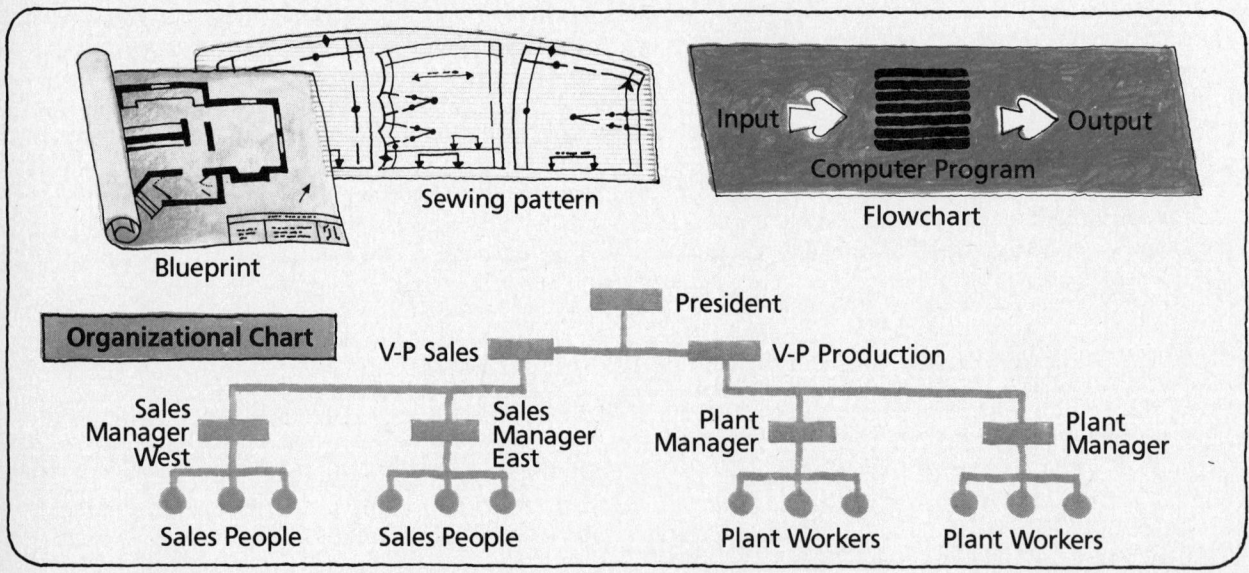

A pattern helps you see how things fit together. Did you know that authors also use patterns? A pattern helps an author organize ideas.

First, seeing a pattern helps you know the author's purpose for writing. Second, the pattern helps you order the ideas in your mind. That helps you understand and remember what you've read.

One pattern you're likely to find as you read is listing. Sometimes the author lists things that are the same. They may be details that explain or describe something. They may be examples. Or they may be reasons for doing something.

Sometimes, the author lists things in a special order. They may be listed from largest to smallest or from least important to most important. Other times, the list may be in no special order.

The author may use clues to help you see the list. Look for words like *most important, next in size, in this list, among other examples,* and *the following.*

Here's an Example

In this passage the author lists the things a person must learn to become a manager.

■ Many workers would like to have their boss's job some day. That is, they would like to become a manager. Some workers think that if they know their job, they can manage others who do the job. But knowing the job is just the first requirement. Managing people takes other skills that must be learned.

A manager must learn what the workers can do. Then the manager can assign jobs to those workers. A manager needs to know about money and how to stay within a budget. Perhaps most important, a manager has to learn about people—not just their names but their needs for job satisfaction and personal challenge.

Can you see the list of things a person must learn to be a manager? A good manager knows (1) the job, (2) the abilities of the workers to do the job, (3) how to handle money and stay within a budget, and (4) the needs of the workers. The author didn't number the list in that way. But there are two clue words to signal the pattern for you: *first* and *most important.* Those terms signal the beginning and end of the list.

Working It Out

Use what you've learned to see the listing pattern in this paragraph.

■ People's last names sometimes tell the work their ancestors did for a living. A person with the last name of Baker, for instance, probably had ancestors who made a living by baking. Other English names that hint at jobs are Hunter, Carpenter, Miller, and Taylor. The German Schmidt is the same as the English Smith. A smith is someone who works with metal like gold or silver. And the name Lemaire is really French for "the mayor."

Answer each question in a few words.

1. What is the main point the author makes about some people's last names?

_____

2. What is the author listing in the paragraph?

   _____

3. Circle a term that clues you to the list in the paragraph.

Writing to Improve Your Reading

Many people keep a journal of ideas and interesting words they read or hear. The journal is like a bank. A person enters words and thoughts in a small notebook to save them for later use. They can be used for writing letters or memos. They also increase the knowledge of ideas and words a person brings to his or her reading.

You can begin a journal of your own now. You may want to work with a friend. It's best to use a small notebook. Note thoughts and words that interest you. Listen for examples of useful ideas as you watch TV or read. Enter the ideas you would like to save in your journal. Your journal may begin to look like this sample:

Peace cannot be kept by force. It can only be achieved by understanding.
— Albert Einstein
serendipity - "lucky accident"

Reading on Your Own

Not all learning is for useful reasons like getting a better job. Learning can be just for fun too. For example, have you ever wondered about your ancestors—the earlier members of your family? Do you think there might be a hero or a princess or a famous inventor in your family's past? Read to find out how you can learn about your family's history. As you read, note how the list helps you organize the information for yourself.

Finding Family Roots

Finding your family roots is like solving a puzzle. It can be work, but it's fun work.

The easist place to start is with your own family. Talk to your parents and grandparents, aunts and great-aunts, uncles and great-uncles. Older family members can tell you many stories about your relations.

In addition, some relatives may have kept old letters and papers. Many families keep records of births, weddings, and deaths in a book such as a Bible. Another place to look is a family album. Names and dates may be written on the backs of pictures there. Often names, dates, and places were sewn onto the backs of old family quilts. Sometimes important facts about a family were even written on the walls of an old home.

If you're interested in finding out still more, turn to government and other official sources. County records of births, deaths, and marriages may tell you more. Government records can also show family ownership of land. If your family has lived in a certain area for a long time, grave markers in a nearby churchyard may show names and dates. Church records may also give information about family relationships.

If you're really serious about learning your family's past, consider joining one of the many clubs for people exploring their family history. Or you can visit one of the special libraries devoted to family histories.

Of course, you can always just hire a genealogist to do all the work for you. But then, that would take all the fun out of the learning too.

Genealogy is the study of family history. A genealogist is a person who studies genealogy for a living.

Thinking About What You've Read

1. What information is the author listing in the article?
   _____
   _____

2. A man wants the easiest way to learn his family's past. What should he do?
   _____
   _____
   _____

3. A woman is very serious about learning her family's past. What two places should she think of turning to?
   _____
   _____
   _____

4. What four kinds of information can you find in county and other government records?
   _____
   _____
   _____

5. Are you interested in learning about your family's past? If so, explain why. If not, explain why not. Try to list at least two reasons.
   _____
   _____
   _____
   _____
   _____

GED Warm-up

Which of the following is the *main* purpose of the author of this article?

(1) to persuade you to learn about your family's past
(2) to inform you on how to learn about your family's past
(3) to entertain you with stories of searching for a family's past

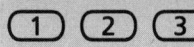

Working with Words

Sometimes you may read a word that you think you know, but the ending is different. The word may have a suffix on it. A suffix is a word part that is added to the end of a word to make a new word.

Here are three common suffixes and their meanings. See how the new word created by a suffix is related in meaning to the main word, or root word.

-**ship** = the condition of being a _____
Friendship is the condition of being a friend.

-**less** = without _____
Something that is *effortless* is done without effort on your part.

-**ment** = the act of _____ing
Your *enjoyment* of something is the act of enjoying it.

For each sentence, use the hint in parentheses to decide which word with a suffix best completes the sentence.

1. Older family members can tell you _____ stories about your relations.
   (count + -less)

2. If you're interested in finding out still more, turn to _____ sources.
   (govern + -ment)

3. Church records may also give information about family _____ .
   (relation + -ship + -s)

4. Government records can also show family _____ of land.
   (owner + -ship)

When you read a word that looks a little strange, see if you can break it into a word you know plus a word ending. If so, put the meaning of the root word with the meaning of the suffix to figure out the meaning of the word.

▲ Looking Back

In this lesson you read about ways in which you can learn about your family's history. You also read how people's family names might reveal the work they once did and how moving up at work might take some special learning.

While you were reading, you saw how authors sometimes organize their ideas by listing them. You also practiced working with suffixes. As you continue to read, look for ideas and words that you would like to keep in a journal.

The Active Reader

Setting a Purpose

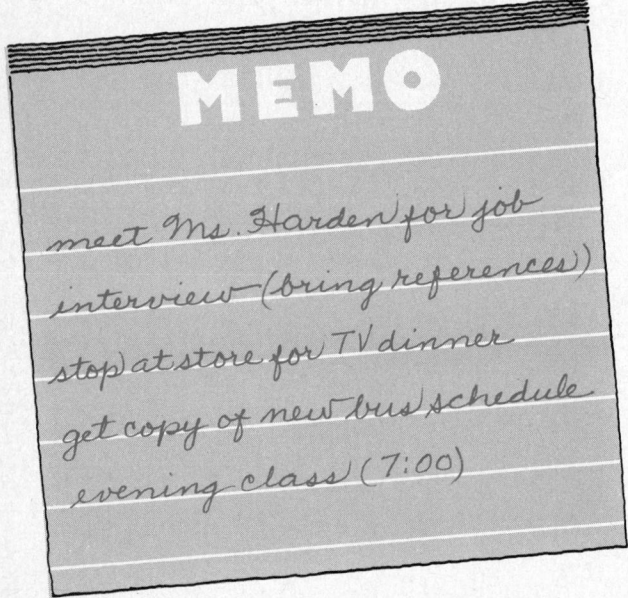

Picture It

Ray knew he had a busy day ahead, so he wrote this list of things he needed to do. By writing the list, Ray set a purpose for himself. The list helped him concentrate on what he needed to do, so he avoided wasting time and energy.

In much the same way, you can become a better reader by setting a purpose each time you read.

Here's an Example

Think about the different types of reading you've done recently. Have you read an ad on a billboard or in a newspaper? Have you used a phone book? Perhaps you had to find out where you could buy something you needed. If so, you may have used the Yellow Pages to learn the name of a store and perhaps its location.

Have you read directions for making a snack or putting together a model? If so, your purpose was to gather information and understand it well enough to know what steps to take.

Have you read a letter from a friend? For that type of reading, your purpose would be to understand the information and opinions your friend wants to share with you.

Since you are reading a textbook right now, you can add still another type of reading to the list of things you've read lately. Often when you read a textbook, the purpose is set for you, either by the authors of the book or by your teacher. You may be told to look for specific information. You may need to find out what happens in a story. You may need to learn an author's beliefs and opinions or the way to do something.

Setting a purpose *before* you read—or keeping in mind the purpose that has been set for you—will help you understand and remember more of what you read.

Working It Out

Think about each of the kinds of reading material listed below. What would your purpose probably be for reading each one? Choose a purpose from the list and write it down. The first one is done for you. (It's hard to imagine anyone reading an income tax form for enjoyment!)

Purposes for reading

- for enjoyment
- for information
- to find out the author's opinions and beliefs
- to find out how to do something

1. instructions for your federal income tax form
   to find out how to do something

2. a love story
   _____

3. a front-page newspaper article
   _____

4. an editorial in a newspaper
   _____

5. a magazine article on why we should protect the environment
   _____

6. a recipe
   _____

7. a comic book
   _____

8. an advertisement
   _____

9. a mystery story
   _____

10. directions for using a VCR
    _____

You can state your purpose for reading in the form of a **question**. For example, suppose you saw an editorial in the newspaper on crime in our streets. You might ask yourself, "What does the author think we should *do* about crime in our streets?" Then, as you read, you can look for the answer to that question.

Below are the titles of some newspaper articles. For each one, write a purpose for reading the article. Write it as a question you hope will be answered.

11. *The Prison System: Cries for Reform*
    _____

12. *Summer Fruits Make Great Salads*
    _____

13. *U.S. President Vetoes Gun-Control Bill*
    _____

14. *Renting May Be Your Best Choice*
    _____

15. *New Fall Cars Are Here!*
    _____

16. *What You Eat Affects Your Health*

Lesson 5 Learning About Your Roots / 45

Part A
Lesson 6

An Exciting Job

In this lesson you will
- read about a man who has an exciting job
- see how authors organize their ideas by putting them in time order
- learn about words that have more than one meaning

Skills for Reading: Time Order

Picture It

As you read this cartoon, find out what happens first, next, and so on.

PEANUTS ®   Charles M. Schulz

Who was in the pool first? You can see that Lucy was. Did you feel sorry for Lucy when she had to move to the bird bath? If you did, part of the reason is that you knew she was in the pool first. The order of events helps make the cartoon funny.

Sometimes authors organize their ideas by noting the order in which events happen. If you notice what happens first, next, and so on, you'll understand the author's message.

One way to discover the time order in your reading is to look for words that are clues. For instance, note words like *first, next, then,* and *last.* Also, words like *before, after, during, soon,* and *meanwhile* are clues to when events take place. Sometimes phrases will tell you the time of day or season of the year in which events happened. These include *in the morning, all evening,* and *last winter.*

Here's an Example

Read the following paragraph. As you read, pay attention to the order in which events happen. The clue words that tell the order are in **bold**.

■ Tina Yount got a new job as a travel agent. **In the morning,** she woke up **early** and dressed in her best suit. **After** breakfast, she caught a bus to the agency. **Before** she began, her boss, Joan Klein, showed Tina how to use the computer. **Once** she had practiced for a while, Tina answered her first call. She was eager to book her first flight.

The clue words tell you the order in which the different events took place.

For instance, *when* did Tina get up? If you read the paragraph again, you'll see that she got up *early in the morning.*

What did Tina do *first,* learn the computer or answer the telephone? If you look back through the paragraph, you'll find *two* places that tell you Tina worked with the computer *before* answering her first call.

Below is a "time line" that shows the order of events in the paragraph you just read.

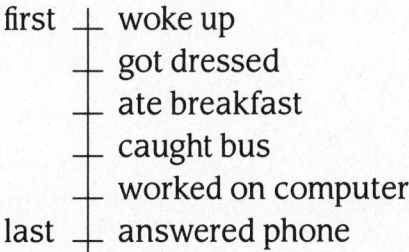

Working It Out

As you read the article below, keep track of the order of events.

■ Wally Amos was like a lot of other young men. He dropped out of high school because he was bored. Wally then joined the Air Force but soon found he could not go much farther without completing his education. So Wally studied hard for the GED Test.

Once Wally had passed the test, he turned to what he did best—cooking. Wally had a good recipe for chocolate-chip cookies. He decided to start his own cookie company. After years of hard work, Wally Amos is a success today. You may have heard of his Famous Amos cookies. Better yet, you may have tasted some.

Answer each question with a few words.

1. What did Wally Amos do right after he dropped out of high school?

_____

Lesson 6 An Exciting Job / 47

2. When did Wally begin studying for the GED Test?

_____

3. Before Wally Amos's cookie company became a success, what did he need to do?

_____

Writing to Improve Your Reading

Creating your own time line can help you keep track of the events in a long article. To make a time line, jot down the main events in the order in which they happen. Leave space between the events. As you read on, you may find that something else happened between them.

You can practice making a time line with the article that follows. To begin, read the headnote (or introduction), the title, and the first paragraph. Here's an example of the time line you could begin just from reading that far.

first — lost hands in accident when 13
— was successful high school athlete

last

As you read *Jay J. Armes, Private Eye,* look for clue words to help you keep track of time order. Jot down in a time line four or five important things that happen. The time line will help you answer the questions that follow the reading.

Reading on Your Own

When Julian Armas was thirteen, he and a friend got hold of some dynamite. They thought it would be exciting to play with. There was an accident, and Julian's hands were blown to pieces. Doctors put hooks on his arms in place of hands, but Julian knew he could no longer reach his goal of becoming a surgeon. Read to find out how his disability did not keep him from doing other exciting work. As you read, note the order of events.

Jay J. Armes, Private Eye

In high school, Julian made the baseball, basketball, and boxing teams. He had dates.

"You are handicapped only if you think you are," he said.

He graduated from high school.

He thought he'd like to be a movie star, so he went to Hollywood. He stayed there six years. He didn't become a star. But in those six years he had small parts in thirty-six movies and twenty-eight TV shows.

Directors liked his big build, black hair, and smile. But one director told him his name didn't sound good for the movies. That's when Julian Armas became Jay J. Armes.

Armes decided he didn't want to be an actor all his life. So he went back to school for a degree in criminology. He wanted to learn why some people get into a life of crime. After Armes got his degree, he headed back to Texas. He knew what he wanted to be. He wanted to be an investigator.

Getting started wasn't easy. Armes rented an office in El Paso. He hired a secretary. He hired ten agents. But then, he tells us, "Nothing happened. I wasn't even asked to find a lost dog."

He learned he'd better go to the people. He couldn't afford to wait for them to come to him. He went out looking for people who needed help. He paid for radio ads.

He found people who had been robbed. Some of them felt the police weren't doing enough to find the robbers and the stolen goods.

He found people whose children had run away from home.

The people looked at Armes's hooks. Some thought he couldn't do the job.

Armes told them, "If I take your case, I will stay on it all the way down the line. If I don't solve it, I won't charge you a cent."

Soon Armes had more work than he could handle. He caught

shoplifters. He caught robbers. He found missing wives, husbands, children, friends, and lovers.

More and more people called on him. He solved cases for kings and presidents. He did jobs for Elvis Presley, Frank Sinatra, and Elizabeth Taylor.

Armes calls his cases "capers." They got tougher and tougher. But, Armes tells us, he has never had a caper he couldn't solve.

Thinking About What You've Read

1. Armes couldn't be a surgeon. He didn't become a movie star. What job did he finally take on?

   _____

2. List some clue words from the story that help you keep track of the order of events.

   _____

3. Number the events listed below to show the order in which they happened in the story.

   _____ Armes became an actor.

   _____ Armes decided he didn't want to be an actor.

   _____ Armes became a private investigator.

   _____ Armes earned a degree in criminology.

   _____ Many people hired Armes to do investigations.

   _____ Armes advertised his business on the radio.

4. Do you think Armes is the sort of person who likes excitement? Give reasons for your answer.

   _____
   _____
   _____

> **GED Warm-up**
>
> When did Armes change his name?
> (1) during one of his "capers" as a private investigator
> (2) while he was working as a movie actor
> (3) when he graduated from high school
>
> ① ② ③

Working with Words

What does the word *date* mean? One answer is that it means a particular day, month, and year. But does that meaning fit with this sentence from *Jay J. Armes, Private Eye*?

   In high school, Julian made the baseball, basketball, and boxing teams. He had dates.

In this paragraph, *dates* has a different meaning. The paragraph is about high school activities. In this situation *date* means going out with a girl.
   Clearly, *date* has more than one meaning. Can you think of another meaning for *date*? (Hint: Think of something to eat.) Write the third meaning on the line below.

_____

Many words in English have more than one meaning. It's just about impossible to know which meaning the author intends unless you see the word in a sentence.
   Following are some sentences from *Jay J. Armes, Private Eye*. Two definitions are given after each sentence. Circle the definition that tells what the **bold** word means as it is used in the sentence.

1. Jay J. Armes never became a **star**.
   leading actor   heavenly light

2. Armes got a **degree** in criminology.
   unit of temperature   college diploma

3. Armes solved a robbery **case**.
   box for storage   problem to solve

4. Jay J. Armes could **handle** any case.
   manage   part of an item to be held

Now practice using context clues to figure out the meaning of these words. Circle the definition that tells what the **bold** word means in the sentence.

5. **Board** the train at noon.
   close up with planks   get on

6. The **board** of education met.
   block of wood   committee

7. Hammer a nail in the **board**.
   block of wood   committee

8. He will **play** the guitar.
   perform music with   act the role of

9. The home team will **play** the Sox.
   perform music   compete against

▲ Looking Back

The article you read in this lesson described how a disabled man went on to succeed at an exciting job. The lesson also showed you how to look for the order of events. You learned how to make a time line to help you remember that order.
   As you continue to read, look for clue words such as *first, next, then,* and *last* to help you see time order. You can make a time line if the order of events is difficult to understand.

The Active Reader

Controlling Your Reading Rate

Picture It
What do these things make you think of?

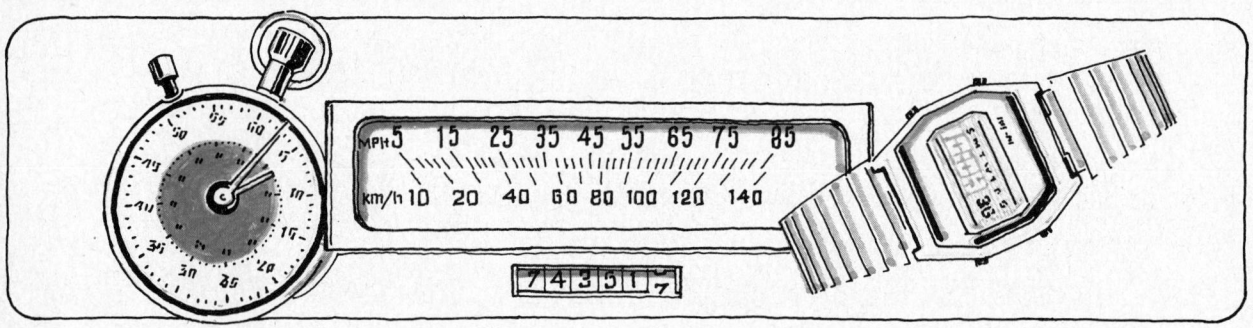

All these things measure rate. Rate is the speed at which you do something. In reading, rate means the speed at which you read. You might be surprised to learn that reading fast is not always best for you. Sometimes speed is helpful, but other times it can work against you. What is important is to be able to change your reading rate.

You've learned that you read for different purposes: to enjoy, to be informed, to get the author's opinions and beliefs, and to learn how to do something. Your purpose for reading helps affect your rate of reading.

Here's an Example
Sometimes you simply want to skim to find a name, a number, or some other piece of information.

For this purpose you can move your eyes very quickly over the lines of print. You don't read everything on the page. Your eyes just try to spot the words or the numbers you're looking for.

When you read for enjoyment, your rate is slower than with skimming. You want to be able to catch the main events. But your rate can still be brisk.

When you read to discover an author's opinions, you need to slow down even more. You want to know all that the author says. You want to know how he or she says it. You want to have time to stop and think, "Do I really agree with this idea? How can it be useful to me?"

When you are reading for information, you'll also want to read slowly and carefully. Even if you can read quickly, you may want to give your mind time to take in the ideas and understand them.

The more practice you have in changing your reading rate, the easier it will become. You can use the paragraphs below for practice.

Working It Out

The sentence above each of the following practice paragraphs tells what your reading purpose should be. Before you begin reading, circle the rate that you think will be best for that paragraph. Then read the selection, keeping to the speed you've chosen.

1. Your purpose is to read for enjoyment. What is the best rate?

   skimming speed   medium speed
   slow speed

   ■ Our cabin had been vacant for a year. It seemed as if mice and bats had taken over. For our first evening, we cleaned as well as we could. Then we fell asleep. About midnight, the dogs woke us with angry barking. Even after they had quieted, I did not sleep well. The same thing happened for two more nights. On the fourth night, I slept with a flashlight nearby. When the dogs barked, I quickly ran and opened the door. A streak of rusty fur parted the bushes. A fox! It held something in its teeth. When day dawned, I discovered what the fox had stolen: the dogs' feeding dish, full of tempting dog food.

2. Your purpose is to find out what percent of cancers may be related to our environment. What is the best rate?

   skimming speed   medium speed
   slow speed

   ■ There are things you can do to help protect yourself and your family from cancer. Scientists have discovered many factors that can cause cancer. Eighty percent of all cancers, in fact, may be related to the environment and to things we eat, drink, and smoke, rather than to factors we cannot control, such as our family background.

3. Your purpose is to understand what a tornado is and when one can occur. What is the best rate?

   skimming speed   medium speed
   slow speed

   ■ In spring and summer, giant thunderstorms with swirling winds form day after day in tornado alley. In perhaps one out of a hundred storms, the swirling winds move downward from the base of a thunderstorm—and a tornado strikes.

   Scientists still do not know quite why this happens. But they have discovered that when warm, moist air from the Gulf of Mexico collides with drier air from the mountains, tornadoes are possible.

Part A Lesson 7

Step-by-step Learning

In this lesson you will

- read how to get a passport, how maple syrup is made, and how to change a tire
- see how authors organize their ideas by writing them as the steps in a process
- find out how the history of some words can help you remember their meanings

Skills for Reading: Steps in a Process

Picture It

Can you tell what product is being made?

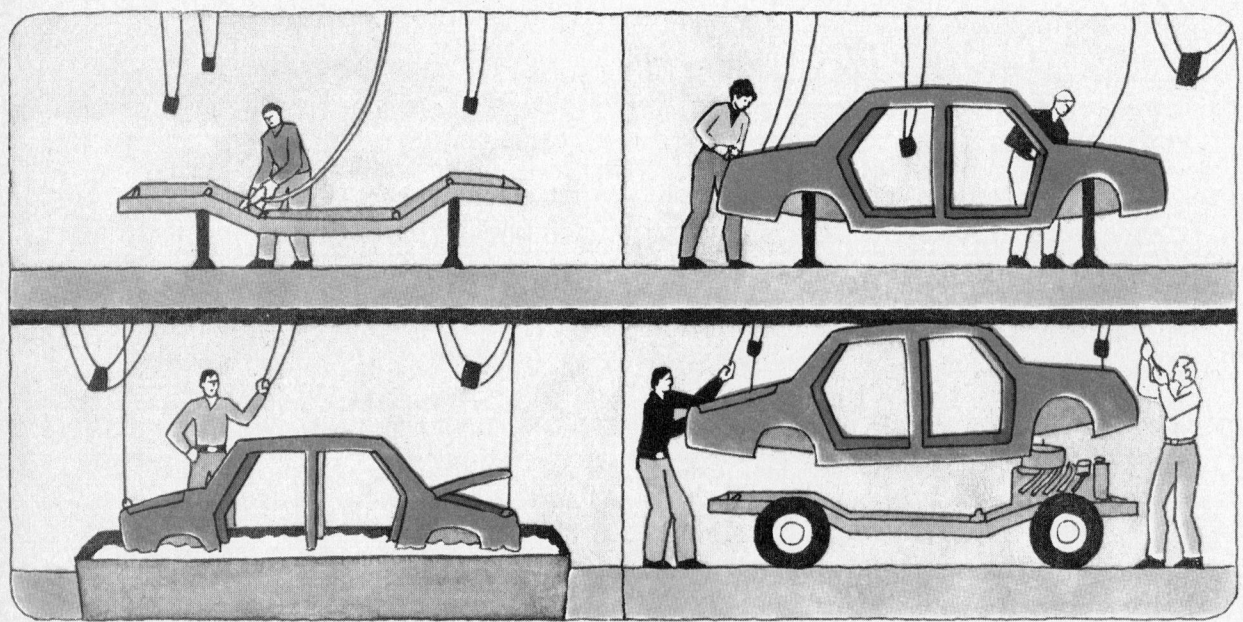

The workers in an assembly line work together to complete a process. Each worker takes charge of one step and then sends the product on to the next person

54 / Part A Reading Skills for Life

on the line. An assembly line is a good way to picture the steps in a process. You can see that each step must follow a certain order, or the product will not be right.

When do you read steps in a process? You do each time you follow a recipe to prepare a food or follow directions for taking medicine. Sometimes the topic of a longer article is a process. When an author writes about a process, he or she will usually organize the steps from first to last. You may have noticed that sometimes an author will even number the steps so that you know which step to take first, next, and so on.

Here's an Example

Read the steps in the process it takes to get a passport. As you read, try to picture each step in your mind. This will help you understand each step.

How to Get a Passport
■ Americans who go to most other countries need to have a passport. Getting a passport is easy as long as you follow the steps.

1. Gather all the papers you need. You must have your Social Security number and proof that you are a citizen of the United States.

2. Get passport photos. You need two photos, exactly the same. The pictures must be two inches by two inches. They can be in black and white or in color. Most photographers' studios can make them. Some travel agencies also have special cameras for passport photos.

3. When all your papers are together, you are ready to apply for the passport. You can apply at your county courthouse or at a large post office. You may want to call first to see how much the fee is. **Then** take the money, papers, and photos to the courthouse or post office. You will be asked to fill out an application form. **Then** you will need to swear that the information you've given is true.

4. Your passport will be mailed to you. In most cases, the wait is about six weeks. It's best to be safe, though, and allow plenty of time.

The steps in the process are numbered. You can see clearly what things you must do before you go to apply for a passport.

Also, the author used clue words to help you understand the order of the steps. The words *When, Then,* and *Then* show the order of some smaller steps within step 3.

Working It Out

Have you ever poured *real* maple syrup over hot pancakes? Some people make maple syrup for a living. The next article tells about the process they follow to make the syrup.

As you read each step in the process, try to picture it in your mind. Then use facts from the passage to answer the questions that follow.

Making Maple Syrup
■ Early in the spring, sap begins to flow in sugar maple trees. That's the time for syrup farmers to collect the sap. First, they drill two or three small holes

slanting up into the trunk of each tree. Next, they drive a metal spout into each hole. A pail hangs from the spout and collects the colorless, tasteless sap.

    The sap is then taken to a sugar house, where it is gently cooked in a large pan. As the water cooks away, the sap becomes thicker and sweeter. About forty gallons of sap will make one gallon of syrup. Finally, the farmers cool the delicious syrup and put it into bottles.

Reread the passage to find the answers to the following questions if you need to.

1. How can you tell which step comes first, next, and last? (Circle two.)
   A. The steps are numbered.
   B. Clue words are used.
   C. The steps are written in the order they should be taken.

2. Why is the time of year important to the process?

   _____

3. Write numbers to show the order in which these steps should be taken.

   _____ The syrup is bottled.

   _____ Spouts are driven into the trees.

   _____ Small holes are drilled into the trees.

   _____ Sap is cooked.

   _____ Sap is collected.

Writing to Improve Your Reading

Do you like to fix up old cars? Do you like to try different recipes? Would you like to decorate a home someday? Would you like to find out more about your own religion? Magazine articles have been written about these and countless other topics. If you don't already clip and save articles that may be useful to you someday, you may want to start. It's easy to make a magazine file. Here's how.

    Whenever you are waiting in a doctor's or dentist's office, for example, or when you have time to read your own magazines, note any article that interests you. Get a copy of the article and place it in a file folder. (If the magazine is yours, you can just cut out the article. If it belongs to someone else, you need to get a photocopy.) Write the title and the date of the magazine across the top of the first page. Add a comment about how the article might be useful. Then write the name of the topic on the file folder and drop the article in.

    If you find other articles on the same topic, you can keep them all together in the same folder. You may want to keep your file folders in a large cardboard box, where you can find them easily and add new articles to them.

    The articles in your file can help you learn to do specific things. They can also help improve your reading in general, because the more you read, the better you get.

Reading on Your Own

You're driving along the highway. Suddenly you feel that something is wrong. Your car jerks and bumps roughly. You are getting a flat tire. Do you know how to change a tire? The following selection describes the process involved. Read to find out what to do first, next, and so on.

How to Change a Tire

Get Ready Drive or push your car well off the highway. Have all passengers get out to lessen the weight of the car. Set the parking brake. Then place a large stone or piece of wood in front of and behind a wheel at the other end of the car. This will keep the car from rolling.

Get Set Take the spare tire from the car. Check to be sure it has enough air. Then get the jack and tire iron. Place the jack under the car next to the tire you must change. Raise the car until the wheel turns freely. Take off the hub cap. Loosen the lug nuts with the tire iron. When all lug nuts have been loosened, remove them and put them in a safe place.

Make the Change Take the old wheel off the car and put the spare on in its place. Put all the lug nuts back on. Tighten them in a cross pattern. That is, when you have tightened one, rotate the wheel and do the one across from it. Now gently lower the car, using the jack. Go back and tighten each lug nut until firm. Put the hub cap back on.

Go—with Caution Put your tools and the tire with the puncture back in the car. If you have a space-saver spare, as many new cars have, do not drive a long way on it. Drive to the nearest service station and have your tire repaired.

Thinking About What You've Read

1. Why couldn't you work on the third set of steps before you complete the second set?
   _____
   _____

2. Circle the *two* reasons that tell why the pictures next to the instructions are helpful.
   A. The pictures attract your attention.
   B. You can see what each tool is like.
   C. You learn the causes of flat tires.
   D. The pictures help you see how the steps fit together.

3. Why should you clear all the passengers from the car?
   _____
   _____

4. What should you do when you take the spare tire from the car?
   _____
   _____

5. Why do you think it is important to read all the steps in a process before you begin working?
   _____
   _____
   _____
   _____

GED Warm-up

Before you loosen the lug nuts on the old tire, you should
(1) drive to the nearest service station
(2) raise the car until the wheel moves
(3) put the spare tire on the car

① ② ③

Working with Words

You might be surprised to know that some of the words you use every day have been around for many hundreds of years. Others are only a few years old.

Learning about the history of some words can help you remember their meanings. The best place to look for the history of a word is in a large dictionary. The history is usually given after the definition.

Below are some words from the article *How to Change a Tire.* Read each word and then complete the sentence that follows. A word history is given for each, but you may want to use a dictionary to find the definitions.

1. *Rotate* means _____ ; it comes from a Latin word that means "to turn."

2. *Caution* means _____ ; it comes from a Latin word that means "beware."

3. *Puncture* means _____ ; it comes from a Latin word that means "to prick."

4. *Car* means _____ ; it comes from a French word that in turn comes from a Latin word meaning "wagon."

▲ Looking Back

All through this lesson you've been learning things step by step. You read about how to get a passport, how maple syrup is made, and how to change a tire. You learned how you can make a file of useful magazine articles. You discovered that a word's history can help you learn its meaning. As you read more and more, watch for examples of writing that tells the steps in a process.

The Active Reader

Visualizing

Picture It

Have you ever heard the saying "A picture is worth a thousand words"? When you read, your mind can "see" a picture of what you are reading about. This is called **visualizing.**

A good way to remember the meaning of the word *visualize* is to recall that it comes from the word *vision,* or "sight."

Visualizing helps you sort out details and see how they fit together. It helps you understand what you read. The pictures in your mind can help you follow the steps in a process and remember their order. Visualizing also helps you follow the action in a story.

You can use all your senses to picture what is happening. Sometimes you will "hear" someone talking to you. Sometimes you will "taste" or "touch" or "smell" the topic you are reading about. As you read, try to form mental pictures that involve *all* your senses.

Here's an Example

Visualizing will help you read this passage about potting house plants. As you read, picture the steps in your mind.

■ A house plant sometimes outgrows its pot. When it does, you will need to repot it. Before you remove a plant from its pot, dampen the soil with a little water. This will help keep the roots from breaking. Then use a garden spade or kitchen knife to loosen the dirt around the edge of the pot. Turn the pot upside down and gently shake it. The plant and the dirt around its roots will slide out. Hold the plant carefully as you slide it into a larger pot. Pour extra dirt around the roots to hold the plant steady. Let the plant sit quietly for a few days.

Did you picture each step in your mind as you read? If you did, it was probably easier to follow the directions for repotting plants.

Working It Out

As you read this article about an unusual bed, form a mental picture of what the paragraph describes.

■ You may think you've seen it all. Well think again. A young man in Japan has invented an alarm bed. The bed is connected to an alarm clock. At wake-up time, the clock and bed go into action. First, the clock rings. Next, a tape recorder plays music. The recorder may also play a tape of your boss telling you to get up. If you go on sleeping the top half of the bed lifts a little. If you're still asleep, a mechanical foot kicks you. If all else fails, the bed lifts up to a slant and slides you right onto the floor.

1. What details in the passage can you hear in your mind? List them.

_____

_____

2. Can you picture the bed? Draw a picture of it below. Don't worry about your artwork. Just sketch the "bed alarm" as you picture it in action. Have fun!

What senses do you use to imagine the details in the next paragraph?

■ It's a hot summer day in the city. Fumes from hundreds of cars and buses make the air heavy. People move slowly along the sidewalk. A group of shoppers stand near a red and yellow hot dog stand. They are waiting for a bus. Far away, church bells ring the hour. Their sound is slow and heavy. Even the bells seem lazy on this hot, still day.

3. What details in the passage help you imagine odors?

_____

_____

4. Which details help you imagine sounds?

_____

_____

5. Which details make you imagine sights?

_____

_____

6. Which detail helps you feel something?

_____

Part A
Lesson 8

On the Job

In this lesson you will
- read about some workers and their jobs
- see how authors organize their ideas by classifying them
- learn how outlining can help you when you read
- use word parts called prefixes to build your word power

Skills for Reading: Classifying

Picture It

This cartoon will show you how Cathy plans to lose weight.

cathy® by Cathy Guisewite

Cathy Copyright 1988 Universal Press Syndicate. Reprinted with permission. All rights reserved.

Do you think Cathy will lose weight with her diet? The empty packages in the last picture show she probably won't.

Cathy says she wants to eat from all the food "categories." Categories are groups. Do you know the four basic food groups? They follow this paragraph. Can you add one more example to each group?

Meat, Fish, and Nuts	Grains	Fruits and Vegetables		Dairy Products
beef	oats	apples	peas	milk
pork	barley	oranges	lettuce	cheese
peanut butter	rice	bananas	celery	eggs

When you put foods into groups, you are **classifying** them. Classifying is sorting the members of a large, general group into smaller groups. Authors often classify when they write.

You'll read many articles that classify things. Certain words can help you spot this pattern. *Kind, group, sort, divide,* and *category* are some clue words.

The author may begin by telling you that he or she is sorting things. A sentence may point out how many groups you should watch for. For example, you might read, "There are three ways to figure your taxes." Then you would look for three ways as you read.

It helps you to know when an author is classifying things. Why? First, the author is telling you the groups are important. Second, the author is telling you the things in the groups are alike. Third, the pattern gives you a way to remember what you've read.

Here's an Example

Joe Linori works at a video rental shop. He decided to write a notice telling customers how to find the tapes they want. This is what he wrote.

■ The tapes in this store are **sorted** into three main **groups:** comedy, action, and drama. Comedies, the first group, can be found on the wall to your left. You'll find everything from family movies to stand-up comedians. Action films, the second group, are in the back. This **category** includes science fiction, Westerns, and thrillers. Dramas, the third group, are on the wall to your right. They range from classics like *Gone with the Wind* to current films on romance and personal relationships.

Joe used a classifying pattern in the notice he wrote. To help his customers see the pattern, he used clue words. Find these words in **bold**: *sorted, groups,* and *category.* These words tell you the writer is classifying things. Joe also used words like *first, second,* and *third* to identify each group.

Working It Out

This article is about Elaine Katz's job. Look for classified groups as you read. Then you can answer the questions that follow.

■ Elaine is like many modern women. She has a job as a manager. She manages a clothes shop in a large mall. Elaine's duties fall into three categories: managing the sales clerks, handling money matters, and controlling the store's stock.

Managing the clerks includes hiring and sometimes firing. Elaine also has to plan the work hours, train new clerks, and solve workers' problems.

Handling money matters includes paying rent to the mall and other bills. It also includes giving the clerks their paychecks. And every day Elaine must record the store's sales. Then she deposits the money in the bank.

Controlling the stock is the part of Elaine's job she likes the most. This group of duties includes ordering new clothes. Elaine also plans sales to push old clothes. And she decides how to advertise these sales.

1. What is the large, general topic that the writer divided into categories?

   _____

2. What clue words that signal classified groups can you find in the article?

   _____

3. What three main categories were discussed in the article?

   _____

   _____

Writing to Improve Your Reading

Have you ever made an outline of an article? If so, you may have decided that outlining is like classifying. In both, you take a large, general topic. Then you divide it into smaller groups.

When you outline, write down the main categories. You can number them for easy spotting. Under each main category, write down the items in that group. You can mark them with letters.

Here's an example of an outline. A woman wrote this outline as she read about Elaine Katz's job.

Elaine's Job Duties

1. Managing sales clerks
   a. Hiring
   b. Firing
   c. Planning work hours
   d. Training new clerks
   e. Solving problems
2. Handling money matters
   a. Paying rent and other bills
   b. Handing out paychecks
   c. Recording sales
   d. Depositing money in bank
3. Controlling stock
   a. Ordering new clothes
   b. Planning sales
   c. Deciding how to advertise

The outline shows you the main categories at a glance. Can you see how? It also shows you which job duties fall within those categories. The outline helps you organize the information in your mind. When you organize information, you can remember it much more easily.

As you read *Finding a Good Job,* think about how you would outline the story.

Reading on Your Own

After the Vietnam War ended, many people from Vietnam came to the United States. It was not always easy for them to find jobs. This story tells about one man's search for a good job. Read to find out how he made himself understood, even though he spoke little English. As you read, see if you can find classified groups.

Finding a Good Job

"Good morning," smiled the lady at the front desk. "Can I help you?"

Mr. Ho smiled back and nodded yes. He hoped this agency would find him work. The last three places he had gone had not helped at all. The lady with the smile led Mr. Ho to Mr. Orr's desk. Mr. Orr looked like a busy man. He liked to do everything fast. He disliked wasting time.

"Want a job?" snapped Mr. Orr. "What kind?"

"Computer," said Mr. Ho. He spoke very carefully. He knew some words in English, but not very many. In Vietnam he had been trained as a computer operator. Then South Vietnam began to lose the war. Everyone's biggest job became just staying alive.

"What kind of computer do you work with?" asked Mr. Orr. "Micro? Personal? A big mainframe?"

At first Mr. Ho misunderstood. He shook his head and said again, "Computer."

"What *kind* of computer work?" asked Mr. Orr again. He spoke loudly, as if shouting would make Mr. Ho understand.

"There are four kinds of computer jobs," explained Mr. Orr. "There are sales jobs, repair jobs, programming jobs, and operating jobs." He thought a moment and then said, "Jobs in sales won't work because of your lack of English." Mr. Ho understood *English* and nodded.

"Can you do repairs?" Mr. Orr ran his fingers through his hair restlessly. "Do you install parts? Fix wiring? Replace parts?" Mr. Ho opened his hands to show he did not understand. "Do you do programming? Do you know any computer language?"

Mr. Ho was becoming worried. He took a pencil and paper. He drew a stick figure of a man placing a large computer tape on a

The United States pulled out of Vietnam in 1973.

Mr. Orr is naming kinds of computers. A "micro"-computer is a small computer. A "personal" computer is for home use. A "mainframe" computer is used by large companies.

Lesson 8 On the Job / 65

computer. Then he drew a figure of a man moving the controls on a computer.

Mr. Orr understood. "You're a computer operator! Now we're getting somewhere!" He slumped back happily in his chair.

Mr. Orr checked his file. "Would you like full-time or part-time work?" he asked.

"Full-time day," said Mr. Ho. "Nighttime for English classes."

"I think we're in business," said Mr. Orr. He handed Mr. Ho a card with an address on it. "Find a friend who speaks English to go with you. I'll call the company for an interview. We can all meet here at a preset time. Good luck!"

Thinking About What You've Read

1. What four types of computer jobs did Mr. Orr mention?
_____

2. What type of job did Mr. Ho have in Vietnam?
_____

3. Why wasn't Mr. Ho able to take a job selling computers?
_____

4. Here is part of an outline of the article you just read. Complete the outline by filling in the blanks. The information you need is in the story.

   Mr. Orr mentions four types of jobs with computers.
   a. Some jobs are for sales people.
   b. Some jobs involve repairing computers.
   c. Some jobs involve programming.
   d. _____

   Mr. Orr mentions two kinds of work hours.
   a. Full-time
   b. _____

5. What are some jobs that would be good for a person in the United States who is learning English? Try to list three.
_____
_____

A Test-Taking Tip

Sometimes an answer looks right because it repeats words from the article. But read closely. It may not really answer the question. Once you choose an answer, read the question again. Make sure the answer you've picked answers the question.

GED Warm-up

How did Mr. Ho finally get Mr. Orr to understand the kind of work he did?
(1) He brought a friend who speaks English.
(2) He drew a picture of what he did.
(3) He explained to him in computer language.

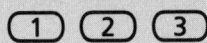

Working with Words

Here are three words you read in *Finding a Good Job*.

    dis**liked**   mis**understood**   pre**set**

Perhaps you had trouble with the whole words. But you probably know the parts of the words in **bold**. They are main words, or root words. They have word parts called prefixes added to them. A prefix is added to the front of a word. That makes a new word. Add the meaning of the prefix to the meaning of the root word. Then you'll understand the new word.

Here are the meanings of the three prefixes on the words above.

dis-	not	He disliked wasting time. = He did not like wasting time.
mis-	wrongly	At first Mr. Ho misunderstood. = At first Mr. Ho understood wrongly.
pre-	before	We can all meet here at a preset time. = We can all meet here at a time set beforehand.

These meanings can help you a lot when you read. Use them to write the meanings of the following words.

1. *preview* means _____
2. *mistrust* means _____
3. *dishonest* means _____
4. *prewar* means _____
5. *displease* means _____
6. *mislead* means _____
7. *preheat* means _____
8. *preschool* means _____
9. *disagree* means _____
10. *disrespect* means _____
11. *misplace* means _____

▲ Looking Back

In this lesson you read about three workers. You learned about three prefixes too. You saw how to outline an article. And you saw how authors classify ideas in their articles. These skills will help you in all your reading.

Lesson 8 On the Job / 67

The Active Reader

Restating

Picture It

You already know about restating. You read about it on page 8. And you've been doing it ever since. Restating is putting someone else's thoughts in your own words.

Restating is useful when you read a complicated idea. You can restate the idea in simpler terms. Restating is also useful when you want to "test" yourself. If you can restate an author's ideas, you can feel sure you understand them.

Here's an Example

Read the first statement about Bill Leonard's job. Then read the second one. It says the same thing in simpler words.

- Bill Leonard's original employment was with a large, influential bank.
- Bill Leonard first worked for a big, important bank.

When you can restate like that, you are a good, active reader.

Working It Out

Here are more sentences about Bill Leonard's work. Read each group. Then put a check next to the restatement that is closer in meaning to the first sentence in the group.

1. Eventually, another bank managed to acquire Bill's bank.
   ____ Bill's bank purchased another bank.
   ____ As time went on, another bank took over the bank Bill worked for.

2. Bill's employment was terminated.
   ____ Bill lost his job.
   ____ Bill fired people who worked for him.

3. Bill concluded that he should found a business of his own.
   ____ Bill thought he should find a better business to work for.
   ____ Bill decided to open a business.

4. Bill has developed a successful business selling automobile parts.
   ____ Selling automobile parts seems to be what Bill does best.
   ____ Bill has a good business selling car parts.

Now read each of these groups of sentences. Cross out the sentence that is *not* a restatement of the first sentence.

5. Vanessa's bicycle simply vanished.
   Vanessa's bike was stolen.
   Vanessa's bike was missing.
   Vanessa's bike could not be found.

6. Vanessa filed a report with law officers.
   Vanessa reported the loss to the police.
   The police were told by Vanessa about the missing bicycle.
   The police reported that Vanessa's bike was stolen.

7. Eventually, Vanessa's companion returned the bicycle.
   Later, Vanessa's friend brought back the bike.
   The bike was brought back in time by Vanessa's friend.
   Vanessa's friend had borrowed her bike for a time.

Restate each sentence below. Use the same idea, but put it in your own words. Try to make the sentence simpler. You can use a dictionary if you'd like.

8. The weather service predicted a violent gale.
   _____

9. Enormous hailstones savagely struck our dwelling.
   _____

10. The precipitation forced us to remain indoors.
    _____

11. The deluge continued throughout the twilight hours.
    _____

Part A Lesson 9

Learning for Living

In this lesson you will
- read about credit cards
- see how authors organize their ideas by comparing and contrasting them
- use context clues to find the meanings of unfamiliar words

Skills for Reading: Comparing and Contrasting

Picture It

Rita Nuncio has an interesting job. She makes costumes for actors in movies. Right now she's making a copy of an outfit worn by George Washington. An actor in a TV show will wear the costume. Rita looked at as many paintings of George Washington as she could find. Then she drew a pattern for the clothes.

Look at the picture again. Do you see ways in which Rita's costume is like the original? You are comparing the two outfits.

Comparing is showing how people, events, or things are alike. An author may use special words to signal a comparison. Some clue words that tell you to watch for a comparison are these:

also, as well as, like, as, and *in the same way.*

Sometimes an author shows ways in which two things are *different.* Then the author is making a **contrast.** Some words clue you to look for a contrast. They include: *however, on the other hand, though, although, while,* and *yet.*

Here's an Example

In this paragraph, two heaters are described. The author shows that one is better than the other by comparing and contrasting them.

■ Grace Pappas needed a heater to keep her room warm. At the store, she found two heaters that she could afford. Both were made by the same company. They were the same size. One heated just as much space as the other. They had the same label to show they had been checked for safety.

On the other hand, they were different in one important way. One of them cost $35 less than the other. The sales person said the cheaper one was last year's model.

Which one do you suppose Grace bought? Recall that they were alike in important ways. They were both safe. Both heated the same amount of space. They were the same size. Yet one cost less money. Don't you think Grace chose the cheaper one? Wouldn't you have done the same thing?

Working It Out

Read this next article about a man choosing food. Ask yourself, "What is being compared and contrasted?"

■ Steve Farmer has his own apartment now. He enjoys shopping and cooking his own meals.

Last week Steve tried two brands of bread: Golden Loaf and Baker's. He found that both taste good. They cost the same. Both have the same number of slices.

Steve read the list of ingredients for each. He was surprised by the difference. Baker's bread was made of flour, vegetable shortening, yeast, and a little sugar. Golden Loaf, on the other hand, was made up of things with very long names. The names sounded like chemicals. Even a little wood fiber was included. None of them seemed like anything Steve wanted to eat.

Write a few words to answer each question.

1. In what three ways are Golden Loaf and Baker's alike?

   _____

   _____

2. How is Golden Loaf different from Baker's?

   _____

   _____

Lesson 9 Learning for Living / 71

Writing to Improve Your Reading

You learned about underlining in Lesson 4. Underlining is a good way to help you remember ideas. As you underline an idea, you read it again. That helps it stick in your mind. And later, the line will help you find the idea easily.

If you want, you can use a highlighter instead of underlining. A highlighter is a colored marker. When you mark *over* the line of type, the words still show through the color. As you move the marker, you read the words over. This helps you remember them. And later, the color will draw your eyes to the idea.

Look at the following article about credit cards. A reader has highlighted the first sentence of the second paragraph. This sentence signals that the author is going to compare credit cards. As you read the article, continue to underline or highlight ideas.

If this is not your book, you can do one of two things: (1) Copy these pages on a photocopying machine. Then underline or highlight on the copies. *Or* (2) just jot down on your own paper the ideas you would underline or highlight.

Reading on Your Own

Credit cards are popular. Nearly everybody has one. There are many different cards to choose from. As you read, find out how comparing and contrasting can help you decide which credit card is right for you. Ask yourself, "How are credit cards alike? How are they different?"

What You Should Know About Credit Cards

It's hard to get along today without a credit card. Is just any credit card right for you? You need to check the facts before you decide.

In some ways all credit cards are alike. In order to get one, you must show that you are responsible. You must prove that you can pay for what you buy. When you get your own credit card, you can use it instead of cash. You can "charge" almost anything, from day-to-day needs to the costs of a trip.

When you use your credit card, the sales person records your credit card number. The amount of money you spend is also recorded. Later, the card company sends you a bill. It's best to pay the bill before the due date. If you don't, the company will charge you interest. This means you will have to pay "rent" on the money you owe. Every credit card company charges interest in this way.

While credit cards are all similar in some ways, there are also important differences. First, you should know that there are three kinds of cards. Bank cards are given by large banks. The banks send the bills and keep track of what you owe. Most bank cards can be used for many different kinds of purchases. Travel and entertainment cards are offered by travel companies and large hotel chains. Often, these cards can't be used in as many places as bank cards. They may also charge higher interest. Retail cards are given by stores and gas companies. A retail card can be used at just the stores or gas stations of one company. If you've never had a credit card before, you may find that getting a retail card is a good place to start. Retail cards often charge less interest too.

Another important difference among credit cards is the amount you must pay to use a card. Some companies charge you a fee each year just to have their cards. Others charge for each purchase or other transaction. Some cards charge much more interest than others. The charge is as low as 12 percent for some cards but as high as 21 percent for others. Some cards charge interest on unpaid bills from the day you make a purchase. Others wait a month or so before they begin charging interest.

With some credit cards, you have the option of letting family members use your card. Not all cards give you that choice. Some charge extra when family members use your card.

Have you ever received a card you did not ask for? If that happens, you can just cut up the card. It is not legal to send people such unsolicited cards. You probably would not want to trust a company that sent you one.

Finally, be sure a company states what to do if your credit card is lost or stolen. Know how much you would have to pay if your card is stolen and used to buy things. If a thief charges things with your card, you should not be held liable, or responsible, for more than fifty dollars of the bills. Of course, you need to notify the card company as soon as you know your card is missing.

Thinking About What You've Read

1. Which of the following statements describes one way in which credit card companies are alike? (Circle A or B.)
   A. They all charge interest on late bills.
   B. They all charge a fee for their cards.

2. Which of the following statements about interest charges is correct? (Circle A or B.)
   A. Retail credit card companies charge greater interest than bank cards.
   B. Different credit card companies charge different amounts of interest.

3. Which of the following statements about credit cards is true? (Circle A or B.)
   A. Some cards are accepted at more stores than other cards.
   B. Once you have a credit card, you may use it at any business.

4. What is one way in which credit cards are different?
   _____

5. Do you think having a credit card would lead you to spend more money? Explain your answer.
   _____
   _____

A Test-Taking Tip

Be sure to read all the answer choices for a multiple-choice question. Read each choice carefully before you decide on one. If you mark an answer without reading them all, you might miss the best choice.

GED Warm-up

What is one way that travel and entertainment cards are different from bank cards?

(1) Travel cards are used anywhere; bank cards are used in banks.
(2) Travel cards are used to buy things; bank cards are used to deposit money.
(3) Travel cards are given by travel companies; bank cards are given by banks.

① ② ③

Working with Words

You sometimes meet words you don't know. All readers do. Like good readers, you can use the **context.** *Context* means "the words and sentences that surround a word." Often the context of a word can help you decide what it means.

Context clues are good to use anytime. They are especially good when you don't have a dictionary nearby. Good readers use context clues first. Then they check their ideas in a dictionary when they get the chance.

There are different kinds of clues. Some examples are shown below.

> A **definition** may be given:
> A *current periodical*—the most recent issue of a magazine—may not be checked out of the library.

Such a definition is often set off with commas or dashes.

> A **synonym** may be given:
> We *unfurled* the flag and then attached the unrolled banner to the pole.

The context shows you that *unfurled* means the same as *unrolled.* They are synonyms.

> **Examples** may be given:
> *Luxury* cars, such as the Rolls Royce and Bentley, are not often seen on the road.

A Rolls Royce and a Bentley are large, rich, comfortable cars. They help you see what *luxury* means: "rich comfort, beyond what you really need."

> **Details** may be given that help you make a good guess:
> The soft knit *balaclava* covered his head, face, and neck.

Note these details: "soft knit" and "covered his head, face, and neck." These details describe a scarf. That's what a balaclava is.

Here are sentences from the article *What You Should Know About Credit Cards.* As you read, use context clues to find the meaning of each bold word. Write a short definition for each.

1. With some credit cards, you have the **option** of letting family members use your card. Not all cards give you that choice.

   Option means _____ .

2. Have you ever received a card you did not ask for? It is not legal to send people such **unsolicited** cards.

   Unsolicited means _____ .

3. If a thief charges things with your card, you should not be **liable,** or responsible, for more than fifty dollars of the bills.

   Liable means _____ .

4. Some card companies charge each time you make a purchase or other **transaction.**

   Transaction means _____ .

▲ Looking Back

In this lesson you read about some choices that consumers made. You read how credit cards can be compared and contrasted. You underlined or highlighted important points. And you used context clues to find the meanings of words. This last skill is especially helpful. You can use it whenever you read.

The Active Reader

Summarizing

Picture It

We have only 30 seconds left. Can you sum up how it feels to win a million dollars?

A **summary** is a short statement—no more than a few sentences. It gives the most important ideas of an article. You can write a summary to check yourself when you read. If you can summarize an article, you've understood its important points.

How do you write a summary of an article? You tell the main idea and the important details. You leave out all extra details, even if they are interesting. A person who has not read the article should be able to read a summary and get all the important ideas from it.

Here's an Example

Read the short article below. Try to note the important details as you read. You'll see how they are used in a summary at the end.

■ As more people use credit cards, more thieves find ways to get their money. Don't be a victim. Follow a few simple rules to protect yourself.

Sign your card in ink as soon as you get it. Write down the number of your card. Put this number in a safe place. You will need to give your credit card company the number if your card is lost.

Then treat the card as you would treat cash. Keep it in a safe place. More than half the credit card thefts are from women's purses. If you carry a purse, keep your credit card zipped or snapped inside it.

Never give your credit card number over the phone unless you are the one who has made the call. You need to know that the person or company you're dealing with is honest.

Following are two summaries of the article you've just read. Note the details in each.

A. A few simple rules help you protect against credit card theft. Sign your card, record the number, and then keep it in a safe place. Avoid giving the number over the phone.

B. Sign your credit card as soon as you get it. If a sales person calls on the phone, do not give your credit card number. A dishonest person could write down your number and then use it to buy things over the phone. You would have no way of knowing this until your bill arrived.

Summary A is better than B. Can you see why? Summary A includes these important details: you should sign a card, keep its number, keep the card in a safe place, and be sure you don't give the number to strangers. It also "sums up" all these details in the first sentence. That sentence gives you the main idea of the article. And summary A does *not* include small details.

Summary B leaves out some important points. It does not mention that you should keep your card in a safe place. It includes small, unimportant details. It has even included some information that did not appear in the article.

Working It Out

The next article is about aid for adult students. As you read, note the most important points. Then see if you can summarize the article.

Money for Your Education

■ The U.S. government has set aside money to help students pay for their education. The money is meant for study after high school. The student can be in college, trade school, or other classes.

The government gives three types of aid. All three provide the student with money. For all three, students must prove they can work hard and get good grades. And for all three, a student must meet certain other requirements.

However, the three types of aid are different in important ways. A grant is money that does not have to be paid back. People who have disabilities can apply for some grants. People who have limited savings may apply for others.

Work-study programs make it possible for people to work while taking classes. In that way, they get both work experiences and classroom learning.

Student loans offer a third type of aid. There are different kinds of loans. Each has its own requirements. Loans are money that you must pay back. You may need to pay interest too. The interest on a student loan is often less than on money borrowed from a bank.

Now see if you can write a summary of the article. Remember to write the main idea. Then include the most important details.

_____
_____
_____
_____
_____

As you study, practice summarizing the articles you read. Writing a summary helps you improve your understanding and your memory.

Part A Lesson 10

The Entertainers

In this lesson you will
- read about a popular comic, a machine that entertains, and a jazz musician
- learn how to infer ideas
- practice your summarizing and context-clue skills

Skills for Reading: Inferring Ideas

Picture It

What is Marmaduke, the big dog, planning to do?

"I hate to think what is going to happen to the poor cuckoo bird when he pops out this time."

In the cartoon, Marmaduke is ready to spring. His eyes are on the clock. When the cuckoo pops out at twelve, what will Marmaduke do?

Everything in the picture leads you to guess that Marmaduke will try to catch the bird. The cartoon doesn't tell you what Marmaduke's plans are. But the look on the dog's face leads you to guess what will happen. So does the child's comment. These details help you make a *good* guess. That good guess is called an **inference.** You **infer** Marmaduke's plan.

Inferring happens in life too. Suppose you see smoke rising from a building. You smell something burning. You hear the snapping sound of flames. No one tells you what is happening. But you *infer* that

78 / Part A Reading Skills for Life

the building is on fire. What you see, smell, and hear leads you to infer what is happening.

Inferring is also an important part of daily life. You infer when you listen to people speak. Sometimes you can guess people's feelings about a topic from the way they speak. Their voices and their faces may give away much more than their words. Suppose you are watching a police movie. As you watch, a robber points his gun. Then he says, "Get out of here or I'll. . . ." The sentence is not finished, but you can infer what the man means. He means that he will shoot!

When you read, you may need to "read between the lines" to learn something important. This means you may need to infer. There are no words between the lines of print. But you can use ideas from what the author says to figure out things that the author *doesn't* say.

Here's an Example

Read this article about the early life of comic Bill Cosby. Then you'll see how you can infer ideas about Bill Cosby.

■ Although he was only nine, Bill became the man of the house when his father left. He tried to help his mother by getting a job. Taking some rags and polish, he went downtown to shine shoes. Two years later, at age eleven, Bill spent his summer as a stockboy in a grocery store. He worked from six in the morning until six at night, with extra hours on weekends. For all that effort, he earned only eight dollars a week. Bill also had a job dusting and cleaning in a local drugstore.

Working hard didn't keep Bill from enjoying himself. Whenever he could, he went out to play with his friends. They called Bill "Cos" or "Cool Cos." Cos and his pals had a good time, even though his neighborhood didn't have many parks and yards. In fact, Bill claims he didn't know there was dirt under the cement until he was all grown up!

Look back at the first paragraph. It explains that Bill had to work at different jobs when he was very young. From this you can infer that Bill's family was poor. He would not have to work if they had money.

Now look at the last sentence of the article. Bill claims he didn't know there was dirt under the cement. From that idea, you can infer that Bill was a city boy. He was used to seeing pavement.

Working It Out

Some entertainers are machines, not people. Read this article about the early days of movies. What can you infer about Edison's invention?

■ In 1887, Thomas Edison and his workers made a camera that surprised the public. Its pictures showed motion. The Edison Company called its new camera a "Kinetoscope." Edison thought it would be good for teaching. His company made only a few motion pictures "for fun." One was the world's first horror film. Sadly for us, it has been lost over the years.

By 1903, other film companies were making movies that told stories. One of the best loved was "The Great Train Robbery." There was no sound. A piano played exciting music to go with the action. The public loved it.

Soon movie theaters called Nickelodeons sprang up all over the country. The name *Nickelodeon* comes from the nickel that people paid to get in. Soon there were more than 5,000 Nickelodeons in the country. The motion picture had become a part of our way of life.

Write a few words to answer each question.

1. Which of the following can you infer about Edison's view of his Kinetoscope? (Circle A or B.)
   A. Edison expected to make a lot of money entertaining people with his Kinetoscope.
   B. Edison did not think the Kinetoscope would become a popular form of entertainment.

2. Does the author wish that Edison's horror film could still be seen? _____ Write the sentence that helped you infer your answer.

   _____

   _____

3. In the last paragraph, the author says, "Soon there were more than 5,000 Nickelodeons in the country." What can you infer from this fact? (Circle A or B.)
   A. People didn't want to pay a lot of money to see the new movies.
   B. Movies became popular very quickly in this country.

Writing to Improve Your Reading

You've just read about summarizing on pages 76–77. A summary is a short statement. It tells the main idea of an article. It also includes the most important details.

If you can write a summary, you know you understand what you read. It's a good way to test your understanding. It's also a good way to help you focus on the main ideas.

Here's a chance to practice summarizing. As you read the next article, note the important points. Then be ready to write a summary of what you've read.

Reading on Your Own

Musician Ray Charles says that "Soul is a way of life—it is always the hard way." His music is known and loved around the world. But life has not been easy for Ray Charles. Read this article to find out how Charles learned music. Read "between the lines" to infer what style of music Charles preferred to play.

Soul Is a Way of Life

When Ray was five, something went wrong with his eyes. They began to secrete fluid. He had pain behind them. He could not see well.

Ray's mother didn't have the money to take Ray to a specialist. The doctor in the town did what he could. He told Ray to stay out of bright lights. He gave him drops to put in his eyes.

A specialist is a doctor who studies and works with one area, such as the eyes.

The drops didn't help. By the time Ray was seven, he was blind. Doctors now tell him he must have had the disease glaucoma. Glaucoma happens when the fluid of the eyes can't drain into the surrounding blood vessels. A specialist might have been able to prevent Ray's blindness.

Some blind children take a long time to adjust. Not Ray. His mother wouldn't let him sit around. "You're blind, not stupid," she told him. "You've lost your eyes, not your mind."

Aretha taught Ray to scrub floors and sweep them. She taught him to chop wood. She told him that someday she would not be there to help him. He'd have to do things for himself. He'd better learn now.

Aretha was Ray's mother.

Aretha had not had much schooling herself, but she taught Ray the alphabet. She taught him to print. She taught him a little arithmetic too.

And Ray learned about music. He learned about it from Wylie Pittman. Pittman had a café near Ray's home.

There was a piano in the café. When Pittman played, Ray came running. Sometimes Pittman would let Ray bang on the piano. He would tell Ray how well he played.

By the time Ray was seven, he could play a few tunes. He liked to sing too.

Ray Charles's name was Ray Charles Robinson. He dropped the last name when he became a performer.

The Robinsons sent Ray to the State School for the Blind in St. Augustine, Florida. There he learned Braille, which is a way of writing and printing. It uses raised dots. Blind people can read by touching these dots.

The state paid for the children's bus fare to the school in September. It paid for the bus fare home in June. It did not pay for visits home at Christmas.

Whitney Balliett is a friend of Ray's. Balliett wrote about the life and career of Ray Charles.

Whitney Balliett wrote in *The New Yorker* magazine on March 28, 1970, "Charles said, 'Somehow my mother always got the money. I remember leaving at Christmas, and there would be two or three kids left at school who wouldn't get home. I didn't want to leave them there alone. I also wanted to see my mother.'"

Ray did well in music at the school. He played pieces by the great masters—Chopin, Mozart, Bach, Beethoven. He liked knowing how to play what they wrote.

When the teacher left the room, Ray played jazz. He took more freedoms with jazz. He could experiment, play it as he pleased.

Thinking About What You've Read

1. What style of music did Ray Charles seem to prefer to play? How do you know? Explain your answer.

2. In what two places did Ray learn about music?

3. Ray's mother told him, "You've lost your eyes, not your mind." What did she mean by that? (Circle A or B.)
   A. Ray should be able to take care of himself.
   B. Ray should not feel sad that he lost his sight.

4. In a few sentences, write a summary of the article.

5. How does Ray Charles's life fit the saying "Where there's a will, there's a way"?

_____
_____

GED Warm-up

After Ray became blind, his mother taught him to scrub floors and chop wood because she wanted him to
(1) be able to take care of himself
(2) stay home with her
(3) do work she had no time to do herself

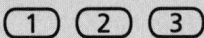

Working with Words

Here's a paragraph about Ray Charles. Read it carefully. See if you can fill in the blanks with the right words.

Ray went to the doctor because he had trouble seeing. The doctor told him to put a few _____ into his eyes. He was
                  1
also told that bright _____ were not
                        2
good for him. The treatment did not work. Ray lost sight in both his

_____ . Today Ray has been told by
     3
_____ that he probably had
     4
glaucoma. His blindness has not stopped Ray, though. He learned to do many

_____ for himself. Best of all, he
     5
learned to give us the gift of music.

If you filled the blanks correctly, each of your answers was a *plural*. That means each named more than one thing. You were using context clues to fill in the blanks. You used the context to figure out two things: (1) the *meaning* of the word that fit each blank, and (2) the *form* of the word. The context told you to add an *-s* to each word to form its plural.

Context clues help you a great deal when you read. They help you know what each word means and how it's being used. That's why good readers always read words *in context*.

▲ Looking Back

This lesson had readings about people and machines that entertain us. You learned that you can infer ideas when you read. You practiced your skill at summarizing. And you practiced using the context as you read.

As you continue to read, watch for times when you need to infer. This skill is useful when you listen to others speak too.

The Active Reader

Self-Questioning

Picture It

Being an active reader means asking questions. As you read, you look for the answers to your questions. That helps you pay attention to your reading. You get more out of what you read. You also are likely to remember better what you read.

Good readers usually preview an article. When you preview, you read the title to find what the article is about. You see if the article has subheads (smaller headings). Subheads show the important points an article tells about its topic. You can also look at pictures and charts before reading.

As you preview, you can form questions. Ask yourself, "What will I probably learn from this article?" Ask other questions about the title, subheads, and pictures. Then start to read and look for the answers to your questions.

Good readers form *new* questions and look for answers all the time. Asking questions and looking for the answers keeps your mind alert and active while you read.

Here's an Example

As you read the following paragraphs, you'll see questions you might ask yourself. First preview the title.

■ Dreams: The "Movies" in Your Mind

What do you think the article will be about? Glance through the article below to see if your guess is right. Next, form one or two questions to help you keep your mind on the reading. The questions below are examples.

What is a dream?
What causes us to dream?

Now read these paragraphs with those questions in mind.

■ A dream is a group of scenes that your mind makes up while you sleep. It is rather like a movie in your mind. Many people feel they can see, hear, smell, and even touch things in their dreams. The things that happen in a dream are imaginary. But they are very real to the dreamer.

Often, the things that you have seen or heard during the day will come into your dreams at night. Feelings of anger or fear may also come into your dreams at night, in the form of nightmares.

Have you found the answers to any of your questions so far? If not, keep those questions in mind as you continue.

Working It Out

Write a question about nightmares that you think the rest of the article might answer.

1. _____

_____

Now read with that question in mind.

■ Nightmares are frightening dreams. The word *nightmare* comes from an old word meaning "fear at night." Nightmares may come when we feel we do not have complete control over our lives. Some psychologists believe that our minds make up nightmares to give us a chance to work out our unhappy feelings.

Was your question answered? If it was, write the answer here.

_____

_____

The next part of the article tells what scientists know about dreams. Write below a question you have about dreams.

2. _____

_____

Now read to see if your question is answered.

■ Some scientists study how we dream. They've found that nearly everyone dreams at night. In fact, they tell us we usually have three to five dreams each night. Most dreams last from ten minutes to half an hour.

As people dream, their eyes move quickly back and forth under closed lids. This is called REM sleep. REM comes from the first letters of the words *rapid eye movement*. The brain works more rapidly during REM sleep. If a person is awakened during REM sleep, he is usually able to remember and describe the dream he was just having. Scientists also tell us that REM sleep seems to help us. In a test, people were awakened each time they began to have rapid eye movement. The people were grouchy and tired the next day.

Was your question answered? If it was, write the answer here.

_____

_____

Active readers ask questions. Asking questions helps you pay attention as you read. The questions are useful, even if you don't always find the answers.

Part A Lesson 11

The Winners

In this lesson you will
- read about the winner of an early auto race
- learn to recognize an author's conclusions
- draw some of your own conclusions when you read
- strengthen your word power

Skills for Reading: Drawing Conclusions

Picture It

The scoreboard shows the Spartans have beat the Pioneers. The players' faces tell the story. Which ones are the Spartans? The players on the left all look happy. You can conclude, or infer, that they are the winning Spartans. The others look unhappy. You can conclude that they are the losing Pioneers.

A **conclusion** is an inference. It is reached after thinking about facts and details. You draw many conclusions each day without realizing it. For example, suppose you look outside and see rain clouds. You probably conclude that you should carry an umbrella that day.

When you read, you also deal with conclusions. Sometimes authors report conclusions they have drawn themselves. At other times, *you* need to draw your own conclusions. You do so in order to understand fully the author's message. You draw conclusions from facts the author gives you.

Here's an Example

Following is a paragraph about a runner. As you read, notice the details. They lead up to the author's conclusion.

■ Cheryl Toussaint had never thought of herself as a winner. Her school grades were low. She had no real goals. Then she joined a team of runners. During her first race her great speed surprised everyone. However, she had run too fast. She fell on the track and had to crawl to the finish line. Training with her team made her strong. It taught her to pace herself. All that hard work paid off. In 1970 she broke a world's record. She won an Olympic race. Cheryl is truly a winner now.

The author's conclusion is stated in the last sentence. Facts and details in the paragraph lead up to that conclusion. The author mentions that Cheryl *crawled* to the finish line in an early race. Later, she broke a world's record. She won at the Olympics. Her actions show that she has the spirit and skill of a winner.

Working It Out

Here's an article about another winner. Try to draw conclusions about Jean-Claude Killy as you read.

■ Jean-Claude Killy began skiing when he was three years old. In the 1968 Olympics this French athlete won three gold medals in the alpine skiing events. Only once before (in 1956) had anyone won all three events in one year.

Killy always loved speed. Nothing thrilled him more than racing down snowy slopes. Yet many things could have kept Killy from becoming a championship skier. Like every skier, he sometimes fell down. During training he broke leg and ankle bones several times. He also became ill and had to stop skiing for two years. Then he became ill again. But none of these setbacks stopped Jean-Claude Killy. . . .

1. What conclusion can you draw about winning three downhill skiing events in the Olympics?
   A. It is very difficult to do.
   B. It is fairly easy to do.

Explain why you drew the conclusion you did.

_____

_____

_____

2. What conclusion can you draw about Jean-Claude Killy's personality?
   A. He was determined and daring.
   B. He was lucky and fun-loving.

Explain why you drew the conclusion you did.

_____

_____

_____

Writing to Improve Your Reading

Do you often stop reading to figure out the meaning of words you don't know? The more words you know, the less often you have to stop and look up meanings. It's clear that learning new words can make someone a better reader.

You can make cards to help you learn word meanings. Each time you come to a word you don't know, write it on a card. Then write the sentence that uses the word so you have its context.

If you can tell the meaning of the word from its context, write the meaning on the back of the card. If the context doesn't help you, find the meaning in a dictionary. Write the meaning on the back of the card.

Then, once or twice a week, look at each word on your cards and say the meaning to yourself. You might want to add these new words to your journal, as well.

As you read *Two-Time Winner* on pages 88–90, make a card for each word that is new to you.

Reading on Your Own

In the early 1900s, cars were called "horseless carriages." Top speed for most cars was 40 miles per hour. But at a new race track in Indiana, drivers pushed their cars to the limit to win the "Indianapolis 500" race. The first man to win that race twice was Tommy Milton. Read to find out what problems he faced on the track. What conclusions can you draw about the early days of auto racing?

Two-Time Winner

Tommy won a hard race in 1921. Then, in 1923, he came back in a racer designed by Harry C. Stutz. Stutz had built the famous Stutz Bearcat sports car. Tommy's racer was painted white. Tommy had decked himself out in white to go with it. He wore new white shoes and white kid gloves. He'd even wrapped the steering wheel with white adhesive tape. Usually, the wheel was wrapped with black friction tape.

Tommy looked great in his new outfit. But he was in for trouble. Early in the race, his hands began to perspire. He had always worn cloth gloves. If they got wet, there was no problem. But the kid gloves began to shrink! Pretty soon, he could hardly close his fingers. And those new shoes were pinching his feet.

Worse yet, the heat was causing the tape on the steering wheel to ooze sticky stuff. The wheel seemed to be covered with molasses. Tommy knew he was in a mess. It was a very dangerous mess for someone whipping along at 90 miles (145 km) per hour.

But, worst of all, there was trouble with the car. Its filler cap gave out. The pit crew didn't have a replacement. A smart mechanic put in an orange that he had pierced with a copper tube. It worked fine, but Tommy wondered how long it would last.

The pit crew members are responsible for keeping the car in good condition and ready for a race.

The orange just had to last, he told himself. He was driving the fastest car on the track. He'd taken an early lead. The Stutz was a sure winner. . . .

If only he could handle that sticky wheel. If only his feet would stop hurting. If only that orange didn't fly apart.

Tommy decided to pit the car. He turned it over to his relief driver, Howdy Wilcox. While Howdy lapped the track, Tommy got rid of those fancy white shoes. He put on a comfortable old pair. Off came the kid gloves. Then he wrapped his hands with friction tape. Now he could handle the steering wheel. But what could be done about that orange?

To "pit the car" is to drive it off the track to where the pit crew is.

He happened to see a spare Stutz parked nearby. There was the answer! Right in front of him! The Stutz had a filler cap just like his. Use it!

He yelled for the crew to remove the cap. The job wasn't easy, because the cap was riveted to the car. But out it finally came. Tommy waved Howdy back to the pits.

Tommy climbed in behind the wheel. The crew attached the cap and tossed the orange aside. They worked quickly. They were finished in just 60 seconds. The Stutz rocketed onto the track.

Howdy had lost the lead. Tommy floored the car. Within minutes, he was back in first place. But he asked himself, "What'll go wrong now?"

To "floor" the car means "to press the accelerator to the floor," or to drive as fast as the car can go.

Lesson 11 The Winners / 89

Nothing! Tommy Milton's troubles were over. His Stutz held the lead for the rest of the way. He shot across the finish line. He became the first man to win the 500 more than once. His average speed was 90.95 miles (146.37 km) per hour.

Thinking About What You've Read

1. Which of the following conclusions about auto racing could you draw from details in the story? (Circle A, B, or C.)
   A. White is not a good color for a racing car.
   B. Fancy clothes can hamper a driver while racing.
   C. The Stutz racer was a better car than the Stutz Bearcat.

2. What details in the second and third paragraphs support the statement that Tommy "was in for trouble"?
   _____
   _____

3. What happened to the gas tank filler cap during the race?
   _____

4. Who was driving the Stutz when other race cars passed it?
   _____

5. Do Tommy's actions show you that he is a winner? Write your own conclusion about Tommy as a race car driver.
   _____

6. If you were going to interview Tommy Milton about the race, what question would you ask first?
   _____

> **GED Warm-up**
>
> What did Tommy do first once he brought his car into the pit?
> (1) told Howdy Wilcox to drive the car
> (2) looked for a cap to replace his broken one
> (3) changed his shoes and gloves
> ① ② ③

Working with Words

A dictionary gives information about words. Each dictionary entry states a word and then gives facts about it. The entry tells you how to spell the word, how to pronounce it, and what it means. Some dictionaries give even more information.

Many words in English have more than one meaning. Large dictionaries often give several meanings for each word. Small pocket dictionaries usually give only the most common meanings.

As you read, you may want to keep a dictionary handy. If you come to a word you don't know, use context clues to try to discover its meaning. Also see if it has a prefix or suffix that can help you decide what it means. If you still don't understand the word, look it up in your dictionary.

Use alphabetical order to find the word in the dictionary. Run your finger down the entries on a page until you find the word you need. Several meanings may be given. Context clues will help you decide which meaning fits the sentence you are reading.

Here are some sentences you can practice with. Use context clues to write the meaning of each **bold** word. Then check your meanings in a dictionary.

1. Tommy had **decked** himself out in white.
   _____

2. He wore white **kid** gloves.
   _____

3. He'd wrapped the steering wheel with white **adhesive** tape.
   _____

4. The tape on the steering wheel began to **ooze** sticky stuff.
   _____

5. A mechanic had **pierced** an orange with a copper tube.
   _____

6. The cap was **riveted** to the car.
   _____

▲ Looking Back

You've read about three winners in this lesson: a race car driver, a skier, and a runner. You've noted conclusions writers made about these winners. You've drawn some conclusions of your own. You've also practiced building your word power.

As you continue to read, think about the conclusions authors draw. See if you agree with them. Ask yourself, "Does the article back up the author's conclusion?"

The Active Reader

Self-Checking and Self-Correcting

Picture It

May received a note from her dentist. She tried to read the note while she was doing other things. She read, "Our records show that your teeth have been cleaned recently. Please make an appointment." May knew that didn't make sense. Why make an appointment if her teeth had just been cleaned.

May put her baby down, turned off the TV, and read the note again. She found that the note really said this: "Our records show that your teeth have not been cleaned recently. . . ." May had read the note a second time. So she was able to check and correct her mistake.

Active readers check their understanding as they read. They do this automatically. They check to see whether the words they are reading make sense. If something goes wrong, they stop. They go back and see why the words are not making sense. They solve many of their own reading problems this way.

Here are some questions you can use. Keep them in mind as you read. They will help you check to be sure you're reading at your best.

- Does this story or article make sense to me? Do I understand what it is about?
- Is there any part I don't understand? How important is it?
- Are there parts of the story or article I should read again? Would that help me understand better?
- Is there someone who could help me understand this better? Should I ask for help?
- Do I need to check the meaning of a word?

You might want to make a bookmark that says, "Does this make sense?" You can keep it in your book. It will remind you to check yourself as you read.

Here's an Example

Hank was reading a magazine article about insect spray. Here is what he read.

■ Dorn's insect spray is a safe way to get rid of bugs. At least, that's what many people think. The truth is that Dorn's uses poisons that have not been carefully checked by the federal government. It may actually be very dangerous.

Hank thought the article said Dorn's is a good insect spray to use. He bought some right away.

Hank made a common mistake. He thought the first sentence of the article was the main idea. He did not ask himself if the article made sense. Instead, he simply accepted the first sentence as the idea he should remember.

Working It Out

A. Laura Davies got a note from her boss. She tried to do exactly what the note said. She read,

Laura:
Please stock each office on this floor with number 2 pencils.

Laura went to the stock room. She took out a box of pencils and put two of them on the desk in each office.

What mistake did Laura make? Look at the note again. Circle the part that Laura should have read again to understand the directions.

B. Al West was reading the paper. The following announcement caught his eye.

■ BTA Bus Company is looking for people who would like to become drivers. The job offers good benefits and good pay. As a trainee, you will be given two weeks of free training, your uniform cap, and a driver's manual.

To apply, you must be at least 21 years old. You must have a clean driving record. You will need to pass a driving test and a written test. You will have to show that you can be patient with bus riders. When you come for your interview, bring three references.

Answer these questions before you read more about Al. Self-check your reading if you need to.

1. What is the announcement about?

_____

2. What is the purpose of the announcement?

_____

Al applied for the job. He was hired. On the first day, he began his training. He was given a cap that matched the bus driver's uniform. But he was surprised he had to pay for his uniform. He thought the announcement had said the uniform would be free.

3. Circle the part of the announcement that Al should have checked more carefully.

4. Are there any words in the article that you didn't understand? If so, write them here. Write a dictionary meaning for each, or use context clues to figure out the meanings.

_____

_____

Part A
Lesson 12

A Zest for Life

> *In this lesson you will*
> - read about people who put extra energy into life
> - study causes and their effects
> - make a chart to keep track of cause-and-effect relationships
> - practice with pronouns

Skills for Reading: Cause-and-Effect Relationships

Picture It
Look at the picture. What happened? Why did it happen?

The window has been broken. That is what happened. It is the effect. Why is the window broken? The worker hit it with the end of the ladder. That is the cause.

An **effect** is what happened. A **cause** is why it happened.

Cause-and-effect relationships happen all the time in daily life. You also find them in many types of reading material.

Here's an Example
As you read about Teddy Stone's plan for the future, look for causes and effects.

■ Teddy Stone loves music. He spends nearly all his free time playing country music or listening to it. His hands seem lonely when he is not strumming his guitar. **Because** music is such a large part of Teddy's life, he chooses friends who like music too.

Since Teddy and his friends love music, they've formed a country band. Teddy is good at managing people. He also has a special gift for arranging songs. So the group has made him the band leader. The members believe all their hard work will **result** in success some day. Until then, they are having fun.

You may have found places where a cause and effect was mentioned. For one, Teddy's interest in music *causes* him to choose friends who also like music.

For another, Teddy is the leader of the band. That is *because* Teddy can manage people and arrange music.

Finally, the band members believe their practice will *result* in their success.

Writers sometimes use clue words to help you spot causes and effects. *Because, since, reason,* and *cause* are clue words that point out a cause. *So, therefore, thus,* and *result* point out effects.

Writers do not always use clue words. When they don't, you can watch for causes and effects yourself. If you're looking for a cause, ask yourself, "Why did this happen?" If you're looking for an effect, ask yourself, "What happened because of this?"

Working It Out

Would you be angry if something of yours was stolen? How might you work off your anger?

In these paragraphs about Muhammad Ali, the boxer, you'll read about such anger. Look for causes and effects as you read.

> ■ The boy was angry. Lean, big-eyed, good-looking, twelve years old. And angry.
>
> Somebody had stolen his bike. He'd gone to the police. Louisville patrolman Joe Martin—Joseph Elsby Martin, badge number 474—talked to the youngster. He'd see what he could do about finding the bike. Meanwhile, Joe Martin had a suggestion to help the boy vent his anger. How about dropping in at the Columbia Gym, on South Fourth Street, and working out?
>
> That's how it began.
>
> The boy's name was Cassius Marcellus Clay, Jr. Today he's Muhammad Ali, and his life, his [boxing] career, began when he started to spend his evenings at the Columbia Gym.

Write a few words to answer each question.

1. What caused the boy to be angry?

_____

2. Why did the policeman suggest that the boy go to the gym?

_____

3. What was the result, or effect, of his working out at the gym?

_____

Writing to Improve Your Reading

A table can help you organize ideas as you read. Here's how to make such a table.

First, preview the article you will read. That will give you an idea of the topic. It will also show you how the information is organized.

Next, make up a table like the one following. Leave spaces for headings.

Leave spaces under each heading for details.

Your preview will help you decide what headings to use. For an article that tells the order of events, the dates or years could be your headings. For an article about causes and effects, your headings could be those in the table at right.

Here is the way you might make a table for the article about Muhammad Ali. What do you think you could write down next under the heading "Cause"? He began his career as a boxer *because* he started to spend his evenings at the gym.

Make a table of effects and causes as you read about painter Clementine Hunter on pages 96–98.

Muhammad Ali

Effect	Cause
Cassius feels angry.	His bike was stolen.
He goes to gym.	Police suggest gym to work off anger.
He becomes a boxer.	

Reading on Your Own

Her parents had been slaves. She never went to art school. When she started painting, she didn't even have her own paints or brushes. Today, her paintings hang in important art galleries. Read to discover how folk artist Clementine Hunter became interested in painting. Find out what events caused changes in her life.

The Story of Clementine Hunter

Clementine Hunter's paintings dance with color and life. They are examples of folk art. Folk art is painting and crafts made by people who have no special art training. Folk artists do not try to follow the example of an art school or artist. They paint everyday people, or everyday "folk."

Clementine Hunter was born in Louisiana in 1887. Because records were not well kept in those days, we do not know the day of her birth. We do know she was more than 100 years old when she died in January 1988.

As a young girl, Ms. Hunter started school. But she had to leave after only three years. Her family needed her to help earn money. Her father taught her to pick cotton when she was eight years old. Picking cotton is not easy work. Pickers must bend over to pluck the soft white puffs off each bush. They work their way slowly up one long row and down the next. They work bent over in the hot sun for long hours each day. There was no time for an eight-year-old girl to play. No time for school. No time for fun.

As years went by, there was less cotton to pick. It was partly because fewer farmers planted cotton. And it was also because machines began to take over part of the work. Clementine Hunter worked at other jobs. Finally she became a cook at the Melrose Plantation.

"A Negro Wedding Scene" by Clementine Hunter, Collection of Anglo-American Art Museum, Louisiana State University, Baton Rouge. Gift of Mr. and Mrs. Lewis A. Bannon.

In the 1930s, Melrose Plantation became a home for artists. Their work caught Ms. Hunter's attention. When the artists left old brushes and paints behind, Ms. Hunter picked them up. She used old scraps of paper or pieces of wood as her canvas. She began painting without help or training. She painted mostly from memory. She painted scenes of the people and places from her childhood in the Louisiana countryside.

Clementine Hunter gave away most of her paintings. She sold some of them. Soon other artists began to notice her talent. Some

An honorary degree is given by a college to show respect to someone. People do not go to school for such degrees. Instead, their lifework has earned them the degrees.

of her paintings were shown in a university gallery. In those days, African American people were not allowed in some university buildings. Because she was African American, Ms. Hunter was not allowed to see her own work displayed. Finally she managed to sneak in. Later, the same university gave her an honorary degree.

In her later years, Ms. Hunter lost her sight. She could no longer paint. The paintings she did complete live after her. She is remembered as an important folk artist—part of our country's past.

Thinking About What You've Read

1. Melrose Plantation became a home for artists. What effect did this have on Ms. Hunter's life?

2. Why did Ms. Hunter quit school after only three years?

3. Why is Clementine Hunter called a folk artist?

4. Why did Clementine Hunter stop painting?

Did your table of causes and effects match some of the questions and answers in items 1–4?

5. Look at the picture on page 97 of "A Negro Wedding Scene" by Clementine Hunter. What stands out in your mind about the painting?

A Test-Taking Tip

Sometimes it helps to rule out wrong multiple-choice answers until the best answer is left. So read all the answer choices for an item. As you see answers you know are wrong, cross them off in your mind. It will be easier to choose from the limited answers you have left.

GED Warm-up

Which of the following is mentioned as a reason that there were fewer jobs for cotton pickers?

(1) People bought clothes made of other materials.
(2) Picking cotton was very hard, unpleasant work.
(3) Machines took over some of the work of cotton pickers.

① ② ③

Working with Words

I, me, he, she, it, we and *they* are called pronouns. They are used in place of the names of persons, places, and things.

Pronouns make our language easier to speak and write. These sentences show how odd we would sound without pronouns. They also show how boring it would be to read an article without pronouns.

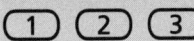 Thelma walked into Thelma's apartment. Thelma sank into Thelma's big, soft chair. Thelma was very tired. Thelma's husband saw Thelma. "Thelma," Thelma's husband said, "Thelma has been working too hard. Why doesn't Thelma ask Thelma's boss for a day off?"

You can see that pronouns are useful. But they can be hard to keep track of sometimes. When you read, be sure to "keep track" of pronouns. Make sure you know the person, place, or thing each pronoun is naming.

Here are some sentences about Clementine Hunter. Practice with pronouns by reading the sentences. Then answer the question that follows each.

1. Folk artists do not try to follow the example of any art school or artist. **They** paint everyday people.
   Whom does *they* refer to?

   _____

2. Ms. Hunter gave **her** paintings away to many people.
   Whom does *her* refer to?

   _____

3. In the 1930s, Melrose Plantation became a home for artists. **Their** work caught Ms. Hunter's attention.
   Whom does *their* refer to?

   _____

4. Pickers must bend over to pluck the soft white puffs off each bush. **They** work their way slowly up one long row and down the next.
   Whom does *they* refer to?

   _____

▲ Looking Back

In this lesson, you read about some famous people in sports and the arts. You also read about a person who is not so famous—yet. While you read, you noted cause-and-effect relationships. You learned how making a table can help you sort out ideas such as causes and effects. And you practiced finding out what word a pronoun refers to.

The Active Reader

Word Maps

Getting Started
When you learn about a new subject, you often need to learn new words. Or you may learn new meanings for old words. You can make a "map" to help yourself see how the new words you are learning fit together.

Here's an Example
Suppose you are reading about different kinds of TV shows. Here are some of the words you read in the article.

game show	soaps	talk shows
sitcoms	network TV	cable TV
public TV	writer	actor
director	producer	

Some of these words are new to you. Others are old words with new meanings. You want to see how these words fit together. To do this, you can make your own "map."

Some of the words name kinds of shows. You can write all the kinds of shows together on one part of your map.

Some of the words name kinds of TV stations. You can write these on another place on your map.

Still other words name people who work on the shows. You can write their names together.

Put all the word groups on one map. Show how they fit together with lines. The drawing below shows you how.

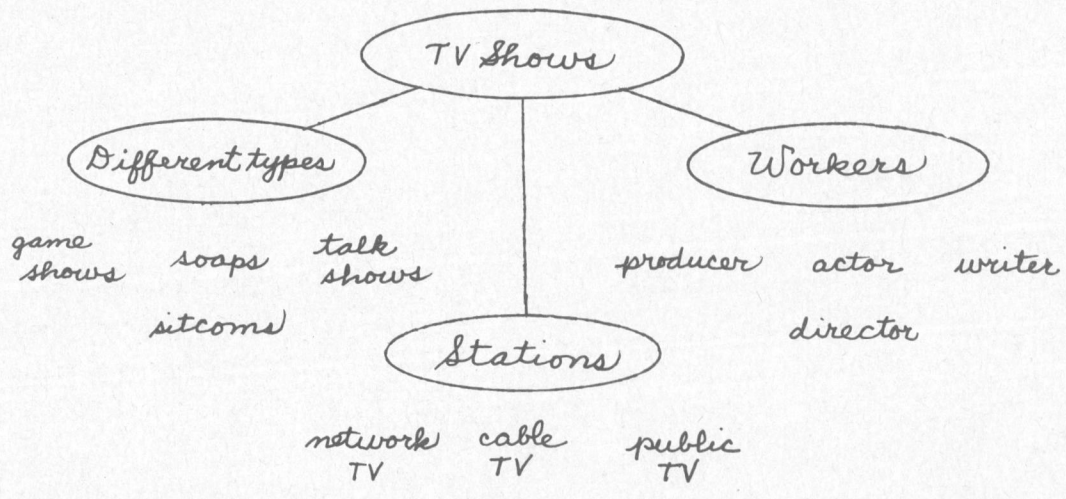

Working It Out

Imagine you have a friend who has just moved to the United States. Your friend wants to learn to drive. He is reading a book about driving, but many of the words are hard for him.

Your friend hands you the article below. He has drawn lines under the words that trouble him. Read the article. Then complete the word map to show how the underlined words fit together.

■ Learning to drive a car is not hard. But learning to drive it safely and wisely can be another matter.

You need to start thinking even before you get those car keys in your hand. Are you the sort of a person who takes risks with your own life and the lives of others? Or can you be sure that you will be a patient, steady driver?

How would you feel if you got stopped for a <u>roadblock</u>? Could you stay cool in a <u>traffic jam</u>? What if another <u>driver cuts in front</u> of you sharply? Could you stay calm?

Another thing to think about is how you might react if you had car trouble. Would you be able to read your oil, electric, and fuel <u>gauges</u>? Could you tell what was wrong if your <u>radiator</u> began to leak? Would you know what to do if a <u>tire</u> began to lose air? You don't need to be a mechanic to drive a car, but you should have some idea of what to do if you have a car problem.

Below, a word map has been started for you. Complete the map with underlined words from the article you just read.

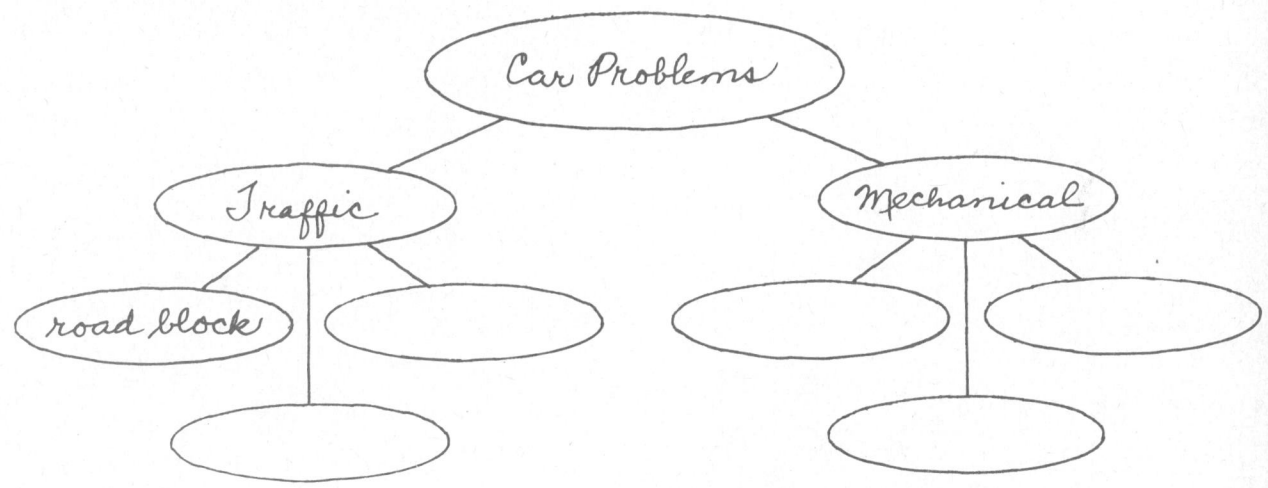

Making a word map is useful when you are reading about something that is new to you. Putting new words into groups helps you see how the words fit together.

Lesson 12 A Zest for Life / 101

Part A
Lesson 13

Keeping Healthy

In this lesson you will
- read some health and grooming tips
- apply information from your reading to new situations
- learn about idioms
- list ideas to help you remember them

Skills for Reading: Applying What You Read

Picture It
What is the man in the drawing reading about?

The man wants to find wild animals. You can see he has followed the book's advice. And he has found two wild animals (though he doesn't know it yet). By following the advice, he has applied what he has read.

Applying what you read means using in your life the ideas you read. You apply ideas each time you follow a recipe. You apply ideas each time you use directions to repair something. Applying ideas is one of the most useful reading skills you can have.

Here's an Example
Read the following article about headaches. You may find some ideas you could use to get rid of a headache some day.

102 / Part A Reading Skills for Life

■ Stress is the cause of most headaches. Tired eyes can cause them too. But headaches can also be caused by more serious problems. They may be a warning of an eye, ear, or tooth problem. They may warn that you are getting the flu. They may be the result of a head injury.

For most headaches, the cure is just to take aspirin. Some people prefer an aspirin substitute. In either case, you should follow the directions on the bottle carefully.

What if you don't want to take medicine? There are other ways to relieve a headache. One easy way is to lie down with a soft pillow under your neck. Close your eyes to rest them. You can also put a hot water bottle on the back of your neck. Or you can gently rub the back of your neck and forehead.

Now you've read some facts about headaches. How could you apply them in your own life?

For one thing, the first sentence says most headaches come from stress. Say that you've been working hard and dealing with many problems. You now know such stress can lead to a headache. So you might decide to take a rest now and then. The rest will help you avoid a headache.

Later, the article suggests ways for easing the pain of a headache. You may want to apply these ideas when you have a headache. To apply them, you would do just what the author says. You would lie down, close your eyes, and rest your neck on a soft pillow.

Working It Out

Here's some information about exercise. The questions that follow will help you apply the ideas you read.

■ Most everyone knows that exercise is good for you. When you exercise, your breathing is easier. Your heart works better. Your muscles are stronger. You feel fit. Did you know that exercise also is good for your mental health? You feel more relaxed. You feel better about yourself.

You *don't* have to punish yourself to keep fit. The trick is to choose an exercise you like. Choose one that works your whole body. Then do it for at least twenty minutes every day or so. It's better *not* to exercise heavily all at once. That can make your heart and muscles work *too* hard. With an exercise such as walking or bicycling, you can begin slowly, for a short distance. Then work up to faster speeds for longer distances. If you do a heavy exercise like weight lifting, check with a doctor before you begin your exercise plan.

Be sure to warm up before exercise, especially heavy exercise. And don't stop suddenly. Slow down gradually at the end.

Use the information you've read to answer the following questions. Circle the letter of the best answer to each question.

1. According to the article, which would NOT be a good way to exercise?
   A. jogging rapidly once a week
   B. swimming every other day
   C. walking up stairs each day instead of using an elevator

Write the information in the article that you used to answer question 1.

_____

_____

2. Iris Lopez is too busy to go to a gym or swimming pool. What could she do every day to get the right kind of exercise at work?
   A. take a walk during lunch break
   B. run up the six stairs to her office
   C. do finger exercises using her computer keyboard

Write the information in the article that you used to answer question 2.

_____

_____

Writing to Improve Your Reading

Making a list of important ideas you read is helpful. It will help you keep your mind on your reading. It will help you remember important facts. And it will help you note ideas you may want to apply in your life.

As you read *How to Care for Your Hair,* list the suggestions you may want to try. Write the list in the margin or on your own paper.

Reading on Your Own

Read this article to find some good ideas you can apply that will make hair care simple and inexpensive.

How to Care for Your Hair

Brushing

Some day, count the number of ads you see for products that make your hair look good. Counting them will open your eyes! Shampoos, sprays, color rinses, hair creams: the list goes on and on. These things can add up in cost. But there's no need to go broke when caring for your hair. Brushing costs nothing once you've bought a good brush. And brushing keeps your hair looking healthy. Hair creams can hold the dust on your hair. They make it look and feel dirty. Brushing takes the day's dust and dirt off your hair. Brushing spreads natural oil evenly over your hair.

The oil protects your hair from drying. It helps hair look rich and shiny. Brushing also helps make blood flow to your scalp. The blood carries important things to your hair to keep it healthy.

Washing

Many people wonder how often they should wash their hair. There is no set rule that works for everyone. For some people, once a week is enough. Others must wash their hair every day. It depends mostly on how naturally oily or naturally dry the hair is. Oily hair needs to be washed more often. It also depends on how long and thick your hair is. It depends on the way you wear your hair. It even depends on where you live. You may live in an area that has lots of dust or smoke in the air. Then your hair will become dirty faster. The best rule is this: Wash your hair as soon as you notice it is dirty.

What kind of shampoo should you choose for your hair? Keep in mind the simplest shampoo is nearly always the best. Today you can find shampoos that have fancy things in them. You can buy shampoos that contain strawberries, milk, eggs, honey, and even beer. The truth is that these extra things do not clean your hair. The detergent or soap itself is what takes away the dirt.

If you use a hair dryer, don't hold it in one place on your head. Keep the stream of hot air moving across your hair, back and forth. The hot air could dry out your hair and skin.

Hair Loss

Do you feel down in the dumps because your hair is getting thin? It is natural to lose a little hair when you brush or wash. New hair grows in quickly. But some things can lead to heavy loss of hair. You might be surprised to know that stress can make you lose your hair. Illness can too. Some types of baldness run in families. Scientists continue to try to find ways to replace hair in bald people. So far, no really good way has been found.

Thinking About What You've Read

1. Which hair-care tip could be followed to save money?
_____
_____

2. Which of the following could a hairbrush company use as a truthful advertising slogan? (Circle A, B, or C.)

   A. Brushing is the healthy way to good-looking hair.
   B. Brush your hair to avoid baldness.
   C. Brush your hair to make it naturally curly.

3. Why should you avoid holding a hair dryer at one place on your head for a long time?
_____

4. According to the article, how often should people wash their hair? (Circle A, B, or C.)

   A. every day
   B. once a week
   C. when it's dirty

5. Which of the following does NOT agree with information given in the article? (Circle A, B, or C.)

   A. Losing a few hairs each day shows you have a scalp disease.
   B. Stress can cause increased hair loss.
   C. Baldness can run in families.

6. Did you write a list of ideas from the article that *you* might want to use? If you did, read the list now. Is there any question *you* have about hair care that was not answered in the article? Write your question here.
_____

106 / Part A Reading Skills for Life

GED Warm-up

1. Which of the following people is correctly applying information from the article?

(1) A woman uses shampoo that contains beer.
(2) A man uses only egg shampoo.
(3) A woman buys a plain detergent shampoo.

① ② ③

Working with Words

An **idiom** is a group of words with a special twist. When words are together in an idiom, they take on a different meaning. An example of an idiom is underlined here.

- I <u>got a kick out of</u> Maria's story.

The idiom *get a kick out of* means "to be amused." With the usual meaning of each word, "to get a kick out of" would be unpleasant. When those words are joined together, their meaning changes. The idiom refers to something fun.

The following sentences contain idioms from *How to Care for Your Hair.* Tell what each underlined idiom means.

1. Counting them will <u>open your eyes</u>!

_____
_____

2. There's no need to <u>go broke</u> when caring for your hair.

_____
_____

3. Do you feel <u>down in the dumps</u> because your hair is getting thin?

_____
_____

4. Can you think of an idiom that you use sometimes? Write it here.

_____

▲ Looking Back

In this lesson you've read suggestions on health and grooming. While you read, you applied ideas and facts. You learned what idioms are. You also read idioms and noted their meanings. Finally, you kept a list to help you note ideas you may want to apply.

As you build your reading skills, think how the information you read can be applied to your life.

The Active Reader

Reading Directions

Picture It

Directions are a part of life. If you don't read instructions, you'll end up like the man above. If you don't follow a recipe right, you won't have dinner. Here are some directions for reading directions!

- Read the directions *all the way through* once. Make sure you understand them. See if they must be followed step by step. Find out if you need any materials on hand.
- Then read each direction one at a time. If you're following steps, do the step after you've read it. Then check it off.

Here's an Example

Part of the directions for a multiple-choice test follow. Read them carefully. Read them the way you would if you were taking the test.

- Work carefully. Do not spend too much time on any one question, though. Be sure you answer every question. You will not have points taken off for wrong answers.

To record each answer, mark a space on the answer sheet beside the number of the question in the test.

Don't make any stray or unneeded marks. If you change an answer, erase your first answer completely. Mark only one answer space for each question. More than one mark will be scored as incorrect.

Working It Out

Here is part of an answer sheet. Compare the way it has been marked with the directions above.

1. ① ● ③ ④ ⑤
2. ① ② ③ ④ ⑤
3. ① ● ③ ④ ⑤
4. ● ② ③ ④ ⑤
5. ① ② ③ ● ⑤

Did the person follow the directions for marking an answer sheet? If not, what was done wrong?

_____

_____

108 / Part A Reading Skills for Life

Part A
Lesson 14

Working for What You Believe

In this lesson you will
- read about people who worked for what they believed
- identify facts and opinions
- work with words that have the same spellings but different meanings

Skills for Reading: Facts and Opinions

Picture It

Do you know which signs you could prove true? Do you know which you could *never* prove? The signs show facts and opinions. You'll want to be able to tell facts from opinions in your reading and in your daily life.

A **fact** is a statement that can be proved true. The proof can come from seeing in real life what the statement is saying. Proof can also come from a film or book you can trust. It can come from people who know a great deal about the subject.

Here's a fact:

- Ronald Reagan was the fortieth president of the United States.

You could prove this fact with an encyclopedia or other book.

An **opinion** is a statement of someone's judgment or belief. There is no way to prove an opinion. Here's an opinion.

- Ronald Reagan was the best president of the United States.

You can't prove this statement. It is someone's judgment. There is no yardstick or tool you can use to measure what is "best" to everyone.

Most reading contains both facts and opinions. To tell a fact from an opinion, just ask, "Is there any way somebody could prove this statement?" You don't need to be able to prove it yourself—just to know that it *could* be proved. If so, it is a fact. If the statement has a word that depends on personal judgment (such as *best, greatest, worst, terrible, silly,* or other similar words), it cannot be proved. Then it is an opinion.

Here's an Example

Read these paragraphs about a growing town. Note the underlined statements. They are a mix of facts and opinions.

- The corner of Main Street and State Road had become very busy. The neighbors grew worried about the heavy traffic. They held a town meeting.

   "We want a stoplight on our corner," one person said. "The corner is not safe," said another. Other comments were made: "It's the worst corner in the state." "There were ten accidents there last year."

   The state highway department studied the corner. It agreed that a stoplight was needed. A stoplight is being put up now.

The first underlined sentence is an opinion. The word *worst* is a personal judgment. What is "worst" to one person may not be to another. So there is no way to prove the statement.

The second underlined sentence is a fact. You could check the fact. You could look at the accident reports at the police department. Or someone might have seen all the accidents.

Working It Out

The article below is about the first woman to serve in the U.S. Congress. Can you find some facts? Can you find one opinion?

- When Jeanette Rankin was born in 1880, Montana was not yet a state. Ms. Rankin grew up to see Montana become a state. She was pleased when Montana was among the first to give women the right to vote.

   In 1915, Ms. Rankin ran for Congress. Many people thought a woman could not win that election. But they were wrong. In 1917, she became the first woman to serve in the House of Representatives.

   Ms. Rankin's most important work in Congress was in the area of women's rights. Many states did not allow women to vote at that time. The year after Ms. Rankin left Congress, the Constitution was changed to allow women to vote.

Read each statement below. Tell if it is a fact or an opinion. If you choose fact, tell how someone might prove the statement.

1. Jeanette Rankin was born before Montana became a state.

   Is this a fact or an opinion? _____

   You could prove this statement by _____
   _____

2. Ms. Rankin's most important work was in the area of women's rights.

   Is this a fact or an opinion? _____

   You could prove this statement by _____
   _____

Writing to Improve Your Reading

Have you ever read an article with names you'd never heard before? Have you ever read, say, a story about Russian people? If you don't know Russian, the names could make it hard for you. It might be hard to keep the different people straight as you read. And you don't know how the names should be pronounced.

Here's a tip you might try as you read *Sequoyah's Talking Pages.* The people in the article have Native American names. Pronounce the names the way it is easiest for you. To keep them straight, write down each name as you read it. Use the margin of the book or your own paper. Then write a few words to tell who that person is. If the name comes up again, you can check your notes to see who the person is.

Reading on Your Own

The Cherokee Native Americans had a spoken language but no written language. Sequoyah was a Cherokee. He saw the letters the settlers sent to each other. He decided to make a written language for his people. Read to find out if Sequoyah reached his goal. As you read, watch for facts and opinions.

Sequoyah's Talking Pages

Sequoyah gathered leaves and bits of bark. He sounded out Cherokee words. Then he drew symbols for each sound. He drew on the leaves with charcoal. He worked at his project for two years.

Then one night a storm tore shingles off the roof. "The roof is half gone," his wife told him. "Go fix it."

"Is it?" he asked. "That reminds me. I haven't made a symbol

Ah-Yoka was Sequoyah's baby daughter.

An oak gall is a large lump on an oak tree. Iron filings are tiny pieces of iron, as fine as dust.

Sequoyah used a symbol for each syllable, or group of sounds. So Sequoyah's system is called a syllabary instead of an alphabet.

for *roof*." And he started to make one on a leaf.

His wife lost patience. She picked up the leaves and bark covered with his symbols. She threw them into the fire. "There!" she screamed. "Now go fix the roof!"

Sequoyah was stunned. Two years' work was destroyed.

"What's happened to you?" screamed his wife. "You used to be a good man before you went crazy over these symbols. You're nothing but a worthless white man. Get out of the house!"

Sequoyah picked up Ah-Yoka and wrapped a blanket around her. He threw another blanket over his shoulders. "Good-bye," he said to his wife. "We're getting out." And he left.

Sequoyah found an old cabin and fixed it up. He hunted with a bow and arrow. When he couldn't hunt, he spent most of his time making symbols for sounds. He made thousands.

One day, he and Ah-Yoka found an old English speller. "Now I have some talking pages," he told Ah-Yoka. "They will help me."

Sequoyah studied the speller. He used the letters to represent Cherokee sounds. There weren't enough letters. So he used some backwards and some upside down. He made up the rest he needed. He reduced the number of symbols to 86. At last, he had a symbol for every Cherokee sound. It had taken him 12 years. . . .

Sequoyah taught his daughter to read and write Cherokee. He decided he must try out his system on other Cherokees.

He copied his symbols on deer hide. He wrote with ink made of oak galls and iron filings. He took Ah-Yoka and started for Cherokee Nation West in Arkansas.

On the way, he met Sally. She was a widow with an 8-year-old son. Sequoyah married Sally in Arkansas. He taught Sally and her son to read and write.

"This is a great thing," Sally said. "It is too great for just us. You must take it to the Cherokee Council in the East."

Sequoyah agreed. He and Ah-Yoka went to show the syllabary to the Council. Sequoyah taught the men in the Council how to read in three days. . . .

Sequoyah trained teachers to teach them. Within a year, thousands of Cherokee people learned to read and write. By 1828, the tribe was publishing a newspaper, *The Cherokee Phoenix*.

Sequoyah was the first Indian to develop a written language without white help. The Cherokee lawmakers honored him. They gave him a silver medal and an income of $500 a year for life.

Thinking About What You've Read

1. Which sentence is an opinion? (Circle A or B.)
   A. "You used to be a good man."
   B. "The roof is half gone."

2. The article says the Cherokees gave Sequoyah $500 a year for life. How could someone check that statement to prove it true?
   _____

3. In whose opinion was Sequoyah's work a waste of time? How do you know?
   _____
   _____

4. What one person in particular had a good opinion about Sequoyah's work? How do you know?
   _____
   _____

5. The Cherokee nation was split into two groups. The groups lived far apart. How could a written language have helped them keep track of old Cherokee traditions?
   _____
   _____

A Test-Taking Tip
Every word in a multiple-choice question counts. Even small words such as *but* and *except* can make a big difference in meaning.

GED Warm-up
Sequoyah worked twelve years on his written language. You can conclude that he did so for each of these reasons <u>except</u>

(1) he wanted to help his people
(2) he wanted to earn $500 a year for life
(3) he had a great interest in language

① ② ③

Lesson 14 Working for What You Believe / 113

Working with Words

Read these sentences out loud if you can.

■ Take a rope and **wind** it around the tree. A gust of **wind** blew the tent over.

Did you pronounce the **bold** word in each sentence differently? In the first sentence, *wind* rhymes with *find*. In the second sentence, *wind* rhymes with *pinned*. The meaning of *wind* is also different. You can tell that from the context of the two sentences. Only the spelling of the word is the same.

Some words are spelled the same but pronounced differently. More important, they have different meanings. When you read, you will come across such words. How can you know which word the writer intended? The answer is to use context clues. The sentence that the word is in and other sentences around it help tell you the meaning.

Use the sentence pairs below to practice this skill. Read each sentence. Then write a few words to tell what the **bold** word means. Use the context to help you.

1. a. He hunted with a **bow** and arrow.
   _____

   b. When the people clap, take a **bow**.
   _____

2. a. He worked at his **project** for two years.
   _____

   b. The slide machine will **project** pictures onto the screen.
   _____

3. a. Thousands of Cherokee people learned to **read** and write.
   _____

   b. Harold **read** the comic strip and laughed.
   _____

▲ Looking Back

You've read about people who worked for what they believed. You've read about the first woman to serve in Congress. You've also learned about Sequoyah. He believed his people should be able to read and write their own language.

As you've read, you've found facts and opinions. You've learned how to help yourself read many foreign names. You've practiced reading some confusing words by paying attention to the context.

As you continue to read, watch for facts and opinions. Be sure you don't mistake an opinion for a fact.

The Active Reader

Taking Notes

Picture It

Did you ever watch the President on TV? If so, you may have seen reporters taking notes. They use the notes later on. The notes help them remember what the President said.

Good readers sometimes take notes too. The notes help them remember what they've read. Taking notes also helps keep your mind on reading. Here are some pointers on taking notes.

- Before you begin to take notes, preview the article. Look at the headings and pictures to see what the article is about. See how it is organized.
- As you read, make notes of the main idea and important details. You may also want to write down important names, places, and dates.
- Keep in mind your purpose for taking notes. Write only the information that you want to understand and remember.
- Keep the notes brief. You can write phrases and abbreviate words.
- Write the notes in your own words.

Here's an Example

Below is an article about life in space and on earth. Read the article with the pointers in mind. Then compare the article with the notes below it.

■ The space program taught us a great deal about living in space. Many of the things we learned have helped us here on earth.

For one thing, scientists made special clothing for the astronauts. The clothing protected them from very high temperatures in space. This same type of cloth now protects firefighters as they save lives and homes from fires.

In space, people must carry a supply of air with them. Small air tanks were first made for astronauts. These same tanks are now used by firefighters. Firefighters sometimes carry air with them into a burning building.

Scientists also had to find out how to wrap food. The food had to be light and easy to carry. It also had to stay fresh for months or even years. The answer to the problem was to freeze-dry the foods. This idea was first meant for space travel. Now many of us make use of it at home. We use freeze-dried coffee and juice. We use dried fruits and meats for hiking or camping.

Here are some notes an adult student took. The first one is the main idea of the article. The others are important details.

Things we've learned about space help on earth.

Invented for astronauts
1. special clothing for high temps help firefighters
2. small air tanks help firefighters
3. freeze-dried food (coffee, juice, fruits, meat)

Working It Out

The next article is about drunk drivers. Use it to practice taking your own notes. You may want to review the pointers first.

■ There is a killer among us. It is not a terrible sickness. It is not an enemy from another country. The killer is the drunk driver.

Each year, drunk drivers injure about 500,000 people. That is enough men, women, and children to make up a large city. Each year, about 24,000 people are killed in crashes caused by drivers who have been drinking.

Take a moment to think about what you've just read. What are the most important points? Note them below.

A. _____
_____
_____

Check the notes you've written before you read on. Did you write the facts and numbers correctly? Now go on to the next part. Take notes on the lines below it as you read.

■ But death is not the only price we pay because of drunk drivers. We pay for repairing cars and property damaged in crashes. We pay higher prices to insure our cars and ourselves. Sometimes people are disabled as a result of a crash. Then they may have high medical costs for life—to say nothing of the many work hours lost.

What can we do about this killer? We can change our ideas about drinking and driving. We can make stronger laws on drunk driving. Our young people must learn never to ride with someone who's been drinking. Most important, we must get the drunk driver off our roads.

B. _____
_____
_____

Part A Lesson 15

Words That Persuade

In this lesson you will
- read about something we have just too much of
- learn what biased writing is and how it might influence you
- learn how words can affect your feelings

Skills for Reading: Noting Bias

Picture It

Each child in the cartoon uses a different word to describe the same thing. But each word stirs up strong feelings. The children make it seem as if the car is beyond repair. The father tells what the damage *really* is. It's just a dent in the bumper.

Bias is a strong feeling. Biased words like *destroyed* and *ruined* show strong feeling. Biased writing gives just one side of a story. Balanced writing is the opposite. Balanced writing presents both sides of a story.

How can you spot bias when you read? First, look at the words that are used. Biased writing uses some words that show approval or disapproval. Words that show approval include *terrific, great, best, super,* or *outstanding.* Some words that show disapproval are *sleazy, dreadful, unfortunate, careless,* or *bad.*

Second, see how much of the story is told. Suppose you were reading an article. The author discussed why smoking should be banned in public places. Biased writing would tell only reasons against smoking. It might mention these: illness from smoke, danger from fire, and the cost of cleaning up after smokers. Balanced writing would mention these reasons. But it would also give the smokers' point of view. It would give both sides.

As a reader, you want to be able to spot biased writing. Then you can judge for yourself whether to trust the author's facts, believe the author's ideas, and agree with the author's opinions.

Here are some questions you can ask yourself. They can help you decide whether to believe what you read.

- Is this statement always true?
- Are any facts given to support the statement?
- Is the statement just one person's opinion?
- Why has this statement been made? Is it intended mainly to give information? Or is it meant to try to get me to do something?
- Who is making this statement? What are the qualifications of this person?

Here's an Example

Here are two paragraphs that tell about the same accident. The first is balanced writing. The second is biased writing.

- Five injuries were reported at the post office this week. All are due to ice at the bottom of the stairs. Three people are in the hospital with broken legs. Two have head injuries. Postmaster Don Swain reports the weather is responsible. Icy rain for three days made it impossible to keep the steps clear. Now, with record cold, normal deicing methods do not work. Swain regrets the injuries. He is stepping up efforts to clear the ice.

Compare the balanced writing above with the biased writing below.

- Five of our citizens lie injured today. Each is a victim of our careless post office. "There is no excuse for having a big patch of ice in front of the post office," says Liz Cato. Liz broke her leg in a fall just below the post office steps. "Sure, we've had bad weather. But why doesn't the post office use salt? It was dreadful! I blame Postmaster Swain. He has not carried out his responsibilities!"

The first article tells both sides of the story. It reports that five people have been injured. It also tells the postmaster's side. He says that bad weather has made it impossible to clear the ice.

Also, the words do not show emotion. They simply tell the facts. The article is an example of *balanced* writing.

In contrast, the second article is biased against the post office. It does not tell the postmaster's side at all. It uses words like "victim," "careless," and "dreadful." These words show strong disapproval. The article is one-sided, biased writing.

Working It Out

As you read the next two articles, ask yourself: Which article is balanced writing? Which is biased in favor of someone?"

■ Alfred N. Hyde, 87, of 395 N. Main, was charged Sunday night with theft. Hyde was found carrying a diamond-covered watch. The watch was reported missing earlier from the Bijou Jewelry shop at 787 S. Main. Hyde is being held, pending bail.

■ He lives alone. His relatives are dead. There is no one to care for him. Alfred N. Hyde is an 87-year-old man with nothing to brighten his life. Tonight he lies in a lonely, dirty jail cell.

With tears in his eyes, Hyde says it is all a mistake. He was caught by the beauty of a watch in the Bijou Jewelry shop. He wanted to see it sparkle in the sun. Police misunderstood and arrested him. There is no one to post bond. No one to help this lonely old man.

1. Which article tells the events from Hyde's point of view?

2. Copy three words or phrases that are meant to make you feel sorry for Mr. Hyde.

Writing to Improve Your Reading

Taking notes on biased writing can be very helpful. Your notes can help you spot facts, opinions, and biased words.

You read some pointers on taking notes on pages 115–116. Here's a chance to practice your note-taking skills. You can take notes as you read the next article. To start you off, here are some notes taken on the first two paragraphs.

garbage dumped for years
no one sees it or smells it
leads to pollution of water

You may want to review the pointers before you begin taking your own notes.

Reading on Your Own

The topic of the following article may surprise you. It's garbage. Actually, it's the problem of what to do with garbage. You may have heard the topic in the news. Cities all over the country are concerned about this problem. The author discusses one way of solving the problem. As you read, note the bias of the author.

Up in Smoke, Down to Ashes

No one gives much thought to garbage. It's not a pleasant subject. For years garbage has simply been hauled out from homes to dumps.

The town dump is usually at the edge of town. No one really sees it there. No one notices the chemicals from the garbage moving down into the ground. The chemicals pollute the groundwater. That water may one day be drunk by someone. No one even smells the dump—unless the wind is blowing from that direction.

City dumps are usually in poor areas of the city. There's a reason for that. Poor people don't have the power to keep dumps out. Some cities even move their garbage to dumps in the country.

Now such dumps are reaching their limits. U.S. cities are being buried in their own garbage. More than half of them will soon fill their dumps. Of course, the dumps were a bad idea in the first place. They pollute. They stink. They take up space. But an idea to solve the problem is even worse.

Burning garbage is suggested by some people. It's suggested by those who get rich from it. Some companies build huge incinerators that burn all garbage together. These companies try to sell their incinerators to local governments. And many local governments are buying.

Now everyone knows that burning gives off two things: smoke and ashes. The smoke from garbage incinerators has toxic substances. This poisonous smoke rises from incinerator stacks and into our air.

An incinerator is something that burns garbage. The word incinerate *means "to burn."*

Toxic means "poisonous." You may have heard this word in the phrase toxic waste *on the news.*

The ash left over is dangerous too. It's even more harmful than the garbage it came from. Scientists have found high levels of lead and other metals in the ash. These metals cause cancer and other illnesses.

What happens to the toxic ash? It's usually put in dumps! Ash takes up less room than solid garbage. And it won't smell the way garbage does. But chemicals from the ash can still move into the groundwater. Also, the ash can be blown away by the wind. Our air, our water, and our land can be poisoned.

We produce tons of garbage each day. That garbage is a problem. But burning it only creates worse problems.

Thinking About What You've Read

1. How does the author feel about the burning of garbage?

2. Write three words or phrases from the article that show the author's bias.

3. Here are some statements from the article. Write *Fact* if a statement is a fact. Write *Opinion* if it is an opinion.

    _____ A. The dumps were a bad idea in the first place.

    _____ B. Now such dumps are reaching their limits.

    _____ C. Chemicals in the ash are poisonous.

    _____ D. An idea to solve the problem is even worse.

4. How can dumps lead to water pollution?

5. The author gives one side of burning garbage. What questions would you like answered before you decide the issue?

A Test-Taking Tip

A question may ask how the author feels about the topic. Or it may ask how the author would feel about a related topic. To answer, you need to figure out the author's bias toward the topic. Then apply what you know. For example, say an author likes one idea. Then he or she will probably like a similar idea. If the author hates an idea, he or she may like an opposite idea.

GED Warm-up

Recycling is reusing material instead of throwing it away. How do you think the author would feel about recycling?

(1) He would probably be for it.
(2) He would probably be against it.
(3) He would probably not care one way or the other.

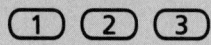

Working with Words

Here are some words that can be used to describe people.

1	2
happy-go-lucky	irresponsible
shy	timid
slender	skinny
flexible	wishy-washy

Which list has words that make a person seem pleasant?

_____

Which list has words that seem insulting?

_____

Each word in list **1** means about the same as the matching word in list **2**. But you probably felt the words in list **1** were kinder and more pleasant.

The two matching words have the same meaning. They both refer to the same basic idea. Their dictionary definitions are the same.

But the feelings that come from these words are different. The feelings of the words in list **1** are pleasant. The feelings of the words in list **2** are not. On the left below are some words from *Up in Smoke, Down to Ashes*. They create strong feelings. Match each word or phrase with the term from the right that means the same thing but does not create the same feeling.

1. dump   smell
2. garbage   make money
3. stink   have too much of
4. get rich   landfill
5. are being buried in waste

▲ Looking Back

In Lesson 15 you read one person's strong opinion about burning garbage. You practiced watching for biased words. You also learned how some words can affect the way you feel.

As you continue to read, watch for biased writing. See how a writer's choice of words can affect your feelings.

The Active Reader

Reading a Newspaper

Getting Started

News. Sports. Notices of events. Ads. Opinions. Weather. Newspapers have something for everyone.

There's a lot to read in a newspaper. In fact, you probably won't want to read it all. The trick is this: Choose the parts that have meaning for you. Look closely at a newspaper. You'll see it's designed to help you get information quickly.

Here's an Example

The contents tell you where to find each type of information. You can turn right to the section you want.

Newspaper articles are printed in narrow columns. You need to stop your eyes only once or twice on each line.

Articles help you get information quickly in another way. The most important facts of a story are given in the first few lines. Those sentences answer these questions:

Who was involved? **What** happened? **When** did it happen? **Where** did it happen? **How** did it happen?

You can read the first few sentences to know the facts. Then you can choose to go on or stop.

Working It Out

Read this news article. Then answer each question that follows.

Office Building Evacuated

■ Hume, Ohio. Poison fumes forced 157 workers to leave the office building at 27 N. Front St. Monday afternoon. The building manager reports the cloud appeared soon after a janitor used two chemicals to unplug a drain on the first floor.

Police and ambulances arrived at the scene two minutes after they were called. Twenty people were taken to nearby hospitals. All but one have been released.

Clint Pavan is the building janitor. He claims the mistake was not his. "I followed the directions to the letter," says Pavan.

1. What event is the article about?

   _____

2. When and where did the event happen?

   _____

3. How did the fumes occur?

   _____

Lesson 15 Words That Persuade / 123

Part A
Lesson 16

Just for Fun

Everybody loves a mystery. The best mysteries are those that happen to real people . . . and maybe a ghost or two. As you read about a troubled airplane, you may begin to wish you had been there to see it all happen.

The Ghosts of Eastern Airlines

The brothers, Wilbur and Orville Wright, brought their airplane to the beach near Kitty Hawk, North Carolina. They had built it themselves. Its body was made of slender sticks. The wings were covered with linen cloth. With its 4-cylinder engine clattering, the plane bounced along the sands. It lifted itself free and sailed through the air one morning. It did the same thing four times before noon. Its best flight saw the plane soar for a distance of 852 feet. The date was an historic one—December 17, 1903. The Wrights had made the world's first flights in a powered aircraft. Those flights marked the birth of the age of aviation.

Almost seventy years later, a giant airplane passed close to the beach at Kitty Hawk. The ship was a Lockheed L-1011. It was powered by three Rolls-Royce jet engines. It was flying from New York's Kennedy International Airport to Miami International in Florida. On board this night of December 29, 1972, were 176 passengers and crew. Like the Wright brothers' plane, the airplane was about to make history—but for a different reason. It was about to give birth to the greatest aviation ghost story of our time.

The flight went smoothly that night. The air was calm. The lights of Miami came into view. The plane began to drop down for a landing. It swept over the Everglades. But the L-1011 never made it to the runway. It crashed into the Everglades. It cut a path 1,600 feet long before finally coming to rest.

The crash took the lives of 99 people. Seventy-seven survivors were rescued. Most of them suffered serious injuries.

Among the dead were two members of the flight crew. One

was the plane's Captain. The other was the Flight Engineer. Both men lived through the crash, but died soon after. The Captain lived for about an hour. He was dead when rescuers finally took him from the shattered flight deck. The Flight Engineer was taken to a hospital. He died of his injuries about thirty hours later.

Ghostly Appearances
In the months following the crash, a number of strange things happened. The Captain and the Flight Engineer were seen time and again. They appeared in ghostly form before pilots, flight officers, stewardesses, and passengers. They were seen on other L-1011s owned by Eastern Airlines. In particular, the ghosts were seen aboard an L-1011 listed in the company records as Plane 318.

Let's consider first the Captain's appearances.

One day, just before Plane 318 taxied out for a flight, the head stewardess counted the passengers. She wanted to make sure that no one was missing. She found an extra passenger on board. It was a man in the uniform of an Eastern pilot. The young woman went to his seat and tried to get his name. The stranger refused to talk. He even refused to look at her. He just sat there and stared straight ahead. The stewardess said he seemed to be in a daze.

Finally, the stewardess called for help. Another stewardess and the ship's pilot arrived at the seat. The pilot looked at the silent man and gasped. The passenger, he said, was the Captain whom he had known quite well.

At that moment, the Captain disappeared. He didn't get up and walk away. He just vanished. Left behind were three very puzzled crew members.

Another time, a stewardess opened a luggage compartment above one of the seats. Her eyes widened. She had flown with the Captain some years earlier. Now she saw his face staring out at her from the compartment. The face vanished after a few moments.

The Flight Engineer appeared even more times than the Captain. During one flight, a woman was riding next to an empty seat. She glanced to her side—and was surprised to find a uniformed man sitting there. She had not seen him sit down. She had no idea where he came from. He sat looking straight ahead. In the next minute, the woman was screaming. The stranger had vanished right before her eyes. Later, the woman was shown a photograph of the Flight Engineer. She identified him as the man in the empty seat.

One night, a crew member went up to the flight deck to give it a final check before the pilot arrived for takeoff. He saw a man sitting at the engineering panel. He recognized the visitor right away—the Flight Engineer. The crew man later said the Engineer told him that he had just checked the panel. He said it was in good working order. Then, as before, the Flight Engineer disappeared.

Galley *means "kitchen" in this context.*

Many times the Engineer appeared in the galley below the passenger's cabin. The galley was lined with ovens used to heat the meals for everyone on board. The oven doors had small windows. Several stewardesses, on looking through the windows, saw the Engineer's face in the glass. One stewardess found an oven door open. She could see the Engineer's face inside it.

Another stewardess came into the galley during a night flight. She found the place damp and cold, even though all the ovens were on. She felt as if someone were in the room with her. Then she caught sight of a ball of mist above the ovens. It was about the size of a grapefruit. She thought it might be caused by steam. But, as she watched, it grew to the size of a basketball. All the while, it shifted and changed shape. At last, it became the face of a man wearing glasses. The Flight Engineer had worn glasses.

A Helpful Ghost

At least twice, the Flight Engineer proved to be a helpful ghost. On one flight, a stewardess found that one of the ovens was not working right. She telephoned the pilot and asked to have someone come and repair it. A man in a flight engineer's uniform appeared a few minutes later. He quickly took care of the problem and departed.

Then another engineer arrived. He looked puzzled when the stewardess explained that someone else had attended to things. He said that he was the only engineer on board. Later, the stewardess looked at the picture of the Flight Engineer. That was the man, she said, who had fixed the oven.

The Flight Engineer's most helpful appearance came during a trip that Plane 318 made to Mexico City. While down in the galley, a stewardess sighted his face in an oven window. Frightened, she hurried out. She told another stewardess of her experience. Together, they went to the galley. An officer from the flight deck joined them a short time later. The three stood and looked at the ghostly face. They could see it very clearly. The face looked troubled. At last, the ghost spoke. He warned them to watch out for fire aboard the plane.

The airplane made its way safely to Mexico City. But, when it took off for a return to the United States, one of its engines stalled. It began to backfire. There was an immediate danger of fire. The pilot quickly stopped the danger. He released a fire-fighting agent into the stalled engine. Then he circled the airport and landed. Mechanics checked the engine. They could find no reason for the stall.

More Mystery

The ghost stories mystified everyone who heard them. Had the stewardesses and pilots really seen the ghosts or had they imagined them?

On the other hand, it certainly seemed that they had seen *something,* no matter what it was. They were all trained airline workers. They were noted for their calmness. They weren't the types to "see things." And there had been times when the ghosts were seen by as many as three people. Each time, the people had all said that they had seen the same thing.

But, on the other hand, who could say what tricks the imagination might play on even the most sensible of individuals?

Eastern Airlines became troubled by the reports of strange things happening. They checked and found that Plane 318 had many of the parts taken from the crashed plane. They removed all those parts. Right away, the ghostly sightings stopped. Who can explain these events? They are still a mystery.

If you enjoyed reading this story, you might want to read others like it. You can find this story and others in the book *Great Mysteries of the Air* by Edward S. Dolan, Jr. The Active Reader on page 129 will teach you how to check for this book at your public library.

The Active Reader

Using a Library

Picture It

A library is a great place to know. Books make up a large part of most libraries. But libraries are not only books. They can include films, tapes, computers, and many other things.

Public libraries allow anyone to use their books, magazines, and reference books right in the library. But to take books, records, and films home, you need a card. It is easy to get a library card. Usually all you need is to give your address. Of course, to keep the card, you must take good care of the materials and return them when they are due.

Each item in a library has a call number. This is like an identification tag. If you know the call number of a book or other item you need, you can find it by using the call number.

Here's an Example
Books
Suppose you decide to borrow the book *Great Mysteries of the Air* by Edward S. Dolan, Jr. You would begin by finding its call number in the card catalog. Cards for books are in alphabetical order. You could look for the title under the letter **G**. Or you could look for the author under the letter **D**.

Write down the call number. Then find the book with that number on the shelves. At first, you might need a librarian to tell you which shelf to look on.

Perhaps you want to read about a subject but don't know the name of a book. Just look up the subject. For instance, you might look up the subject *Air Disasters* or *Mysteries.* Then you would find the cards for all the books in the library on that topic. You could look through them and choose any you find interesting.

Magazines and Newspapers

Recent magazines and newspapers are usually on display in a library. You can find older magazines on the shelves. They will be bound together in books.

If you want to read an article in an older newspaper, you may need to use microfilm. All the papers for a week are kept on a reel of film. You need to put the film on a viewing machine to read the paper. The first time you use microfilm, ask a librarian to help you find and use the film.

Reference Books

Reference books cannot be borrowed. They must be used in the library. Here is how they will help you:

- A **dictionary** gives the meanings of a word. It tells how to pronounce the word. It may give the word's history.

If you need to know what a foreign word means, you can look it up in a foreign language dictionary. For instance, a German-English dictionary would give you the English meaning for German words.

- An **encyclopedia** gives facts about a wide range of subjects. It's a good place to start when you want a general overview of a subject.
- An **atlas** is a book of maps. Some atlases have road maps. Others show counties, states, or countries.
- **Almanacs** list facts and figures about topics that might come up in conversation. Almanacs may list the capitals of states or dates of eclipses. They often give wise sayings, folk remedies, weather forecasts, or even recipes.
- **Books of quotations** are useful when you need to write a speech or essay. You may want to begin by quoting what a well-known person said about the subject. Books of quotations list interesting sayings, usually grouped by subject.

Working It Out

Look at the reference books listed above. Which book would be most likely to have the answer to each question? Be sure to write the name of the book, not the answer to the question. (For some questions, more than one answer is possible.)

1. What city is the capital of Maine?

_____

2. How does the human heart work?

_____

3. What is the best road to take from New York City to Boston?

_____

4. What English word means the same as the Spanish word *escuela*?

_____

5. What is a good quote for opening a speech about love?

_____

6. What does the word *quandary* mean?

_____

7. When can we expect the next eclipse of the moon?

Measuring What You've Learned

This test has 5 reading selections and 23 questions. It will help you see how much you've learned. Read each selection carefully. Then answer the questions about it. This test is not timed, so don't feel you have to hurry. When you've finished, you can check your answers on page 243.

Read the article. Then circle the best answer for each question that follows.

We like to feel safe. We lock our doors. We wear seat belts in a car. We pay our police and fire departments to keep us safe. Why, then, do we *love* to be frightened by scary movies?

One look at the movie page of your newspaper tells what America will pay to watch: scary stories. Here is a movie about people trapped in a burning building. Next to it is a movie about a family of "living" dead people. Another is a tense story about a spy who lives among savage enemies. And many favorite movies are about haunted houses.

The best movies, according to investors, are the most frightening ones. Even movies for children must have moments of fear to be "successful."

1. Which of the following best tells the main idea? (Circle one.)
   A. Everyone likes to feel safe.
   B. Scary movies are popular.
   C. Scary movies are bad for children.

2. Which of the following is a detail the author uses to support the main idea?
   A. Most drivers use seat belts.
   B. Newspapers advertise many movies.
   C. Scary movies make a lot of money.

3. Why does the author mention that children like scary movies?
   A. to show that all ages like scary stories
   B. to show that people are the same
   C. to explain why adults like scary stories

4. What does the word *successful* mean in the third paragraph of this article?
   A. famous
   B. getting the best reviews
   C. making the most money

5. Which of the following best tells the author's purpose?
   A. to inform the reader about how to know whether or not a movie is good
   B. to persuade the reader to avoid scary movies and books
   C. to entertain by describing how nearly everyone likes scary stories

Read the article. Then circle the best answer to each question that follows.

Have you ever wondered where and when money was first used? Thousands of years ago, people did not use money. Instead, they traded things like salt, shells, or food for what they needed. For example, a family raising chickens might trade eggs in order to get cloth for clothing.

We know that about 2,500 years ago some people began using money. Coins were used in the land that is now western Turkey. The coins were made of a mixture of silver and gold. They were shaped like beans. Each coin had a stamp on it. The stamp showed what the coin weighed. People did not have to weigh a coin each time it changed hands.

For hundreds of years, coins were the only type of money in use. Then, about 1,300 years ago, the Chinese began to use paper money. People in Europe heard that the Chinese used paper money. But the Europeans did not understand how paper could have so much value. They continued to use gold, silver, and coins as their money until about the 1400s. Even then, paper money was made by banks and not by governments.

By the late 1800s, paper money had become more common all over the world. In Canada, soldiers were given their compensation, or pay, in the form of playing cards. Each card was marked to be worth a certain amount of money. Today, nearly everyone is willing to use paper money. In fact, most of us can't seem to get enough of it!

6. The author tells the history of money to show that
   A. money has changed over the years
   B. people have always used money
   C. trade is better than using coins

7. Which of the following statements is true?
   A. Coins and paper money came into use about the same time.
   B. Americans invented paper money.
   C. Paper money was used in China long before it was used in America.

Read the two summaries below and decide which is the best. Then answer the questions that follow.

(A) People have not always used money. Before they used money, people traded goods to get what they needed.

(B) Early people used trade instead of money. Coins were used as early as 2,500 years ago. Paper money was used in China about 1,300 years ago.

8. Paragraph B is a better summary than A because
   A. B gives only the most important facts from the article
   B. A fails to give any of the important facts
   C. A gives many details that were not mentioned in the article

9. Which of the following sentences should be added to paragraph A?
   A. Coins were used about 2,500 years ago, and paper money followed later.

B. Paper money was used about 2,500 years ago, and coins followed later.
C. For a long time, Europeans felt that paper could not be used as money.

10. The word *compensation* in this article most nearly means
    A. salary
    B. honor
    C. rules

Read the article. Then circle the best answer for each question that follows.

If the early settlers came to visit America today, they would have many surprises. What might surprise them most is that nearly all American homes have a bathtub or shower.

You see, the Puritans who settled New England did not approve of bathing. They felt it was a sin to go without clothes, even to take a bath! They also brought to this country the idea that bathing was unhealthy. For many years, the Europeans had believed that bathing would lead to illness. They used perfume to smell good. They used powder to cover dirt. It is said that England's Queen Elizabeth the First had more than an inch of makeup on her face when she died.

Today, of course, our ideas about baths are quite different. We feel that keeping clean leads to good health. We often think of a bath as a way to relax. The backyard swimming pool—another form of bathing—is a popular American luxury. We can only wonder what the Puritans might say if they could see a group of us relaxing together in a wooden hot tub!

11. Which of the following conclusions can reasonably be drawn from the article?
    A. Soaking in a hot tub is good for your health.
    B. Puritans did not keep their homes very clean.
    C. Our ideas about bathing have changed over the years.

12. Based on information in the article, you can conclude that
    A. soap is a very recent invention
    B. Queen Elizabeth the First did not wash her face often
    C. Queen Elizabeth the First was sick all her life

13. Puritans avoided bathing because
    A. their water was polluted
    B. their climate was too cold
    C. they felt nakedness was sinful

14. As a result of not bathing, many people in the days of Queen Elizabeth had to
    A. live alone
    B. wear very heavy clothes
    C. wear perfume and powder

15. On the basis of this article, you can infer that if the Puritans who settled our country came here today, they would probably be
    A. disapproving of today's beach clothing
    B. eager to swim in a public swimming pool
    C. pleased that many schools give swimming lessons to their students

Read the article. Then circle the best answer for each question that follows.

If you had met Mohandas Gandhi as a child, you might have felt he would never come to much. He was tiny. His ears stuck out. Everyone knew he was afraid of the dark. No one could have guessed that this person one day would have the power to end a bloody civil war in his own country, India.

In his early years, Gandhi did poorly in school. He asked his family to send him to England to study law. He became a good student there. He began to see that his own mind was a powerful tool for him.

Back in India, he could not find much work. He was too shy to talk in court. He worked in South Africa for many years.

When Gandhi and his family went back to India, there was trouble all over. Many people wanted to fight to be free of England. Gandhi showed them peaceful ways to get what they wanted.

First, Gandhi taught people to make cloth so they did not need to buy it from England. England lost a lot of money. Then Gandhi talked people into making their own salt instead of buying it from England. England lost more money.

Gandhi was now a strong leader of his people. He wanted India to be free. But instead of fighting, he fasted. He did not eat for many days. The English were afraid to let him starve. They feared his many followers would rise up. So they gave in to some of his demands.

Finally, in 1947, India became free. But there were still problems. The people of India were fighting each other. Those of the Hindu religion were killing Moslems. Moslems were killing Hindus. Gandhi said he would not eat until the killing stopped. He fasted for weeks. When he was nearly dead, he heard the good news—Hindus and Moslems had stopped killing. They did not want Gandhi to die. Tiny, shy Gandhi had brought peace to his country.

16. Which of the following old sayings best describes Gandhi's idea of how to fight?
    A. The pen is mightier than the sword.
    B. An eye for an eye and a tooth for a tooth.
    C. Don't fire your guns until you see the whites of your enemies' eyes.

17. Which action would Gandhi most likely not take to fight racism in the United States?
    A. organize a boycott of stores that don't hire blacks
    B. arrest and jail shop owners who don't hire blacks
    C. urge blacks to open their own stores to create more jobs for blacks

18. The word *fast* in this article most nearly means
    A. speedy
    B. tightly fastened
    C. go without eating

Read the letter. Then circle the best answer to each question that follows.

This letter was mailed to everyone who uses the Wilton County Public Library.

Dear Library Patrons,
A new Esperanto Club is starting here at the library. We invite you to join us. Everyone can have fun in this new club. We believe you will learn some important things and meet interesting people too.

Esperanto, as you may know, is an international language. Esperanto was invented in 1887 by a man named Dr. Lazarus Zamenhof. He invented it so that people of all countries could speak together and understand each other.

Through Esperanto, scientists from different countries can share ideas. Companies can conduct business all over the world. Perhaps some day Esperanto can lead to world understanding and peace.

Esperanto is easy to learn. At our meetings, club members will learn and practice this interesting language. It is a terrific way to meet great new friends and have a good time. You do not have to pay for books or lessons. Yet you can gain a great deal. Please do yourself a favor. Come and join our Esperanto Club.

19. Which statement is a fact, not an opinion?
    A. Everyone can have fun in this new club.
    B. Esperanto was invented in 1887 by a man named Dr. Lazarus Zamenhof.
    C. Esperanto is easy to learn.

20. Which statement contains words meant to make you want to join the club?
    A. A new Esperanto Club is starting here at the library.
    B. Club members will learn and practice Esperanto.
    C. This is a terrific way to meet great new friends and have a good time.

21. The letter is an example of biased writing because it
    A. gives a one-sided view of the Esperanto Club
    B. does not tell when and where the first meeting will be held
    C. tries to persuade people to do something that might be harmful

22. The author's purpose is to
    A. persuade people to join the new Esperanto Club
    B. entertain people by telling about Esperanto
    C. inform people about a new club

23. In this letter, the word *international* most nearly means
    A. across the ocean
    B. within one nation
    C. between two or more different nations

You can check your answers on page 243.

Your Test Results

Here's a table like the one for Measuring What You Know. It shows you three things: (1) the test question number, (2) the main skill each question tests, and (3) the lesson that teaches that skill.

Which skills did you do well on? Which skills do you still need to practice? You can use the table to plan which lessons to review.

Question	Skill	Lesson
1	Main Idea	1, 2
2, 3	Supporting Details	3
5, 22	Author's Purpose	4
4, 10, 18, 23	Word Meanings	6
6, 7	Seeing Patterns	5–9
8, 9	Summaries	9–10
11, 12	Drawing Conclusions	11
15	Inference	10
13, 14	Causes and Effects	12
16, 17	Applying Ideas	13
19	Facts and Opinions	14
20, 21	Biased Language	15

Part B
Reading Skills for Literature

In **Part B,** you will build skills in reading literature. Some of the readings are taken from magazines, newspapers, essays, or reviews. Some are taken from short stories or novels. A few are taken from plays that appeal to modern readers like you. And you will read several humorous and serious poems.

You may be nervous about reading literature. But keep in mind that you have one important asset: your reading *experience.* Do you read newspaper columnists or movie reviews? Then you have experience in reading nonfiction. Do you read stories or watch TV? That experience will help you read fiction and plays. Do you listen to song lyrics? That can help you read poems.

These lessons will build on that experience. They will give you tools for reading literature. You probably will enjoy the stories you read.

Measuring What You Know

You can test your reading skills in this short survey. There are 3 reading selections and 13 questions. The survey is here to help you. It will show you what you already know. It will also tell you what you need to study.

Read each selection carefully. Then answer the questions about it. Take your time. When you're finished, check your answers on page 236. The table on page 141 will help you plan your study time.

Directions: Choose the <u>one best answer</u> to each question.

<u>Items 1–5 refer to the passage below.</u>

I did not often get angry. I like to think it is not in my nature. Also, like all reporters, I got close to an awful lot of tears and pain and injustice. If a reporter reacts to all he sees, he will stay angry most of the time. But the Medgar Evers case hit me harder than most things I had seen. . . .

Brutality and violence were not new to me. But this was different. Evers had been murdered on his doorstep. His children were desolated by what had happened. Here someone had lain in the grass, snakelike, across from a man's home, had waited for him to climb the steps to his porch and in front of his family had shot him in the back and then had slithered away. I felt great waves of anger. I also thought about how this despicable act must make the country look.

A man named Byron de la Beckwith was arrested, and later tried, twice, for the murder of Medgar Evers. Both trials resulted in hung juries so, in the eyes of the law, he was and is an innocent man, although there have been persistent reports that Beckwith went around the state boasting that he had killed Evers.

1. What is the main idea of the *entire* passage?
   (1) Byron de la Beckwith probably murdered Medgar Evers.
   (2) The murder of Medgar Evers was so awful that it made the writer angry.
   (3) The writer is a reporter who did not often get angry.
   ① ② ③

2. The reporter thinks of himself as the kind of person who usually
   (1) keeps his emotions under control
   (2) stays angry most of the time
   (3) works hard to fight injustice
   ① ② ③

138 / Part B Reading Skills for Literature

3. The first paragraph tells about the author's anger. The author explains this anger in the rest of the article by
   (1) listing all the things he saw that made him angry
   (2) telling the story of Medgar Evers's death from beginning to end
   (3) contrasting Medgar Evers's goodness with his murderer's crime
   ① ② ③

4. Why is Byron de la Beckwith considered innocent of murdering Medgar Evers?
   (1) because he did not really commit the crime
   (2) because two different juries could not find him guilty
   (3) because the police did not believe he murdered Evers
   ① ② ③

5. What does the word "tried" mean in the line "Byron de la Beckwith was arrested, and later tried, twice, for the murder"?
   (1) tested
   (2) made an effort
   (3) put on trial
   ① ② ③

Items 6–9 refer to the passage below.

Roy sighed and picked up [his bat] Wonderboy. He slowly walked up the steps.

"Knock the cover off of it," Pop yelled.

"Attention, please," the P.A. man announced. "Roy Hobbs, number forty-five, batting for Baily."...

Glancing at the wives' box, Roy saw that Memo had her head turned away. He set his jaw and advanced to the plate....

He couldn't tell the color of the pitch that came at him. All he could think of was that he was sick to death of waiting, and tongue-out thirsty to begin. The ball was now a dew drop staring him in the eye so he stepped back and swung from the toes.

Wonderboy flashed in the sun. It caught the sphere where it was biggest. A noise like a twenty-one gun salute cracked the sky. There was a straining, ripping sound and a few drops of rain spattered to the ground. The ball screamed toward the pitcher and seemed suddenly to dive down at his feet. He grabbed it to throw to first and realized to his horror that he held only the cover. The rest of it, unraveling cotton thread as it rode, was headed into the outfield.

6. How did Roy feel as he stood at home plate?
   (1) eager to start playing
   (2) angry at his coach
   (3) hungry and thirsty
   ① ② ③

7. Which of these lines from the story helps show that it takes place at a baseball game?
   (1) "Memo had her head turned away"
   (2) "There was a straining, ripping sound"
   (3) "Roy Hobbs, number forty-five, batting for Baily"
   ① ② ③

8. What happens to the ball that Roy hits?
   (1) It is caught by the pitcher and thrown to first base.
   (2) It flashes in the sun and cracks the bat.
   (3) The cover flies off, and it begins to unwind.
   ① ② ③

9. What detail does the author include to help create a feeling of drama as Roy hits the ball?
   (1) A few raindrops fall.
   (2) The crowd roars.
   (3) A tremendous thunderclap sounds.
   ① ② ③

Items 10–13 refer to this poem.

When I Heard the Learn'd Astronomer

When I heard the learn'd astronomer,
When the proofs, the figures, were ranged in columns before me,
When I was shown the charts and diagrams, to add, divide, and measure them,
When I sitting heard the astronomer where he lectured with much applause in the lecture-room,
How soon unaccountable I became tired and sick,
Till rising and gliding out I wander'd off by myself,
In the mystical moist night-air, and from time to time,
Look'd up in perfect silence at the stars.

10. What does the poet do on the night he describes in the poem?
    (1) learns all about stars so he can become an astronomer
    (2) leaves a lecture and walks into the night by himself
    (3) becomes sick and tired of the world and everyone in it
    ① ② ③

11. What is the *main* point the poet is telling you?
    (1) An astronomer was talking about stars.
    (2) Taking a walk when you feel sick can help.
    (3) You appreciate nature more by experiencing it than by studying it.
    ① ② ③

12. How does this poem make you feel at the end?
    (1) thoughtful
    (2) excited
    (3) cheerful
    ① ② ③

13. What does the word "figures" mean as it is used in the second line of the poem?
    (1) numbers
    (2) shapes
    (3) people
    ① ② ③

You can check your answers to this test on page 236.

Using the Results

This table shows you the *main* skill tested by each question in Measuring What You Know. Did you have problems with some questions? If you did, find those questions on the table. You'll see which skills you need to practice. You'll also find which lessons teach those skills.

Did you find the lessons that teach the skills you need to practice? You can study those lessons carefully. You will want to work through every lesson in the book, of course. This will strengthen the skills you already have. The reading practice will help you not only read more smoothly but also build your word power.

When you have finished all the lessons in this book, you'll take another test. The results of that test will show you how much you have improved on each reading skill.

Question	Skill	Lesson
1	Main idea	2
2	Supporting details	2
3	Seeing patterns	3
4	Cause and effect	4
5	Understanding vocabulary	3, 8
6	Character	6, 7, 10
7	Setting	6, 7, 10
8	Plot	6, 8, 10
9	Author's craft	9
10–12	Understanding poetry	11
13	Understanding vocabulary	3, 8

Part B Lesson 1

Reading Nonfiction

> *In this lesson you will*
> ■ read some examples of nonfiction literature
> ■ learn about the purposes of nonfiction

What Is Nonfiction?

Picture It

If you read newspaper or magazine articles, you read nonfiction. Nonfiction is writing that is about facts and ideas. It deals with real events, real people, and real things. Newspaper and magazine articles are just one type of nonfiction you can read. Nonfiction *literature* offers you even more kinds of writing to choose from.

Here's an Example

Biographies are one kind of nonfiction literature. A **biography** is the story of one person's life told by another person.

This paragraph is from a biography of Thomas Jefferson, the third President of the United States.

■ He had no love for the legal profession, but from the time he began practicing law in 1767, Thomas Jefferson was a very successful lawyer. His work grew from sixty-eight cases his first year to more than four hundred annually just a few years later. But he regarded a lawyer's work as part of the "dark side" of life. Reading and learning were far more important to him.

In the paragraph you read facts about a real person—Thomas Jefferson. You also learned of some ideas Jefferson had about lawyers.

142 / Part B Reading Skills for Literature

Autobiographies are a special kind of biography. An **autobiography** is the story of a person's life told by *that* person, not someone else. Like all types of nonfiction, autobiographies deal with real people and events. In Lesson 4 you'll get to read a selection from an autobiography.

Essays are another kind of nonfiction literature. In an **essay,** an author tells you his or her thoughts and feelings about a topic. The topic can be anything in the world. Here are the first two paragraphs of a funny essay. The topic is etiquette, or manners.

> ■ Have you noticed a strange thing about etiquette books? They are all written for grownups. *Us.*
>
> I really don't understand it. Most adults have lovely manners; it's a pleasure to have them around. Ask an adult to hand you your glasses and he says "Here they are, dear." He doesn't put them behind his back and say "Guess which hand?" And when you give him a birthday present he doesn't burst into tears and say "I already *have* Chinese checkers!" What I wish is that Emily and Amy and the others would get to work on the real trouble area—people under twelve.

The author gave you her thoughts on etiquette books. She talked about how *real* adults and *real* children act.

Authors of **journals** and other kinds of personal writing try to share their experiences with you. Here's an example from a journal a woman kept on a trip through the West.

> ■ I step out of the car and take a short stroll away from the road. The dark green pines sway against the sky. The evergreen forest fills my lungs. From off in the distance comes the ever-present rush of a rocky mountain stream. Across the valley, the peaks of the Front Range command the scene.
>
> How can someone look at such a sight and think "oil" or "development" or "money"? Such sad, blind people must not alter the scene. Our children and their children must also be able to see the green pines sway, smell the evergreen forest, hear the ever-present rush of a stream. . . .

Why Do People Write Nonfiction?

Authors of nonfiction have a purpose, or reason, for writing. You learned about their purposes in Part A. Sometimes they write to inform you. At other times they write to convince, or persuade, you about something. And sometimes authors just want to entertain or amuse you.

Here's an Example

Look again at the paragraph from a biography of Thomas Jefferson. Notice that the paragraph gives you information about Jefferson and how he felt about lawyers. The author's main purpose is to inform you about Jefferson.

Now look at the two paragraphs from the essay about manners. Can you see how the author gives some funny examples of children's bad manners? Do you agree that the author's main purpose is to entertain you?

Finally, reread the travel journal. The author gives reasons for enjoying the wilderness. The main purpose is to persuade you that some wilderness should be saved.

Working It Out

Read each of the following nonfiction passages. Decide what the author's purpose was for writing it. You can choose from the list below.

Purposes for Writing

- to inform
- to entertain
- to persuade

1. I strongly support the idea of working your way up on the job. My first job here at the Tip Top Restaurant was as a dishwasher. Then I worked as a bus girl, waitress, cashier, cook, and an assistant manager. Recently I was promoted to the job of restaurant manager. Because I have done every job in the restaurant, I know how to keep things running smoothly. I know all the employees and what I can expect from each one.

   The author's main purpose is _____.

2. [B]asketball is a hunting game. It lasts for forty minutes, and there are ten men on the court, so the likelihood is that any one player, even a superstar, will actually have the ball in his hands for only four of those minutes, or perhaps a little more. The rest of the time, a player on offense either is standing around recovering his breath or is on the move, foxlike, looking for openings, sizing up chances, attempting to screen off a defensive man. . . .

   The author's main purpose is _____.

3. If children through the age of five could ride free on the trolley, what father's child would ever turn six?
   "When will I be six, Pa?"
   "When you get off the trolley."

   The author's main purpose is _____.

Looking Ahead

In the following pages, you'll read some of the types of nonfiction literature discussed in this lesson. You'll learn skills that will help you understand what you read. You can look for the main idea in a passage. You can look for a pattern in what you read. You can change your reading speed to suit the kind of passage you're reading.

You'll also find that the more you read, the more your reading skills will improve. The best way to become a better reader is to practice reading. And a good way to practice is with interesting nonfiction literature.

Part B
Lesson 2

Living Simply

In this lesson you will
- read a passage about beach living
- find the main idea and supporting details
- outline to help you find the main idea
- learn how to figure out the meanings of words that sound alike

Skills for Reading: Main Idea and Supporting Details

Picture It

What is the topic of this picture? That is, what is the picture about?

The topic of the picture is a race. The picture shows a woman winning the race. That's the main idea of the picture. It's the most important point that the picture shows.

To get the point of a picture, you need to figure out its main idea. To get the author's point in nonfiction, you also need to figure out the main idea.

You already know about main ideas from Part A. There you learned how to figure out the main idea of a reading passage. You also learned how to find the supporting details. These details are the small pieces of information that tell more about the main idea.

To help you figure out the main idea and supporting details, remember to ask yourself the following questions:

Lesson 2 Living Simply / 145

1. In a word or two, who or what is the passage about? That is, what is the **topic?**
2. What is the author's most important point about the topic? In other words, what is the **main idea?**
3. What details tell more about the main idea? That is, what are the **supporting details?**

Here's an Example

You know that you need to find the topic of a passage before you can figure out the main idea. One way to find the topic is to look for an important word that is repeated. Then ask yourself: "Does this word tell me who or what the passage is about?" If the answer is yes, you've found the topic. If the answer is no, you'll need to look for another important word and ask yourself the same question.

In the following paragraph, the words *diary* and *diaries* are used four times. These words tell you what the paragraph is about. Diaries are the topic of the paragraph.

■ Anne Frank was a German Jewish girl who kept a famous <u>diary</u>. From her <u>diary</u> we've learned how her family hid from the Nazis in an attic apartment for two years during World War II. People in all situations of life have kept <u>diaries</u>. Some were famous, such as Thomas Edison, the inventor, and that great American wit and writer, Mark Twain. But others were ordinary people who used their <u>diaries</u> to express their thoughts and feelings about their everyday lives.

After you've identified the topic of a passage, you need to figure out its main idea. You already know that the main idea is sometimes given in one sentence.

This is the case in the following paragraph. The topic is early American women. The main idea is given in the first sentence.

■ Early American women had few rights. There were almost no colleges for women, and most professional careers were closed to them. A married woman could not own property. Instead, any property she had legally belonged to her husband. In addition, American women were barred from voting in all elections.

The following outline shows the topic, main idea, and supporting details of the paragraph you just read. Notice how the supporting details tell more about the main idea.

Topic: Early American women
  Main Idea:
  Early American women had few rights.
   Supporting Details:
   1. few colleges for women
   2. most careers closed to women
   3. married women couldn't own property
   4. women couldn't vote

You may also recall that sometimes the main idea is not given in a sentence. If it isn't, you can figure it out for yourself. First think about the details in the passage. Then decide which is the most important point the author is making about the topic. You can then put that idea into a sentence of your own.

For example, look again at the paragraph about diaries. The main idea isn't given in a sentence. But the details give information about diaries and the kinds of people who have kept them. You could therefore say the main idea is: Famous and ordinary people alike have kept diaries.

Working It Out

If you like dogs, you'll probably like this paragraph about a dog. After you've read it, answer the questions.

■ Charley likes to get up early, and he likes me to get up early too. And why shouldn't he? Right after his breakfast he goes back to sleep. Over the years he has developed a number of innocent-appearing ways to get me up. He can shake himself and his collar loud enough to wake the dead. If that doesn't work he gets a sneezing fit. But perhaps his most irritating method is to sit quietly beside the bed and stare into my face with a sweet and forgiving look on his face; I come out of deep sleep with the feeling of being looked at.

1. What is the topic of the paragraph?

_____

2. Underline the sentence that gives the main idea.

3. What are three details that support the main idea?

_____

_____

_____

Writing to Improve Your Reading

You've learned that writing your own outline can help you find the topic, main idea, and supporting details of a passage. Begin by making a blank outline, as shown below.

Topic:

   Main Idea:

      Supporting Details:

As you read the following passage, fill in as much of the outline as you can. Follow the example given on page 146. Your outline will help you answer the questions on pages 149–150.

Reading on Your Own

The following passage comes from a book called Gift from the Sea. *This book was written by Anne Morrow Lindbergh. As you read, fill in the blank outline that you just copied.*

Beach Living

One learns first of all in beach living the art of shedding; how little one can get along with, not how much. Physical shedding to begin with, which then mysteriously spreads into other fields. Clothes, first. Of course, one needs less in the sun. But one needs less anyway, one finds suddenly. One does not need a closet-full, only a small suitcase-full. And what a relief it is! Less taking up and down of hems, less mending, and—best of all—less worry about what to wear. One finds one is shedding not only clothes—but vanity.

Vanity is too much pride in the way one looks.

Next, shelter. One does not need the airtight shelter one has in winter in the North. Here I live in a bare sea-shell of a cottage. No heat, no telephone, no plumbing to speak of, no hot water, a two-burner oil stove, no gadgets to go wrong. No rugs. There were some, but I rolled them up the first day; it is easier to sweep the sand off a bare floor. But I find I don't bustle about with unnecessary sweeping and cleaning here. I am no longer aware of the dust. I have shed my Puritan conscience about absolute tidiness and cleanliness. Is it possible that, too, is a material burden? No curtains. I do not need them for privacy; the pines around my house are enough protection. I want the windows open all the time, and I don't want to worry about rain. I begin

Puritan means "very strict."

148 / Part B Reading Skills for Literature

to shed my Martha-like anxiety about many things. Washable slipcovers, faded and old—I hardly see them; I don't worry about the impression they make on other people. I am shedding pride. As little furniture as possible; I shall not need much. I shall ask into my shell only those friends with whom I can be completely honest. I find I am shedding hypocrisy in human relationships. What a rest that will be! The most exhausting thing in life, I have discovered, is being insincere. That is why so much of social life is exhausting; one is wearing a mask. I have shed my mask. . . .

I love my sea-shell of a house. I wish I could live in it always. I wish I could transport it home. But I cannot. It will not hold a husband, five children and the necessities and trappings of daily life. I can only carry back my little channeled whelk. It will sit on my desk in Connecticut, to remind me of the ideal of a simplified life, to encourage me in the game I played on the beach. To ask how little, not how much, can I get along with.

Martha was a woman in the Bible who complained when her sister Mary listened to Jesus instead of helping with the household chores.

Hypocrisy means "dishonesty" or "phoniness."

A whelk is a sea snail. Here the word refers only to the snail's shell.

Thinking About What You've Read

1. The topic of the passage is _____
2. Tell in your own words what beach living teaches the author about clothes.
   _____
   _____

3. Circle the letter of the main idea of the passage.
   A. Beach living teaches a person not to worry about dirt and dust.
   B. Beach living teaches a person how little he or she really needs.
   C. An airtight house is not needed for beach living.

4. Circle the letters of two details that support the main idea of the passage.
   A. One does not need a closet-full.
   B. The most exhausting thing in life . . . is being insincere.
   C. No curtains. I do not need them for privacy.
   D. I want the windows open all the time.

5. List at least two things you own that you really don't need. Explain why you could get along without each one.

___

GED Warm-up

Why does the author at first wear fewer clothes?

(1) The weather is sunny and warm.
(2) She did not bring enough clothing.
(3) There is no one around to see her.

① ② ③

Working with Words

Read the following pairs of words. How are the words in each pair alike? How are they different?

sun   son   there   their   too   two

The words in each pair are pronounced the same but have different meanings. They also have different spellings.

When words like these appear in sentences, the surrounding words, or context, help you decide which meaning is correct. The spelling also is a clue to the word's meaning. Being able to figure out the correct meaning of words that sound alike helps you understand what you read. You probably did just that when you read sentences like "one needs less in the sun" in *Beach Living*.

The following sentences are also from *Beach Living*. Circle the word that correctly completes each sentence. If you need help, you can check a dictionary.

1. _____ learns first of all in beach living the art of shedding.
   One   Won

2. No rugs. There were _____ , but I rolled them up the first day.
   sum   some

3. It is easier to sweep the sand off a _____ floor.
   bear   bare

4. But I find I don't bustle about with unnecessary sweeping and cleaning _____ .
   here   hear

5. Washable slipcovers, faded and old—I hardly _____ them.
   sea   see

▲ Looking Back

In this lesson you read about what a person can learn from living on the beach. You also reviewed how to find the topic, main idea, and supporting details of a passage.

Whenever you read nonfiction, you'll find it helpful to figure out the main idea. When you know the main idea, you know what the author is trying to tell you. This communication is what reading and writing are all about.

The Active Reader

Setting Your Own Purpose

Picture It

Carol bought a new bicycle for her son. Look at the picture. What is Carol reading? What do you think her purpose for reading is?

You've learned that authors have purposes for writing and readers have purposes for reading. You have a purpose for reading each time you sit down with a magazine, a newspaper, or a nonfiction book.

Here's an Example

Like Carol, you've probably read an instruction manual to find out how to do something. That is one purpose for reading.

Reading for enjoyment is another purpose. When you read a good true story, you're usually reading for enjoyment. You're also reading to find out what happened to the people in the story.

Reading for information is another important purpose. You might, for example, read an article to get information about new treatments for cancer. Sometimes you read to find out the writer's thoughts or opinions about something. Journals and personal essays tell you the writer's thoughts or opinions.

You'll find it helpful to take a moment to think about your purpose *before* you begin to read. This will help you focus on what you hope to get out of your reading. It will also help you understand better what you read.

Working It Out

In the following passage, the author gives his thoughts and opinions about personal letters. Decide on a purpose for reading the passage. You can write your purpose below or on your own paper.

_____

_____

Lesson 2 Living Simply / 151

Now read the passage with your purpose in mind.

■ There is something special about a personal letter. It's better than a phone call, no matter what the telephone company says. A phone call disappears into the air as soon as the receiver is put back on the hook. A good letter can last a lifetime.

Some of my most precious possessions are letters that have been written to me sometime in the past. I don't have a single memorable phone call stored in a box in my attic or basement. I've never thrown away a good letter and, like any real treasure, I don't even have to look at them to enjoy having them. I *know* I have them. The telephone calls come and go. They make no permanent impression on me and have no place in my memory.

A personal letter is a good thing because you say things you can't say in a crowd and might not even say to the person face to face. If you feel like it, a letter allows you to take yourself and your thoughts more seriously than you would dare take them in conversation. And you can say things without interruption.

1. Reread the purpose you wrote for reading the passage. Did you meet your purpose?
   _____

2. What did you find out that you expected to find out?
   _____
   _____
   _____

3. Did you find out something that you didn't expect to find out? If so, what?
   _____
   _____
   _____

If you're walking to a store, you don't start out without first knowing the way. You could waste a lot of energy otherwise. Reading is like walking. It takes energy. And it's a waste of energy to start reading without knowing *why* you're reading. So before you begin to read, think about "where you want to go." That is, think about your purpose for reading.

152 / Part B Reading Skills for Literature

Part B
Lesson 3

Staying Young

In this lesson you will
- read a selection about a young-thinking grandmother
- review some patterns authors use to organize their writing
- take notes to help you identify a pattern
- use context clues to figure out unfamiliar words

Skills for Reading: Seeing Patterns

Picture It

In this picture, how are the items on the shelves organized?

Grocers put all the canned vegetables in the same section. You can see that all the different brands of each vegetable are grouped together. The same is true for all the other kinds of food in the store.

Organizing items in this way makes your shopping quicker and easier. Can you imagine how confusing it would be if the canned vegetables were scattered throughout the store?

Grocers organize their shelves to make it easier for you to shop. And authors organize their ideas to make them easier for you to understand. You've already learned some patterns of organization that authors use. In this lesson, you'll review three patterns that are often used in nonfiction literature. Recognizing these patterns will help you understand and remember the nonfiction passages you read.

Lesson 3 Staying Young / 153

Here's an Example

Listing is one pattern that authors use in nonfiction. An author might list examples or reasons or pieces of information. In the following paragraphs, the author lists examples of the sounds you would hear in the forest at evening.

■ In the evening the sounds change. As the setting sun turns the lake into a sheet of glittering gold the yodeling laugh of a loon floats across from the . . . opposite shore. Overhead the pines and the spruce sigh in the soft evening breeze, and around the point a beaver slaps the water as he dives. . . .

And if you are lucky, really lucky, when night settles over the forest and lake, you may hear the grandest and most chilling sound in the American wilderness: the howling of the wolves.

How many different sounds did the author list? Go back and count if you need to.

Did you count four sounds in the list? The sounds of a loon, the trees, a beaver, and the wolves were listed.

Authors also use **comparisons and contrasts** to organize their writing. Remember that comparison points out how two or more things are alike. A contrast points out how they are different.

You already know that one way to find comparisons and contrasts is to look for signal words or phrases. *Like, also, both, similar,* and *the same as* are often used in comparisons. *Unlike, but, however, on the other hand, only,* and *different* are often used in contrasts.

In the following paragraph, the author contrasts the hunting of wolves in winter and summer. He also contrasts wolves as hunters and humans as hunters.

■ In the north woods the wolf hunts for deer and moose. During winter, when the lakes are frozen, weak or sick animals fall easily to a pack of wolves. In summer, however, the moose spends most of its time in or near the water, where it has the advantage. Thus, unlike the human hunter who seeks the best trophies, the wolf actually helps improve the quality of the moose herd by killing only the weaker members.

The underlined words help you see the contrasts in this paragraph.

Time order is another way authors of nonfiction literature organize their writing. In this next paragraph, the author tells you a true story from beginning to end.

■ Sigurd Olson, who has lived in these woods all his life, tells of a time he was followed by a pack of wolves while snowshoeing across a frozen lake. He knew that at a point where the lake narrowed they might swing around to intercept him, and he had nothing but a pocket knife for protection. Sure enough, when he reached this point there they were. From 50 feet away the wolves stared at him, motionless. Olson stared right back. After a few minutes the wolves turned and went away. Olson is certain that the only reason they did not attack was because he did not show his fear. . . .

As you read the story, you can follow the order of events, from the point when the wolves follow Olson to the point when they leave.

Working It Out

In each of the following paragraphs, decide which pattern of organization was used. Choose a pattern from the list provided.

Patterns of Organization

- listing
- comparison and contrast
- time order

1. An exciting and colorful man, Babe Ruth packed fans into baseball stadiums as readily as he walloped pitches out of them. In 22 major league seasons Ruth sent the ball beyond the outfield wall a total of 714 times. In contrast, quiet Hank Aaron, by the sheer presence of his skill and dignity of manner, fought the prejudice of those in the stadium too small to see beyond the color of a man's skin. And in his 21st season, Aaron hit his 715th home run, breaking Babe Ruth's record.

Pattern: _____

2. Getting information about Germans lost in World War II was difficult for several reasons. First, many village records of births, marriages, and deaths were destroyed in the war. Second, some of the people who were killed had no identification on them. Third, the children who had become separated from their parents were often too young to know their own names. The war, it seems, continued to cause suffering and loss even after its official close.

Pattern: _____

3. The *Eagle* was less than 500 feet from the moon when Armstrong realized that they were about to land in the large, forbidding West Crater, so called because it was four miles west of their target. He flew beyond it, but this . . . meant that he was rapidly running out of fuel; he had to decide immediately whether to turn about there or risk crashing. In that instant two lights on the panel in front of him glowed. They read LUNAR CONTACT. The *Eagle* had made it.

Pattern: _____

Writing to Improve Your Reading

Writing can help you discover the pattern of organization in a reading passage. First, list the three patterns you reviewed in this lesson on a sheet of paper: listing, comparison and contrast, and time order. Leave plenty of space after each numbered item.

As you read *Young at Heart,* think about which pattern of organization the author is using. If you find evidence of any pattern, jot down notes about it. For example, if you find a list, note the items in the list under number 1. If you find comparisons or contrasts, record these under number 2.

Here's an example of how this works. Let's say you are reading the headnote before the story **Young at Heart** in Reading on Your Own. As you read, you notice some events given in time order. You could jot down the following notes under number 3.

3. time order — was born in Vietnam
came to the U.S.
wrote a book about his village

Reading on Your Own

When you read the name of a person from another country, don't worry if you can't pronounce it. You can still read and enjoy the rest of the story.

Huynh Quang Nhuong was born and raised in a small village in Vietnam. After coming to the United States, he wrote a book called The Land I Lost. In this book he remembers his village and the people who lived there. Below is a passage from Mr. Huynh's book. In it, he remembers his grandmother. As you read, look for the pattern of organization the author uses. Make notes about that pattern to help you.

Young at Heart

When she was eighty years old my grandmother was still quite strong. She could use her own teeth to eat corn on the cob or to chew on sugar plants to extract juice from them. Every two days she walked for more than an hour to reach the marketplace, carrying a heavy load of food with her, and then spent another hour walking back home. And even though she was quite old, traces of her beauty still lingered on: Her hands, her feet, her face revealed that she had been an attractive young woman. Nor did time do much damage to the youthful spirit of my grandmother.

One of her great passions was theater, and this passion never diminished with age. No matter how busy she was, she never missed a show when there was a group of actors in town. If no actors visited our hamlet for several months, she would organize her own show in which she was the manager, the producer, and the young leading lady, all at the same time.

My grandmother's own plays were always melodramas inspired by books she had read and by what she had seen on the stage. She always chose her favorite grandson to play the role of the hero, who would, without fail, marry the heroine at the end and live happily ever after. And when my sisters would tell her that she was getting too old to play the role of the young heroine anymore, my grandmother merely replied: "Anybody can play this role if she's young at heart."

Thinking About What You've Read

1. What two examples does the author use to show that his grandmother was still strong?

   _____

   _____

2. What three parts of the grandmother's physical appearance showed she had once been pretty?

   _____

3. What three jobs did the grandmother take on in her own shows?

   _____

4. Your answers to the first three questions can help you answer this question: What pattern of organization does the author use several times in the first two paragraphs?
   A. listing
   B. comparison and contrast
   C. time order

5. In what ways can an older person today stay "young at heart"?

_____
_____
_____
_____
_____
_____

A Test-Taking Tip

When you answer a multiple-choice question, make sure you use information from the passage, not just your own ideas and opinions. Reading *all* the choices before you select one can keep you from picking the first answer just because it sounds as if it could be right.

GED Warm-up

Even at a very old age, the grandmother kept her love for
(1) her home village
(2) the marketplace
(3) the theater
(4) the United States

① ② ③ ④

Working with Words

You've already worked with synonyms and context clues. Like any other reader, you'll sometimes come across an unfamiliar word when you read. To figure out its meaning, first look for any context clues given in the sentence or passage. Then try replacing the unfamiliar word with a word you know—a word that could be a synonym of the unfamiliar word. Here's an example.

■ Jan put on comfortable shoes and took a **stroll** through the park.

The clues in the sentence—"shoes" and "through the park"—tell you that *stroll* has something to do with walking. Try replacing *stroll* with *walk*. Do you agree that *walk* makes sense in the sentence?

Read each of the following sentences from "Young at Heart." Use any context clues given in the sentence to figure out the meaning of the **bold** word. Circle the word that is a synonym for the underlined word. Be sure it makes sense in the sentence.

1. She could use her own teeth to chew on sugar plants to **extract** juice from them.
       eat   remove   fill

2. And even though she was quite old, traces of her beauty still **lingered**.
       hoped   disappeared   remained

3. One of her great passions was theater, and this passion never **diminished** with age.
       grew   lessened   aged

4. If no actors visited our **hamlet** for several months, she would organize her own show.
       village   house   party

▲ Looking Back

In this lesson you reviewed three different patterns authors use to organize their writing. You also took notes to help yourself discover a pattern in a reading selection. In addition, you read several nonfiction passages and practiced using context clues.

Good readers try to identify the pattern of organization used in any material they read. Recognizing such patterns will help you understand and remember what you read.

The Active Reader

Varying Your Reading Rate

Getting Started

Would you read a cartoon at the same speed that you read a book? Of course not. The rate at which you read depends on why you are reading.

Here's an Example

Before you begin reading a book or a selection, it's a good idea to preview it. In **previewing,** you glance quickly at the table of contents, headings, and pictures. You want an idea of what the material is about.

Sometimes your purpose for reading is to find a particular fact. In this case, you skim the material. **Skimming** is moving your eyes very quickly over the lines of print until you find what you want.

Reading for details takes much longer than previewing or skimming. Your purpose is to understand *all* the writer's ideas. You read slowly to be sure you understand every detail.

Sometimes you read for details and still miss some of the author's points. When this happens, you'll probably want to reread certain parts of the material carefully and skim over others. In **rereading,** your purpose is to understand certain ideas better.

Working It Out

Suppose you have an article about vacationing in Disneyland. Four purposes for reading the article are listed below. Decide which reading rate is best for each purpose.

Reading rates

- previewing
- skimming
- reading for details
- rereading

1. to find out current air fares to Disneyland

2. to find out why the writer thinks vacationing in Disneyland is enjoyable

3. to find out whether you want to read the whole article

4. to understand better why you might like to go to Disneyland

Part B Lesson 4

Conquering Fear

In this lesson you will
- read a passage about a young man overcoming his fear
- find cause-and-effect relationships
- underline and label to help you find causes and effects
- learn about figures of speech

Skills for Reading: Cause and Effect

Picture It

Look at the picture. What happened? Why did it happen?

Mud was splattered on the man's coat. That is what happened. It's the *effect*. *Why* was mud splattered on the coat? The bus hit a mud puddle. That is the *cause*.

If you can find causes and their effects when you read, you'll understand how the events in a passage are related.

Spotting cause-and-effect relationships will help you in your everyday reading *and* on the GED Test.

In Lesson 3, you learned that writers sometimes use clue words that signal cause-and-effect relationships. *Because, since,* and *reason* are clue words that may signal causes. *So, therefore, thus,* and *as a result* may signal effects.

Keep in mind that writers do not always use clue words. But even without clue words, you can still find cause-and-effect relationships. When looking for a cause, ask yourself, "Why did this happen?" When looking for an effect, ask yourself, "What happened because of this?"

Here's an Example

Read the following sentences. The first sentence tells you *why* something happened (the cause). The second sentence tells you *what* happened because of this (the effect). Notice that no clue words are used.

■ Bill was late for work five times in the last month. Yesterday, he was fired.

Also keep in mind that a cause can have more than one effect. And an effect can have more than one cause. For example, read the following paragraph. The first sentence tells what happened: Grace retired at age forty-five. That is the effect. The next three sentences tell why this happened. These are all causes.

■ It wasn't surprising that Grace was able to retire at age forty-five. She made a great deal of money in the stock market. Her grandfather died and left her a large sum of money. A book she wrote became a best-seller and was later made into a movie.

Working It Out

As you read the following paragraph, look for cause-and-effect relationships. Then answer the questions. Be sure you base your answers on the information in the paragraph.

■ The Vietnam War had far-reaching effects in the United States. It was the first foreign war in which U.S. combat forces failed to achieve their goals. This hurt the pride of many Americans and left bitter and painful memories. . . . Most [Vietnam] veterans adjusted smoothly to civilian life. But the war left others with deep psychological problems. . . . Both Congress and the public became more willing to challenge the President on U.S. military and foreign policy after the Vietnam War.

1. Why did the Vietnam War hurt the pride of many Americans?

   _____
   _____

2. What types of problems did the war cause for some veterans?

   _____

3. How did the Vietnam War come to affect the President's ability to make policy?

   _____
   _____

Writing to Improve Your Reading

As you read, be on the lookout for cause-and-effect relationships. When you find a cause or effect, underline it. Then label it in the margin.

The passage *Poetry and Jujitsu* below shows how this works. In the first paragraph, an effect has been underlined and labeled in the margin. In the second paragraph, a cause has been underlined and labeled. The same thing has been done in the third paragraph. Arrows have been drawn from the two causes to their effect.

162 / Part B Reading Skills for Literature

Note that you need to read all three paragraphs in order to identify the two causes and their effect. Until you do so, it isn't clear that the author is living alone because his parents are away.

As you read *Poetry and Jujitsu,* look for other causes and effects. If this is your book, underline and label them. Then draw arrows to show how the causes and effects are related. If this is not your book, you can list the causes and effects on your own paper. Draw arrows between them.

Reading on Your Own

This passage comes from the autobiography of a Russian poet named Yevgeny Yevtushenko. It takes place in 1944, when the Soviet Union was fighting with the United States against Germany in World War II. In the passage the author describes an experience that taught him an important lesson. As you read the passage, look for cause-and-effect relationships.

Poetry and Jujitsu

In 1944 I was living alone in an empty apartment in a small quiet Moscow street. . . .

My parents were divorced. My father was somewhere in Kazakhstan with his new wife and their two children. I seldom received letters from him.

My mother was at the front. She had given up her work as a geologist to become a singer and was giving concerts for the troops.

My education was left to the street. . . .

The ruler of our street . . . was a boy of about sixteen who was nicknamed Red.

Red's shoulders were incredibly broad for a boy of his age.

Red walked masterfully up and down our street, his legs wide apart and with a slightly rolling gait, like a seaman on the deck of his ship.

From under his peaked cap, always worn back to front, his forelock tumbled down in a fiery cascade, and out of his round pockmarked face, green eyes, like a cat's, sparkled with scorn for everything and everyone crossing his path. Two or three lieutenants, in peaked caps back to front like Red's, trotted at his heels.

Remember not to let names of people from other countries trip you up. You can keep reading without knowing how to pronounce the name.

Jujitsu is a Japanese form of wrestling.

effect
cause
cause

The author was eleven at this time.

Red could stop any boy and say impressively the one word "money." His lieutenants would turn out the boy's pockets, and if he resisted they gave him a real beating.

Everyone was afraid of Red. I too was afraid. I knew he carried heavy brass knuckles in his pocket.

I wanted to conquer my fear of Red.

So I wrote a poem about him.

This was my first piece of journalism in verse.

By the next day the whole street knew the piece by heart and relished it with triumphant hatred.

One morning on my way to school I suddenly came upon Red and his lieutenants. His eyes seemed to bore through me. "Ah, the poet," he drawled, smiling crookedly. "So you write verses. Do they rhyme?"

Red's hand darted into his pocket and came out armed with its brass knuckles; it flashed like lightning and struck my head. I fell down streaming with blood and lost consciousness.

This was my first payment as a poet.

I spent several days in bed.

When I went out, with my head still bandaged, I again saw Red. I struggled with instinctive fear but lost and took to my heels.

I ran all the way home. There I rolled on my bed, biting my pillow and pounding it with my fists in shame and impotent fury at my cowardice.

But then I made up my mind to vanquish it at whatever cost.

I went into training with parallel bars and weights, and after every session I would feel my muscles. They were getting harder, but slowly. Then I remembered something I had read in a book about a miraculous Japanese method of wrestling which gave an advantage to the weak over the strong. I sacrificed a week's ration card for a textbook on jujitsu.

A ration card was needed to buy food.

For three weeks I hardly left home—I trained with two other boys. Finally I felt I was ready and went out.

Red was sitting on the lawn in our yard, playing Twenty-one with his lieutenants. He was absorbed in the game.

Fear was still in me and it ordered me to turn back. But I went up to the players and kicked the cards aside with my foot.

Red looked up, surprised at my impudence after my recent flight.

He got up slowly. "You looking for more?" he asked menacingly.

As before, his hand dived into his pocket for the brass knuckles. But I made a quick jabbing movement, and Red, howling with pain, rolled on the ground. Bewildered, he got up and came at me, swinging his head furiously from side to side like a bull.

I caught his wrist and squeezed slowly, as I had read in the book, until the brass knuckles dropped from his limp fingers. Nursing his hand, Red fell down again. He was sobbing and smearing the tears over his pockmarked face with his grimy fist. His lieutenants discreetly withdrew.

That day Red ceased to rule our street.

And from that day on I knew for certain that there is no need to fear the strong. All one needs is to know the method of overcoming them. There is a special jujitsu for every strong man.

What I also learned that day was that, if I wished to be a poet, I must not only write poems but also know how to stand up for what I have written.

Thinking About What You've Read

1. Why was everyone afraid of Red?

_____

_____

2. Draw a line from each cause in column A to its effect in column B.

A	B
Red struck Yevtushenko on the head.	Yevtushenko spent three weeks learning jujitsu.
Yevtushenko decided to conquer his fear of Red.	The brass knuckles dropped from Red's fingers.
Yevtushenko squeezed Red's wrist.	Yevtushenko was knocked out.

3. What two things did Yevtushenko learn from his experience?

_____

_____

4. Have you ever conquered your fear of someone or something? Describe your experience.

___

GED Warm-up

What effect did Yevtushenko's poem have on Red?

(1) It amused him.
(2) It had no effect on him at all.
(3) It bored him.
(4) It made him quite angry.

① ② ③ ④

Working with Words

A simile compares two unlike things that are similar in some way. Similes are signaled by the word *as* or *like*. Authors use similes to make their writing clearer and more interesting.

The simile in the following sentence is in **bold** type.

- The old man's hands were **as rough as sandpaper.**

In this simile, the writer is comparing two unlike things: a man's hands and sandpaper. These things have something in common: they are both rough. Did you notice that the word *as* signals the simile?

Here's another sentence in which the simile is in **bold** type.

- The children ran through the house **like a herd of wild horses.**

Children and wild horses are the two unlike things being compared. What is similar about them is the way they run. The writer used the word *like* to signal the simile.

See if you can spot similes in these sentences from *Poetry and Jujitsu*. Underline the simile in each sentence. Then tell what two unlike things are being compared. Finally, explain what the two things have in common.

1. Red's hand darted into his pocket and came out armed with its brass knuckles; it flashed like lightning and struck my head.

___

2. Bewildered, [Red] got up and came at me, swinging his head furiously from side to side like a bull.

___

▲ Looking Back

In this lesson, you learned more about cause-and-effect relationships. You also learned how to underline and label to help you find causes and effects. In addition, you learned how to find and understand similes.

In all your reading, be on the lookout for cause-and-effect relationships. Understanding them will help you get more out of your reading.

166 / Part B Reading Skills for Literature

The Active Reader

Summarizing

Picture It

Can you summarize this cartoon? In a sentence or two, explain what you see happening.

_____

_____

"MOM, HOW MUCH SHOULD I CHARGE FOR CHICKEN LEGS?"

Dennis has invited five friends in for a snack. He is charging them for their food and drink.

These two sentences give the most important ideas of the cartoon. They are a good summary of what's happening. You've learned that a summary tells the main events in a story or the most important idea in an article.

A good summary is brief. It includes only the most important events or ideas from the selection. Here are some unimportant details about the cartoon. Can you see why they would be left out of a summary of the cartoon?

1. Dennis's mother has just come into the kitchen.
2. Two boys are eating sandwiches.
3. A girl is eating a chicken leg.
4. Dennis has poured a glass of milk.

When you write a summary, you can take certain steps to make sure you include only the most important ideas.

Here's an Example

The first step in summarizing is to make sure you understand the selection.

Reread the passage **Beach Living** on pages 148–149. Do you understand all the ideas the author presents? If you don't, reread the parts you don't understand.

The second step is to find the most important ideas of the selection. Here are some ideas from *Beach Living.* Which sentences give the most important information?

■ (1) Beach living teaches a person how few possessions he or she really needs. (2) One doesn't need many clothes at the beach. (3) At the beach, one worries less about what to wear. (4) A bare sea-shell of a cottage is all the shelter one needs at the beach. (5) It is easier to sweep the sand off a bare floor. (6) Beach living teaches a person to shed pride and hypocrisy in human relationships. (7) The most exhausting thing in life is being insincere.

Sentences 1, 2, 4, and 6 give the most important ideas of the selection. Sentences 3, 5, and 7 are not important enough to be included in a summary.

The third step is to write the most important ideas down in a summary statement.

The last step in summarizing is to reread your summary. Make sure you didn't repeat yourself. If two sentences contain related ideas, try combining them into one sentence. Also, make sure you didn't leave out important ideas.

If possible, ask someone who hasn't read the passage to read your summary. If the person understands it, you know you've written a clear and complete summary.

Here's a summary of *Beach Living.* It's based on the ideas listed above. Notice how the writer has combined sentences 2 and 4 into one sentence.

■ Beach living teaches a person how few possessions he or she really needs. One needs only a few clothes and a simple shelter at the beach. In beach living, one learns to shed pride and hypocrisy in human relationships.

Working It Out

Reread the selection about personal letters on page 152. Then do the exercises below.

1. Circle the sentence that should be included in a summary of this selection.
   A. Telephone calls come and go.
   B. A personal letter is special for several reasons.
   C. Some of my most precious possessions are letters.

2. Circle the sentence that is *not* important enough to include in a summary.
   A. I've never thrown away a good letter.
   B. A letter is something you can keep, unlike a phone call.
   C. You can say things in a letter that you might not say in person.
   D. In a letter, you can say things without interruption.

3. Now you can practice your summary skills. If you need to, read the selection on page 152 again. Then write a summary of the selection on a sheet of paper.

4. Now reread your summary. Decide whether you repeated yourself or left out important ideas. If so, you may want to revise your summary.

Part B
Lesson 5

Reading Commentary

In this lesson you will
- read about the beginnings of a popular music group
- learn what commentary is
- discover the author's tone
- use context to understand special terms

What Is Commentary?

Suppose you see a movie one night. The next day, a friend asks how you liked the movie. "Great," you say. In other words, you *comment* on the movie.

Many people write down their comments. They comment about movies, TV shows, books, paintings, and other art forms. You can read their comments in newspapers and magazines. Can you see why this kind of writing is called *commentary*?

Think of the skills you've learned to read nonfiction. You can use those skills to read commentary too. That's because commentary is one kind of nonfiction. Other skills also help you understand commentary. One such skill is discovering the tone of the writing.

Skills for Reading: The Author's Tone

Picture It

Suppose your friend asked two other persons about the movie you saw. Which person do you think said each comment below?
"I thought I'd die from the excitement."
"I thought I'd die of boredom."

The woman thought the movie was exciting. The man thought it was boring. You could probably match the comments with the people. The look on their faces shows you their feelings.

When you talk with people, the look on their faces and the tone of their voices show how they feel. When you read, you can't see or hear the author, of course. But you can still tell how authors feel about their subjects. You can infer their tone by the words they use.

Here's an Example

The paragraph below is a commentary on a movie. You can tell the author likes the movie. The words he uses to describe it show you. As you read, pretend the author is speaking the words to you. Ask yourself, "How would the author say these words?"

> ■ **Invasion of the Body Snatchers** (1956): Pods from space take over people's bodies. This creepy horror movie is a classic. The terror builds slowly but surely in this thriller. It's perhaps the best of the 1950s science fiction films. Don't miss it!

These words let you know the author likes the movie: "classic," "thriller," and "perhaps the best." Such words help set the tone of the commentary. The tone is praising because the author likes the movie so much. The tone could also be called approving. It could even be called enthusiastic. An enthusiastic person is excited about something he likes. The author seems excited about the movie when he says, "Don't miss it!"

Sometimes a commentary is approving but more serious. The author respects the artist and quietly praises the artist's work. You can detect this kind of tone in this next commentary. It's about the artist Georgia O'Keeffe.

> ■ "Filling space in a beautiful way—that is what art means to me." And that is what Georgia O'Keeffe did from the time she was growing up in Wisconsin in the late 1800s to her death in New Mexico in 1986.
>
> O'Keeffe is best known for her paintings of flowers, bones, mountains, and clouds. She is also known for her independent, extraordinary spirit. . . .
>
> When O'Keeffe died in 1986, she was ninety-nine years old. She had painted for almost seventy years, always filling space in beautiful ways—ways that were hers alone.

Sometimes writers don't like a work of art. Then their writing will have a disapproving tone. The commentary may sound angry. The writer may even make fun of the artist.

Below is a commentary with a disapproving tone. These words help set that disapproving tone: "Still another," "boring," and "never create suspense."

> ■ Still another "new" Perry Mason TV show will air this Sunday. Once more, Raymond Burr plays the boring, near-perfect lawyer. These shows never create suspense because Mason never loses. So why watch?

Sometimes a writer doesn't show how he or she feels. The writer may just describe an artist's work. Or the writer may discuss both the good points and the bad points. The writer lists the points in an even, fair way. This kind of tone is called objective. Here's another paragraph about the artist Georgia O'Keeffe. In this piece, the writer has an objective tone.

> ■ O'Keeffe's fascination with bones developed in the Southwest. She painted them often, believing them to be beautiful shapes and symbols of the

desert she loved so much. She also painted New Mexico's red hills and found them a challenge to paint, partly because they eroded so quickly and seemed to change colors so often. The hills changed colors in her paintings, too, varying from pink to red to purple to orange.

Working It Out

Here's a commentary about a mystery called *The Five Blades.* Read it carefully. Try to infer how the writer feels about the book.

■ Characters are, of course, needed for any good story. And the characters in Graham's new mystery *are* interesting. The problem is not their interest but their number. The first forty pages introduce about forty characters. The mystery itself takes second billing. It first appears on page 42. It rears its head every so often after that. Then it is weakly solved on page 237. Meanwhile, the reader is left trying to keep track of countless characters.

1. What word and phrases help show how the writer feels about the book?

   _____
   _____

2. How would the writer's face look if she were saying those words and phrases aloud?

   _____
   _____

3. What is the tone of this piece of commentary?

   _____

Writing to Improve Your Reading

Often a writer says both good things and bad things about a work of art. You can list the good and bad points as you read. Then you will understand the commentary better. Such a listing can also help you infer the writer's tone.

For example, one man read the commentary under Working It Out. As he read, he made the following list. He restated the good and bad points.

<u>Good</u>
1. interesting characters

<u>Bad</u>
1. too many characters—hard to keep track of
2. mystery seems unimportant
3. weak ending to mystery

The list helped the man in two ways: (1) He could see the writer had more bad things to say than good. (2) He could infer a disapproving tone.

The next commentary has both good and bad points. You can list the points as you read.

Lesson 5 Reading Commentary / 171

Reading on Your Own

The commentary below is from a book about the Beatles. The writer shows his feelings about the Beatles. He shows his feelings about Elvis too. And about rock music in general. As you read, try to infer his tone.

The Birth of the Beatles

Nobody really took much notice [of popular music], at least not boys in Britain of John Lennon's age. Pop music, up to the mid-1950s, . . . had no connection with real life. It all came from America and was produced by very show-businessy professionals in lovely suits with lovely smiles who sang lovely ballads. . . .

Then three things happened. On April 12, 1954, Bill Haley and his Comets produced "Rock around the Clock." It took a year for it to have any effect on Britain. But when it did, as the theme song of the film *Blackboard Jungle,* rock and roll hit Britain. . . .

The second event occurred in January 1956 when Lonnie Donegan produced "Rock Island Line." This had little connection with the wild rock music, despite the title. What was new and interesting was the fact that it was played on the sort of instruments anyone could play. Lonnie Donegan popularized skiffle. For the first time, anyone could have a go, with no musical knowledge or even musical talent. Even the guitar, the hardest instrument in a skiffle group, could be played by anyone who mastered a few simple chords. The other instruments, like a washboard, or tea-chest bass, could be played by any idiot.

The third and in a way the most exciting event in pop music in the fifties . . . was Elvis Presley. He also appeared in the early part of 1956. By May his "Heartbreak Hotel" was top of the charts in fourteen different countries.

In a way it was obvious that someone like Elvis should happen. You just had to look at Bill Haley . . . to realize that this new exciting music, rock 'n' roll, had eventually to have an exciting singer to go with it. Rock was the music which excited all kids. Elvis was the exciting singer singing the exciting songs. "Nothing really affected me until Elvis," [John Lennon once said]. . . .

> Elvis was the first to hit the new teenage market. . . . He wasn't singing phoney, slushy ballads, with a nice smile or a quiet cry, . . . but outright provocative, . . . exciting songs. Kids everywhere felt it was aimed at them.
>
> All the Beatles, like millions of lads of the same age, were affected. They all have the same sort of memories, of groups springing up in every class at school and in every street at home. There were overnight about a hundred dances in Liverpool. . . . It was the first time for generations that music wasn't the property of musicians. Anyone could get up and have a go. It was like giving painting sets to monkeys. Some of them were bound to produce something good sometime.

Provocative means "arousing."

Thinking About What You've Read

1. What three things happened that led to the forming of the Beatles and other groups in Britain?
   _____
   _____

2. According to the author, why did skiffle become popular?
   _____

3. How did John Lennon feel about Elvis?
   _____

4. Circle *all* the words in this list that could be used to describe the tone of the whole commentary. If you listed good and bad points as you read, use your list to help you.

   enthusiastic   uncaring   angry   respectful
   admiring   excited   scornful   objective

5. The author writes, "The most exciting event in pop music in the fifties . . . was Elvis Presley." Check the fact below that helps the author back up this statement.
   ____ Presley appeared in the early part of 1956.
   ____ "Heartbreak Hotel" was popular in 14 countries.
   ____ It was clear that someone like Elvis would appear.

A Test-Taking Tip

You already know about synonyms. They are words with similar meanings. Often more than one word can describe a writer's tone. For example, *positive* and *approving* are synonyms. They could describe the same article.

A multiple-choice question may ask you about the author's feelings. Think of one or two words that describe the tone. Then look for your answer among the choices. If you can't find it, look for a synonym of the word.

GED Warm-up

How does the author seem to feel about popular music in the *early* 1950s?

(1) scornful
(2) admiring
(3) objective
(4) angry

Working with Words

Is there a special field that interests you? For example, do you like to watch sports? Are you a good cook? Do you have a hobby? If so, you know some words that many other people don't. That's because every field has its own special words. Football has "first down" and "tight end." Cooking has "simmer" and "marinate."

Each of the arts also has its special terms. You may read such terms when you read commentary. If you don't know the meaning of a term, you can use the context to help you.

For example, look back at the commentary on the Beatles. You may not have known the word *skiffle*. But the word was used in phrases like these: "popularized skiffle" and "instrument in a skiffle group." The context helps you understand that skiffle is a kind of music.

Sometimes the context groups two words. One word you don't know and one word you do. For instance, look again at the commentary on the Beatles. It talked about "the other instruments, like a washboard, or the tea-chest bass." From the context, you can figure out what a tea-chest bass must be. A tea-chest must have been a household item, as a washboard was. And it was used as a musical instrument, as a washboard was.

Here are some phrases from *The Birth of the Beatles.* Write down the meaning of each term in **bold.** Use the context. Turn back to the reading if you need to.

1. "Heartbreak Hotel" was **top of the charts** in fourteen different countries.

   _____

2. He wasn't singing phoney, slushy **ballads.**

   _____

▲ Looking Back

You've read about the beginning of the Beatles. You learned what commentary is and how to read it. You inferred the tone of pieces of commentary. And you used the context of special terms to understand them. These last two skills will help you with all your reading. That's because different tones and special terms are found in many kinds of writing.

The Active Reader

Judging the Author's Qualifications

Picture It
Look at these pictures.

Which person would you believe? You probably said the scientist. Why? Because the scientist is an expert on outer space, has studied facts, and has used those facts to draw a conclusion. The UFO lover has not.

Most people have opinions on many subjects. A *valid* opinion, however, must be based on knowledge of the subject. *Valid* means "well-founded; sound; just."

You don't want to trust an opinion that is not valid.

Commentary gives a writer's opinion about a work of art. You can decide if you want to accept that opinion. But first, you'll want to know the author's background. You'll want to be sure the author knows about the subject. Then you can decide if his or her opinion is valid.

Here's an Example

The following two opinions are about a new play. You'll probably trust the first opinion more than the last.

■ *From a drama critic:* Wilson's new drama is the second in a planned series of three. It combines strong staging with powerful acting. It beautifully continues the story from the first play.

■ *From a car salesperson:* My wife and I won two tickets to this play. It was awful. Nothing made sense. I haven't been to a play in years. I won't be going back to one, either.

Drama critics have studied and seen many plays. They know what to look for in a play. Their background and knowledge make them qualified to write commentary.

Of course, a car salesperson may also be interested in the theater. The person may have studied drama and may attend many plays. These are qualifications for writing drama commentary. But this car salesman admitted he hasn't "been to a play in years." He is *not* qualified.

Working It Out

Suppose you're a newspaper editor. You have to hire people to write the following articles. For each article, choose the person you think would be the *most qualified* to write the commentary. Circle the letter of your choice.

Subject of Commentary	Choice of Authors
1. a new exhibit at an art museum	a. a person who frames artwork b. a student of the history of painting
2. a book about fighting in the Vietnam War	a. a Vietnam veteran b. a writer of romantic stories
3. the effect of the Beatles on popular music	a. a twenty-year-old Beatles fan b. a fifty-year-old popular musician
4. a collection of poems	a. someone who enjoys reading poetry b. someone who knows the poet
5. a TV mini-series	a. the star of the mini-series b. a television critic
6. the skills a dancer needs	a. a dance instructor b. a fan of the ballet

Part B
Lesson 6

Reading Fiction

In this lesson you will learn
- what fiction is
- how to tell the difference between fiction and nonfiction

What Is Fiction?

Picture It

This drawing shows a scene from a story. You'll read part of the story below. The people and events may seem real. But they are not. The story is an example of fiction. **Fiction** is a story that comes from an author's imagination.

Works of fiction have characters, a setting, and a plot. The **characters** are the people in the story. The **setting** is where and when the story takes place. The **plot** is the series of events that make up the action of the story.

Here's an Example

The fictional passage below comes from a book written by Willa Cather. The passage tells a story about three characters.

■ One Saturday night Mr. Harling had gone down to the cellar for beer. As he came up the stairs in the dark, he heard scuffling on the back porch, and then the sound of a vigorous slap. He looked out through the side door in time to see a pair of long legs vaulting over the picket fence. Ántonia was standing there, angry and excited. Young Harry Paine, who was to marry his employer's daughter on Monday, had come to the tent with a crowd of friends and danced all evening.

Afterward, he begged Ántonia to let him walk home with her. She said she supposed he was a nice young man, as he was one of Miss Frances's friends, and she didn't mind. On the back porch he tried to kiss her, and when she protested—because he was going to be married on Monday—he caught her and kissed her until she got one hand free and slapped him.

The characters are Mr. Harling, Ántonia, and Harry Paine. The setting is Mr. Harling's back porch on a Saturday night.

The plot is the series of events described in the passage: First, Ántonia and Harry attended a dance. Afterward, Harry walked Ántonia home. When he forced a kiss on her, she slapped him. Then Mr. Harling saw him run away.

Notice how the plot helps you learn about the characters. Harry's behavior seems odd for a man about to be married. Perhaps he really cares for Ántonia. Or maybe he's just a flirt. Ántonia's behavior shows something about her. She's not the kind of woman who fools around with someone else's fiancé.

Fiction or Nonfiction?

Getting Started

It's good to know if a story is true or not. In other words, you'll want to know if you're reading nonfiction or fiction.

One way is to ask yourself, "Is this work based on fact? Does it describe real events, people, or things?" If it does, it is nonfiction. Works of nonfiction sometimes have photographs. Photographs let you know that the work deals with real people, events, or things.

Another clue to nonfiction is the use of subheadings. Subheadings often are printed in dark type.

If the people and events in a story come from the author's imagination, you're reading fiction. Fictional works sometimes have drawings or paintings. But photographs are seldom used. That's because the people and events in fiction are not real.

Another clue to fiction is the use of conversations between people. The author may even take you inside the characters' minds. You'll read their feelings and thoughts.

Here's an Example

The following two passages both have to do with the wind. The first passage is nonfiction. It's based on fact. Notice how it could easily have photographs with it.

▪ Wind is air in motion. Wind can move so slowly that leaves on a tree seem to stand still. Or it can move so fast that houses are smashed and large trees fall. Strong winds can hurl great ocean waves against the beach, flooding the land.

The next passage is fiction. The people and events come from the author's imagination. Notice the conversation between two characters. Also notice that you read the *thoughts* of one of the characters.

■ Karen looked out her kitchen window and saw garbage spread all over the back yard. She went upstairs and woke her husband, Rich.

"Honey, the wind blew our garbage cans over," said Karen. "There's garbage everywhere, and I'm late for work."

"I'll pick it up later," said Rich. "You go on to work." Then he turned over and tried to go back to sleep. Why did Karen have to wake me up? he thought. Why didn't she just leave me a note?

Working It Out

Read this next passage. Look for clues that help you figure out if it is fiction or nonfiction. Then answer the questions that follow.

■ Morris awoke, soured by the long afternoon sleep. He dressed, combed his hair with a broken comb and trudged downstairs, a heavy-bodied man with sloping shoulders and bushy gray hair in need of a haircut. He came down with his apron on. Although he felt chilly he poured out a cup of cold coffee, and backed against the radiator, slowly sipped it. Ida sat at the table, reading.

"Why you let me sleep so long?" the grocer complained.

She didn't answer.

"Yesterday's or today's paper?"

"Yesterday's."

He rinsed the cup and set it on the top of the gas range. In the store he rang up "no sale" and took a nickel out of the drawer. Morris lifted the lid of the cash register, struck a match on the underside of the counter, and holding the flame cupped in his palm, peered at the figure of his earnings. Ida had taken in three dollars. Who could afford a paper?

Nevertheless he went for one, doubting the small pleasure he would get from it. What was so worth reading about the world?

1. Which of the following are included in the passage? (You can circle more than one.)
   A. an exact conversation between people
   B. real people and real events
   C. characters, a setting, and a plot

2. Is this passage fictional or nonfictional? How do you know?

_____

_____

▲ Looking Ahead

In this section, you'll read a variety of fictional selections. You'll learn more about character, setting, and plot. You'll also learn about the different kinds of problems characters face.

As you work on your skills, don't forget to enjoy the selections themselves. You're about to read some really good stories!

Part B Lesson 7

A Man of Honor

In this lesson you will
- read a short story about an old man who values his honor
- learn more about character and setting
- practice taking notes about a story
- review the use of word parts to help you figure out word meanings

Skills for Reading: Character and Setting

Getting Started

Characters are the people in a story. When you read fiction, you can learn about characters in various ways. One way is to notice what the author tells you about them. For example, the author may describe how someone looks. The author may also tell you someone is kind, or greedy, or smart.

Sometimes authors do not tell you directly what characters are like. Instead, they show you. For example, they may tell you what someone did or said. Based on this information, you can draw conclusions about that person. Authors also may tell you what one person says or thinks about another. This is another way you can learn what a character is like.

Besides characters, works of fiction also have a setting. The setting is where and when the story takes place. Sometimes an author will tell you the setting of a story. At other times, the author will expect you to figure it out. To do so, you must use clues in the story.

Here's an Example

Read the following passage about a computer company's problem. Think about the characters and the setting.

- Jack Weaver came out of the vitals of Multivac looking utterly worn and disgusted.
  From the stool, where the other maintained his own stolid watch, Todd Nemerson said, "Nothing?"

"Nothing," said Weaver. "Nothing, nothing, nothing. No one can find anything wrong with it."

"Except that it won't work, you mean."

"You're no help sitting there!"

"I'm thinking."

"Thinking!"

Nemerson stirred impatiently on his stool. "Why not? There are six teams of computer technologists roaming around in the corridors of Multivac. They haven't come up with anything in three days. Can't you spare one person to think?"

Notice how the author describes what the characters do and say. Using this information, you can draw conclusions about what the characters are like. Jack Weaver keeps snapping at Todd Nemerson to *do* something. Thus, you might conclude that Weaver is short-tempered and impatient. Nemerson sits and thinks about the problem. Thus, you might conclude that he is a thoughtful person.

The author does not describe the setting in this passage. But he does give you clues about it. You know that the action takes place near a machine called Multivac. This machine is some kind of computer. You know this because the author refers to "teams of computer technologists roaming around in the corridors of Multivac." The fact that Multivac has corridors means that it must be quite large. The story takes place sometime after the invention of computers.

Working It Out

Here's a chance to practice focusing on character and setting. Read this passage about a woman leaving a grocery store. Then answer the questions.

■ It's ten o'clock, closing time, when I push my loaded shopping cart out of the supermarket. The parking lot is almost deserted. There is only one delivery truck by the side of the building and a few cars near the exit, mine one of them. Not a person is in sight.

I start thinking, *How stupid to have parked so far away. The lot wasn't full when I drove in. Just habit, I guess. I've parked near the exit ever since the car was rammed that day. It seemed safer. It never seemed far, either. Now it looks a mile away. I'd better get a move on.*

1. When and where does the story take place?

   _____
   _____

2. Why does the woman always park near the exit?

   _____
   _____

3. How is the woman feeling?

   _____
   _____
   _____

Reading on Your Own

This short story is about an old man who values his honor more highly than money. As you read, pay special attention to the characters and the setting.

Gentleman of Río en Medio

It took months of negotiation to come to an understanding with the old man. He was in no hurry. What he had the most of was time. He lived up in Río en Medio, where his people had been for hundreds of years. He tilled the same land they had tilled. His house was small and wretched, but quaint. The little creek ran though his land. His orchard was gnarled and beautiful.

Río en Medio (rē′ō en me′dyō), the name of a town, meaning "River in the Middle."

The day of the sale he came into the office. His coat was old, green and faded. . . . He also wore gloves. They were old and torn and his fingertips showed through them. He carried a cane, but it was only the skeleton of a worn-out umbrella. Behind him walked one of his innumerable kin—a dark young man with eyes like a gazelle. . . .

There was a great deal of conversation, about rain and about his family. He was very proud of his large family. Finally we got down to business. Yes, he would sell, as he had agreed, for twelve hundred dollars, in cash. We would buy, and the money was ready. "Don Anselmo," I said to him in Spanish, "we have made a discovery. You remember that we sent that surveyor, that engineer, up there to survey your land so as to make the deed. Well, he finds that you own more than eight acres. He tells us that your land extends across the river and that you own almost twice as much as you thought." He didn't know that. "And now, Don Anselmo," I added, "these Americans are *buena gente*, they are good people, and they are willing to pay you for the additional land as well, at the same rate per acre, so that instead of twelve hundred dollars you will get almost twice as much, and the money is here for you."

Don *means "Mr." or "Sir" in Spanish.*

Buena gente *means "good people."*

182 / Part B Reading Skills for Literature

The old man hung his head for a moment in thought. Then he stood up and stared at me. "Friend," he said, "I do not like to have you speak to me in that manner." I kept still and let him have his say. "I know these Americans are good people, and that is why I have agreed to sell to them. But I do not care to be insulted. I have agreed to sell my house and land for twelve hundred dollars and that is the price."

I argued with him but it was useless. Finally he signed the deed and took the money but refused to take more than the amount agreed upon. Then he shook hands all around, put on his ragged gloves, took his stick and walked out with the boy behind him.

A month later my friends had moved into Río en Medio. They had replastered the old adobe house, pruned the trees, patched the fence, and moved in for the summer. One day they came back to the office to complain. The children of the village were overrunning their property. They came every day and played under the trees, built little play fences around them, and took blossoms. When they were spoken to they only laughed and talked back good-naturedly in Spanish.

I sent a messenger up to the mountains for Don Anselmo. It took a week to arrange another meeting. When he arrived he repeated his previous preliminary performance. He wore the same faded cutaway, carried the same stick and was accompanied by the boy again. He shook hands all around, sat down with the boy behind his chair, and talked about the weather. Finally I broached the subject. "Don Anselmo, about the ranch you sold to these people. They are good people and want to be your friends and neighbors always. When you sold to them you signed a document, a deed, and in that deed you agreed to several things. One thing was that they were to have the complete possession of the property. Now, Don Anselmo, it seems that every day the children of the village overrun the orchard and spend most of their time there. We would like to know if you, as the most respected man in the village, could not stop them from doing so in order that these people may enjoy their new home more in peace."

Don Anselmo stood up. "We have all learned to love these Americans," he said, "because they are good people and good neighbors. I sold them my property because I knew they were good people, but I did not sell them the trees in the orchard."

Preliminary *means "coming before the main action."*

This was bad. "Don Anselmo," I pleaded, "when one signs a deed and sells real property one sells also everything that grows on the land, and those trees, every one of them, are on the land and inside the boundaries of what you sold."

"Yes, I admit that," he said. "You know," he added, "I am the oldest man in the village. Almost everyone there is my relative and all the children of Río en Medio are my *sobrinos* and *nietos*, my descendants. Every time a child has been born in Río en Medio since I took possession of that house from my mother I have planted a tree for that child. The trees in that orchard are not mine, *Señor,* they belong to the children of the village. Every person in Río en Medio born since the railroad came to Santa Fe owns a tree in that orchard. I did not sell the trees because I could not. They are not mine."

There was nothing we could do. Legally we owned the trees but the old man had been so generous, refusing what amounted to a fortune for him. It took most of the following winter to buy the trees, individually, from the descendants of Don Anselmo in the valley of Río en Medio.

Sobrinos are nephews and nieces.
Nietos are grandchildren.

Thinking About What You've Read

1. What was the old man wearing on the day of the sale?
   _____
   _____

2. What can you conclude about the man from his clothes?
   _____

3. Reread the first paragraph of the story. Underline the three sentences that describe the old man's house and land.

4. Circle the words that describe the old man. Refer to the notes you took about him.
    proud   greedy   honest   polite   dignified   dishonest

5. Why do you think Don Anselmo refused the extra money?
   _____
   _____
   _____

GED Warm-up

Which words best describe the Americans?

(1) jealous and unkind
(2) nasty and greedy
(3) fair and reasonable
(4) careless and thoughtless

① ② ③ ④

Working with Words

A prefix is a word part that is added to the beginning of a word. A suffix is a word part that is added to the end of a word. Knowing the meanings of prefixes and suffixes can help you figure out what words mean. The suffixes *-er* and *-or,* for example, mean "a person or thing that does something." Thus, a farmer is a person who farms. An inspector is a person who inspects.

Here are some common prefixes and suffixes, with their meanings.

Prefixes

re-	again
un-, in-, im-	not

Suffixes

-able	able to be
-er, -or	a person or thing that does something
-ion	the act or process of doing something

Read the following sentences. The underlined word in each sentence has a prefix, a suffix, or both. Circle the correct meaning of each word.

1. You remember that we sent that surveyor, that engineer, up there to survey your land.
   A. the act of surveying
   B. a person who surveys

2. They had replastered the old adobe house.
   A. plastered again   B. not plastered

3. It took months of negotiation to come to an understanding with the old man.
   A. the act of negotiating, or bargaining
   B. a person who negotiates, or bargains

4. Behind him walked one of his innumerable kin.
   A. able to be numbered, or counted
   B. not able to be numbered, or counted

▲ Looking Back

In this lesson you learned more about character and setting. You also took notes on a story's characters and setting. In addition, you learned how to use prefixes and suffixes to figure out word meanings.

When you read fiction, it's important to pay attention to the characters and setting. Doing so will help you remember what you have read. Authors use many methods to tell you about the characters and setting.

The Active Reader

Visualizing

Picture It

Creating pictures in your mind is called visualizing. It can help you understand and remember more of what you read. As you read stories, try to picture the characters and settings. Also try to picture the action.

Here's an Example

Look at the two men. Which man could be Don Anselmo?

The man on the left could be Don Anselmo. Did you picture him like this as you read the story?

Working It Out

In Lesson 7 you read about a woman leaving a grocery store. Read again the description of the parking lot.

■ It's ten o'clock, closing time, when I push my loaded shopping cart out of the supermarket. The parking lot is almost deserted. There is only one delivery truck by the side of the building and a few cars near the exit, mine one of them. Not a person is in sight.

Circle the picture that could be the parking lot described in the passage.

Part B
Lesson 8

Courage

In this lesson you will
- read a story about a man who faces a difficult decision
- learn about plot and conflict in stories
- use context clues to figure out word meanings

Skills for Reading: Plot and Conflict

Getting Started

In Lesson 6 you read about **plot.** You learned that plot is the series of events in a story. A story won't be interesting unless the plot has a **conflict.** A conflict is a struggle or problem.

Think about this for a moment. Say everyone in a story is happy. They all go to the beach for a day. They all have a great time. Then everyone goes home. That's not very interesting, is it?

Now add a shark to the plot. Suppose children are swimming. A shark fin appears. The children's father must overcome his own fear to save his family. That's a little more interesting, isn't it? The shark and the man's fear provide conflict. Once the man saves his children, the conflict has ended, and the story is over.

Stories can have different kinds of conflict. One kind of conflict is a struggle between characters. For example, two men might try to win the same prize.

Characters can also struggle against nature. Suppose you read a story about being lost in a desert. The characters in such a story face a conflict with nature.

Characters can also struggle within themselves. For example, a person can try to reach goals or overcome fears. He or she can struggle to do what is right.

You can't really enjoy a story without understanding its plot and conflict.

Here's an Example

Reread the passage about Ántonia and Harry on pages 177–178. The conflict is between Ántonia and Harry. Harry wants to kiss Ántonia. But she doesn't want to kiss him.

The plot includes this series of events: First, Ántonia and Harry attend a dance. Afterward, Harry walks Ántonia home. When he forces a kiss on her, she slaps him. Then he runs away. That is the way their conflict is settled.

Working It Out

Reread the story on pages 182–184. Pay attention to the plot and conflict as you read. Then answer these questions.

1. Why did the people who bought the ranch complain?
   A. They thought the price was too high.
   B. The children of the village played in their orchard every day.
   C. There was no fruit on the trees.

2. How did the person telling the story try to settle this conflict?
   A. He chased the children away.
   B. He called the police.
   C. He asked Don Anselmo to speak to the children.

3. How did Don Anselmo deal with this conflict?
   A. He said there was nothing he could do.
   B. He told the children not to play in the orchard.
   C. He cut down the trees in the orchard.

4. How was the conflict settled?
   A. Don Anselmo was sued by the new owners.
   B. The new owners bought the trees from the children.
   C. The new owners left the ranch.

5. What kind of conflict does this story contain?
   A. a conflict among characters
   B. a conflict within a character
   C. a conflict with nature

Writing to Improve Your Reading

The events in a plot are often in time order. You learned on page 47 about making a time line to keep track of time order. Read that section on page 47 again. Then make a time line of the events in the next story yourself.

Reading on Your Own

Here's a good short story. It's about a man who must do something difficult. As you read the story, think about the events that make up the plot. Also think about the conflict that the man faces. This will help you understand and enjoy the story.

Fetch!

The last thing George Dixon expected, or wanted, to meet in an apartment on the 17th floor was this enormous Great Dane with an old tennis ball in his mouth. When Professor Werner called, "Come on in," and George opened the door, the only thing that greeted him was that dog, who knocked him back against the wall.

"Play with the dog, Dixon. I'll be out in a minute," the professor said from somewhere back in the apartment.

With that dog you did what that dog wanted you to do: Throw the ball so he could go galloping around and bring it back to you.

George had a lot more on his mind than playing with a dog. Six of his friends in Werner's archeology class already had been interviewed for the job and been turned down. Now it was his turn and he wanted to rehearse his speech, but this dog was jumping all over him and the furniture, dropping the drool-soaked ball on his best pants.

Then the idea came and George took the slimy ball and held it up. "OK, Fido, you're so smart, go get this one."

Instead of throwing the ball, George rolled it gently across the floor and, with great satisfaction, watched it roll under a low Oriental chest placed beneath an open window.

The Great Dane bounded across the room, his tail knocking a vase of flowers off a table.

The dog did not stop, nor even slow down.

With sudden horror George watched him leap from the floor. He cleared the top of the chest and went on, stretched out, flying. Outside a gentle rain was lit by the streetlights far below. The enormous dog sailed out into the rainy darkness. For what seemed a century to George the body of the dog seemed to float in the air. Then it slowly sank out of sight, falling down through the rain.

The Great Dane did not make a sound as he fell toward the pavement 17 stories down.

For a moment George just sat there, paralyzed with agony for the dog.

Then he was on his feet running, looking only at the open, dark, and empty window.

Something grabbed his arm, stopping him in mid-stride and spinning him around.

"Come on!" Professor Werner said. "I'm late for an appointment so we'll talk in the elevator."

"Wait!" George begged, trying to pull his arm free.

"Come *on!*" the professor ordered, yanking him to the door.

"No! Wait!" George said, but the professor pulled him out of the room and locked the door.

Without a word Werner dragged George to the elevator, shoved him into it, and pushed the button for the lobby.

It was only after the elevator began to sink that George really understood the enormity of the thing. In his mind's eye he could still see that beautiful dog sailing out into the darkness and, in his body, almost feel the long, dreadful fall. . . .

Slowly, as the elevator dial went past 10 and 9 and 8, George tried to erase the picture of that dog and to think about himself: this job he wanted so badly, this interview on which everything depended.

Had it been his fault? A dog had made a mistake and leaped out an open window. Had that been his fault? Was he to blame for that? Did he have to admit it?

Should he lose this job because of a dog? A dead dog.

George realized slowly that the professor had been asking him a direct question.

The elevator dial read 3.

"Dixon," the professor asked again, "what's your definition of courage?" It took all his mental strength to force his mind to pay attention. "Courage, sir? Er. Courage? I guess it's doing the right thing when you don't have to. Even though no one is watching. Nobody saw anything."

Werner laughed. "That's a definition I'd never thought of. But it's not bad. Anyway, this expedition you and I are going on is going to take a lot of it."

You and I. That's what he'd said. *You and I.*

People would be standing in the rain now, looking down at that beautiful dog lying crushed on the wet pavement.

The elevator stopped and the doors slid silently open.

As Werner started out, George pushed the CLOSE DOORS button and then turned and put both hands on Werner's shoulders, pushing him back against the wall.

"I killed your dog," George said.

Werner stared at him.

"I was playing with him. Throwing the ball. He went out the window. Just out. Into the rain."

Werner said nothing as he pushed George's hands aside and

then walked to the front of the elevator and pushed the 17 button.

The elevator going up made no sound at all and Werner stood in silence with his back to George.

"He was a beautiful dog," George said. "I'm sorry."

Werner said nothing as the doors opened and he stepped out. Without looking at George or waiting for him, he walked down the silent corridor, unlocked the door, reached in and turned on the lights and then, at last, turned and waited for George.

Feeling sick, and seeing again that dark, open window, George walked slowly into the room.

A great, moving weight struck him from behind, knocking him down flat on his face.

For a moment he just wanted to lie there, his face down on the carpet, his body waiting for more of the attack he knew he deserved.

Then something gently nudged him and he turned his head.

There was the Great Dane with that soggy tennis ball in his mouth, his tail flailing away, knocking things off a table.

"It was a mean thing to do to you, Dixon," Werner said. "But I need to know what sort of man I'm taking on this dangerous expedition."

George put his arms around the dog's neck and then got to his feet.

"There's a balcony outside that window," Werner said, smiling. "And this mutt loves to show off."

Thinking About What You've Read

1. What did George think had happened to the Great Dane?

_____

2. What important decision did George have to make?
    A. whether to ask Professor Werner for the job
    B. whether to accept the job with Professor Werner
    C. whether to tell Professor Werner what had happened to the dog

3. What kind of conflict did George face?
    A. a conflict with nature
    B. a conflict with another character
    C. a conflict within himself

4. How was this conflict settled?
   A. George told the professor he had killed the dog.
   B. George didn't say anything to the professor about the dog.
   C. George told the professor he didn't want the job.

5. Do you think George made the right decision? Why or why not?

_____

_____

GED Warm-up

What actually happened to the Great Dane?

(1) He landed on the balcony outside the window.
(2) He never really jumped through the window.
(3) He was merely injured as a result of the fall.
(4) He survived the fall unhurt.

Working with Words

You've been working a lot with context clues. Using context clues is a great way to improve your reading. Here's a short review of one kind of clue.

Sometimes an author tells you the meaning of a hard word. Here's an example.

■ The travel agent wrote an **itinerary,** a plan for our trip.

The comma is a clue in this sentence. It tells you an explanation of *itinerary* will follow. You can tell an itinerary is a plan for a trip.

Read the sentences below. The bold word in each sentence is from *Fetch!* Use context clues to figure out the meaning of the word.

1. Ms. Higgins teaches **archaeology,** the study of ancient life and culture.

_____

2. At first, we didn't understand the **enormity,** or great size, of the problem.

_____

3. The scientists are planning an **expedition,** a voyage made for a special purpose.

_____

▲ Looking Back

In this lesson you read a story about how a young man faced a conflict within himself. You learned about plots and conflicts in general. You also used context clues.

When you read fiction, think about the conflict the characters face. Notice how this conflict is settled. The conflict is what makes the story interesting.

The Active Reader

Predicting Outcomes

Picture It
Look at the picture. What do you think will happen next?

The woman will probably step on the skate and fall down the stairs. Did you predict that this might happen?

To predict means to tell what you think might happen next. You often predict events in your daily life. You base your predictions on your experience and your common sense.

Suppose your car's gas tank is almost empty. But you don't stop for gas. It's easy to predict that your car will soon stop running. You know this will happen because a car cannot run without fuel.

Good readers also predict. They guess what is going to happen next. Their predictions are based on what has already happened. They also use their experience and common sense.

When you're able to predict, you know you've been paying close attention to the story. You also know you're using your experience and your common sense. If you cannot predict, you may need to read the story more carefully. Or you may need more background information in order to understand it.

Here's an Example
Look again at the story *Fetch!* on pages 188–191. Suppose you had read only the first ten paragraphs of the story. You might make these predictions.

- George will tell the professor the truth.
- George will say nothing to the professor.
- George will jump out the window himself.

After you make predictions, think about which are most likely to be correct. George may be honest enough to tell the professor the truth. Or he may pretend that nothing has happened. So, the first and second predictions might be correct. George isn't likely to jump out of a window because of a dog. So, the third prediction is probably not correct.

The next step is to read to find out if your prediction is correct. You found out George told the truth about the dog.

If a prediction you make is not correct, ask yourself why. Did you miss some clues in the story? Did you forget to use your experience or common sense? Do you need more background information in order to understand the story?

Working It Out

Here's the beginning of a story. It's about a man who wants to come to America. Read it carefully.

■ It was four years ago, although it seems like a lifetime. My neighbors and I, Janos Hurok, huddled near a stove in the town store. The store owner pulled from his coat pocket a creased, worn American newspaper. He said angrily, "Possessing this newspaper is against the law! The government wants us to read only what they print!"

He then began reading from the newspaper. "In America, the government ensures the rights of its people—the rights to life, liberty, and the pursuit of happiness. These rights no one can take away."

It was then that I decided I must go to America. I wasn't permitted to leave the country. But I knew where I could get forged traveling papers and a ticket for a ship going to America—for a price. I decided to see the secret agent from the resistance movement that steadily fought for freedom. I could be sent to prison or executed, but I was determined.

"Did you bring the money?" asked the agent.

"Yes," I said. "My father gave me most of his savings. And I sold my furniture, my clothes, and a few tools. But how do I know these papers and the ticket are good—that I won't get caught?"

"You can't know—until it is too late. But, my friend, remember we both search for freedom. We just each go about it in a different way. Now be careful in your journey. And good luck."

1. Do you think the traveling papers and the ticket are good? Why or why not?

   _____

   _____

2. Make at least two predictions about what might happen next.

   _____

   _____

Now read the rest of the story.

■ The secret agent seemed to be an honest man. In any case, I had no choice but to trust him. That trust was rewarded several weeks later, when my ship sailed into New York Harbor. I nearly burst with joy as I looked upon the Statue of Liberty for the first time. My new life in America was about to begin!

Was one of your predictions correct? If it wasn't, look at the story again. What clues did you miss? Did you need more background information?

Part B
Lesson 9

Making the Most of What You Have

In this lesson you will
- read a story about a blind beggar
- study *how* the author tells you the story
- use margin notes
- use context clues to figure out words with opposite meanings

Skills for Reading: The Author's Craft

Picture It

The first picture shows a romantic scene. A couple is having dinner. You're an outsider looking at them.

The second picture is the same scene. But it's from the man's point of view. Notice how you see part of the scene through *his* eyes.

Can you see how the information you get depends on the point of view? In other words, it depends on whose eyes you're looking through.

The same is true of a story. The author chooses someone to tell you the story. That person is the **narrator.** The narrator

Lesson 9 Making the Most of What You Have / 195

tells you the story from his or her point of view. The information you get as a reader depends on the narrator's point of view. That is why the author's choice of a narrator is important.

Sometimes the narrator is a character in the story. This is like the second picture on page 195. The narrator will use the word *I*. Here's an example from a story you've just read.

> ■ It was then that I decided I must go to America. I wasn't permitted to leave the country. But I knew where I could get forged papers. . . .

A character-narrator also tells you his or her thoughts. But you won't learn the thoughts of other characters. That's because the narrator can't know those thoughts.

Often the narrator is a person outside the story. This is like the first picture on page 195. The narrator will use words like *he, she,* and *they*. Here's an example of an outside narrator.

> ■ She was fifty-one, nine years younger than he, her thick hair still almost all black. But her face was lined, and her legs hurt when she stood too long on them, although she now wore shoes with arch supports.

Sometimes an outside narrator can tell you the thoughts of all the characters. Sometimes he or she will tell you the thoughts of only one.

The narrator is just *one* choice the author makes. For example, the author also chooses a feeling for the story. The author can excite you by writing about thrilling events. Or the author can make you feel sad by writing about unhappy events. Often the author may even change your feelings during a story.

It's good to understand the choices an author makes. The choices help the author craft the story. Understanding this craft helps you *enjoy* the story.

Here's an Example

Do you remember the story ***Fetch!***? You can reread the story on pages 188–191.

The narrator in the story is an outside person. The narrator tells you George's thoughts. These thoughts help you see that George is afraid. He doesn't want to tell the professor the truth.

The outside narrator did *not* tell you Professor Werner's thoughts. That's why the ending may have surprised you. You couldn't know the dog was still alive. But Professor Werner knew all along.

Did you feel nervous for George during the story? Did you feel relieved at the end? If you did, the author created those feelings in you. He did this by crafting a nervous, tense situation. Then he wrote a happy ending.

Working It Out

1. Reread "Gentleman of Río en Medio" on pages 182–184. Is the narrator a character or an outsider? How can you tell?

_____
_____
_____

2. Reread the passage on pages 180–181. How does the author make you feel with this passage?
   A. happy
   B. hopeful
   C. tense

Writing to Improve Your Reading

When you read, you sometimes come across ideas you don't understand. When this happens, it's good to make a note of it. If you own the book you are reading, you can make a note in the margin. If the book is not yours, write your notes on a sheet of paper.

Here's an example of how this works. Look at the second paragraph in the story below. Let's say you don't understand what *half-furtive* means. You can't seem to figure it out using the context. So you circle the word and put a question mark in the margin. This will remind you to look it up later in a dictionary.

Here's another example of how to use margin notes. Note the third paragraph in the story below. The last sentence describes Mr. Parsons's pity for blind creatures as "foolish." You may wonder *why* it is foolish for Mr. Parsons to pity the blind. You can circle the word *foolish* and write "Why is it foolish?" in the margin. Perhaps you'll find out as you read the story.

As you read the story below, make notes in the margin. When you finish reading, go back to those notes. If necessary, you can reread parts of the story to understand the ideas better.

Reading on Your Own

The following story is about being blind. Notice what the narrator chooses to tell you. Think about how the author surprises you at the end. Making margin notes will help you follow the narrator's story. Note in the margin when you begin to feel a little tense and eager for the story to end.

A Man Who Had No Eyes

A beggar was coming down the avenue just as Mr. Parsons emerged from his hotel.

He was a blind beggar, carrying the traditional battered cane, and thumping his way before him with the cautious, half-furtive effort of the sightless. He was a shaggy, thicknecked fellow; his coat was greasy about the lapels and pockets, and his hand splayed over the cane's crook with a futile sort of clinging. He wore a black pouch slung over his shoulder. Apparently he had

Traditional *means "usual."*

?

Splayed *means "stretched out."*

Why is it foolish?

Guv'nor *is a slang way of saying "Governor." The beggar calls Mr. Parsons "guv'nor" to show respect because Parsons is in a higher social class.*

Inquisitive *means "nosy."*

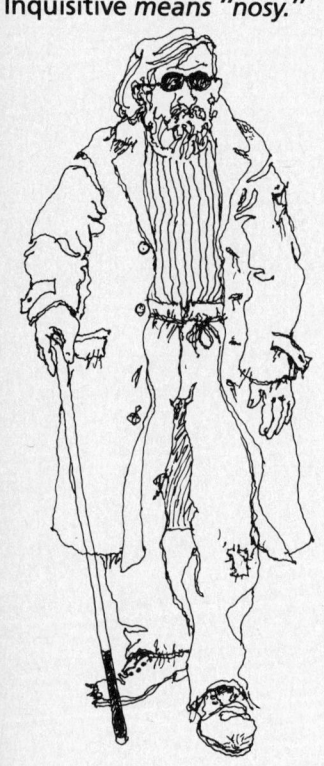

something to sell.

The air was rich with spring; sun was warm and yellowed on the asphalt. Mr. Parsons, standing there in front of his hotel and noting the *clack-clack* approach of the sightless man, felt a sudden and (foolish) sort of pity for all blind creatures.

And, thought Mr. Parsons, he was very glad to be alive. A few years ago he had been little more than a skilled laborer; now he was successful, respected, admired . . . Insurance. . . . And he had done it alone, unaided, struggling beneath handicaps. . . .

He took a step forward just as the tap-tapping blind man passed him by. Quickly the shabby fellow turned.

"Listen, guv'nor. Just a minute of your time."

Mr. Parsons said, "It's late. I have an appointment. Do you want me to give you something?"

"I ain't no beggar, guv'nor. You bet I ain't. I got a handy little article here"—he fumbled until he could press a small object into Mr. Parsons' hand—"that I sell. One buck. Best cigarette lighter made." . . .

Mr. Parsons sighed and felt in his vest pocket. He brought out two half dollars and pressed them into the man's hand. . . . He hesitated, not wishing to be boorish and inquisitive, even with a blind peddler. "Have you lost your sight entirely?"

The shabby man pocketed the two half dollars. "Fourteen years, guv'nor." Then he added with an insane sort of pride: "Westbury, sir. I was one of 'em."

"Westbury," repeated Mr. Parsons. "Ah, yes. The chemical explosion. . . . The papers haven't mentioned it for years. . . ."

"Just think about it, guv'nor. There was a hundred and eight people killed, about two hundred injured, and over fifty of them lost their eyes. Blind as bats—" He groped forward until his dirty hand rested against Mr. Parsons' coat. . . .

"You want to know how I lost my eyes?" cried the man. "Well here it is!" His words fell with the bitter and studied drama of a story often told, and told for money. "I was there in C shop, last of all the folks rushing out. Out in the air there was a chance, even with buildings exploding right and left. A lot of guys made it safe out the door and got away. And just when I was about there, crawling along between those big vats, a guy behind me grabs

198 / Part B Reading Skills for Literature

my leg. He says, 'Let me past, you—!' Maybe he was nuts. I dunno. I try to forgive him in my heart, guv'nor. But he was bigger than me. He hauls me back and climbs right over me! Tramples me into the dirt. And he gets out, and I lie there with all that poison gas pouring down on all sides of me, and flame and stuff. . . ." He swallowed—a studied sob—and stood dumbly expectant. He could imagine the next words: *Tough luck, my man. Now, I want to—* "That's the story, guv'nor."

   The spring wind shrilled past them, damp and quivering.

   "Not quite," said Mr. Parsons.

   The blind peddler shivered crazily. "Not quite? What do you mean, you—"

   "The story is true," Mr. Parsons said, "except that it was the other way around."

   "Other way around?" He croaked unamiably. "Say, guv'nor—"

Unamiably means "in an unfriendly way."

   "I was in C shop," said Mr. Parsons. "It was the other way around. You were the fellow who hauled back on me and climbed over me. You were bigger than I was, Markwardt."

   The blind man stood for a long time, swallowing hoarsely. He gulped: "Parsons, I thought you—" And then he screamed fiendishly: "Yes. Maybe so. Maybe so. But I'm blind! I'm blind, and you've been standing here letting me spout to you, and laughing at me every minute! I'm blind."

   People in the street turned to stare at him.

   "You got away, but I'm blind! Do you hear? I'm—"

   "Well," said Mr. Parsons, "don't make such a row about it, Markwardt. . . . So am I."

Thinking About What You've Read

1. How does the narrator surprise you at the end?

2. How does the feeling of the story change after Mr. Parsons reveals who he is?
    A. The feeling becomes joyful and funny.
    B. The feeling becomes tense and angry.
    C. The feeling becomes hopeful and relieved.

3. How did Mr. Parsons and Markwardt become blind?

4. What kind of work does each man do now?

5. What was wrong with the story Markwardt told Mr. Parsons?

6. Go back through the story. What clues does the author give you that Mr. Parsons is blind?

   Did you make margin notes about any of these clues?

200 / Part B Reading Skills for Literature

GED Warm-up

Why did Markwardt tell Mr. Parsons about the accident?

(1) He knew Mr. Parsons was blinded in the same accident.
(2) He liked to tell stories.
(3) He thought Mr. Parsons was a newspaper reporter.
(4) He hoped Mr. Parsons would give him more money.

① ② ③ ④

Working with Words

In Lesson 8, you reviewed one kind of context clue: definitions. Sometimes a definition is a synonym—a word with a similar meaning. Antonyms are another kind of context clue. Antonyms are words that have opposite meanings. Here are some examples.

| hot/cold | rich/poor |
| agree/disagree | fresh/stale |

Writers sometimes give you an antonym for a hard word. This helps you figure out the word's meaning. Here's an example.

■ The first attempt to climb the peak was futile, but the second attempt was successful.

The clue word *but* tells you that *successful* is an antonym for *futile*. So, *futile* means "unsuccessful."

As you read, watch for antonyms that can be used as context clues. Also be on the lookout for the following clue words and phrases. They often are used to signal antonym context clues.

but   instead   not   on the other hand

Read the sentences below. Use context clues to figure out the meaning of each **bold** word. Circle the correct meaning.

1. Our old neighbors were quite **boorish.** Our new ones, on the other hand, are very polite.

   stupid   rude   lazy

2. I thought the woman would be **shabby,** not well-dressed.

   ragged   pretty   tired

▲ Looking Back

In this lesson you read a story about two blind men. You learned about the choices an author makes. You also learned how to use margin notes. And you practiced using antonym context clues.

When you read fiction, think about the feeling the author creates. Notice whether the feeling stays the same or changes. Also notice who is telling the story. Is the narrator a character or an outsider?

The Active Reader

Self-Checking

Picture It

Fairfax Road Next Right EXIT ONLY

Joan got off the highway at Fairfax Road. After lunch she looked for an entrance back onto the highway. There wasn't any. Joan had not read the sign carefully. If she had, she would have seen the words "Exit Only." She would have known there was no entrance.

When people read, they sometimes miss important information. They may also run into other reading problems. You can cut down on these problems. You can check yourself as you read.

One way to check yourself is to stop after every few paragraphs or pages. Ask yourself, "Do I understand what I've read?" Rate your understanding on a scale of 1 to 10. If your rating is less than 6 or 7, you need to find out why.

Here's an Example
Here's a checklist of questions you can use when you read.

_____ Does this story make sense to me?
_____ Is there any part I don't understand?
_____ Are there parts of this story I should read again?
_____ Is there any information I should look up in a reference book? Or is there someone who could help me understand this better?
_____ Do I need to check the meaning of any words in a dictionary?

Working It Out
Check yourself as you read this paragraph. Use the questions in the checklist.

■ It was another heavy morning, already hot and breathless, but in the wood the air was cooler and smelled agreeably damp. Winnie had been no more than two slow minutes walking timidly under the interlacing branches when she wondered why she had never come here before. "Why, it's nice!" she thought with great surprise.

1. What was Winnie doing?

2. Underline any part you had to reread in order to understand it.

Part B
Lesson 10

Reading Drama

In this lesson you will
- read drama
- learn how to understand lines of speech and stage directions
- work with pronouns

Skills for Reading: Speech and Stage Directions

Picture It

Do you think drama doesn't play a part in your life? Think again.

When you watch a TV show or movie, you're often watching drama. Reading drama takes the same skills that watching drama does. But reading drama also requires other skills.

You learned about characters, setting, and plot in fiction. Drama has all those ingredients too. In drama, though, they are written down in a special way. A written drama is called a script. In a script, the lines of speech and stage directions tell about the characters, setting, and plot. Part of a script is shown below.

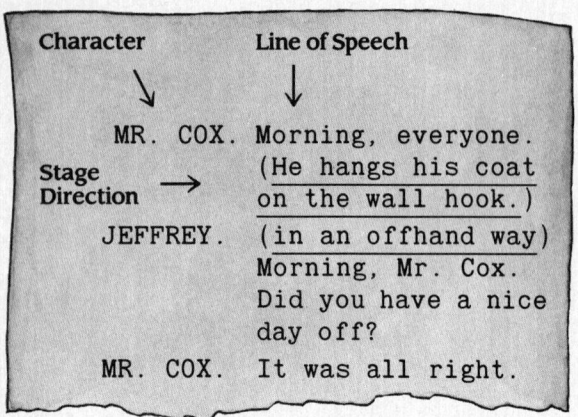

The lines of speech are all the words the characters speak. The stage directions describe the characters, their actions, and the setting. Stage directions are in *italic* type and placed in parentheses.

To connect a drama with real life, you can visualize as you read. You've learned about visualizing. You can read more about it on page 210. You may want to read those pages before you go on. Visualizing is the *best* way to understand a drama.

Here's an Example

Below is part of a script from a play called *The Man Who Came to Dinner*. Try to visualize as you read. This will help you understand the stage directions and lines of speech.

WHITESIDE. Miss Preen. Miss Preen.... Answer the door, will you?
(MISS PREEN, *obviously annoyed, hurries to the door.... She is carried into the room in the arms of a pixie-like gentleman, who is kissing her over and over.*)

THE GENTLEMAN CARRYING MISS PREEN. I love you madly—madly! Did you hear what I said—madly! Kiss me! Again! Don't be afraid of my passion. Kiss me! I can feel the hot blood pounding through your varicose veins.
MISS PREEN *(through all this).* Put me down! Put me down, do you hear! Don't you dare kiss me! Who are you! Put me down or I'll scream. Mr. Whiteside! Mr. Whiteside! . . .
WHITESIDE. Banjo, put that woman down. That is my nurse, you mental delinquent.

There are three characters in this part of the play: Whiteside, Miss Preen, and the gentleman. You find out that the gentleman's name is Banjo. That's the name Whiteside calls him in his last set of lines.

The stage directions tell you these actions: The gentleman comes through the door. He takes Miss Preen up into his arms. Then he kisses her.

The lines of speech tell you he loves her. Miss Preen is shouting, "Put me down." The stage direction "*(through all this)*" tells you she is speaking at the same time he's kissing and carrying her. Finally, Whiteside explains that Miss Preen is his nurse. You can infer that the man thought Miss Preen was someone else.

Can you see how the stage directions and lines of speech carry out the story of a drama?

Working It Out

Here's part of a script. It's from a play and movie called *Mr. Roberts.* The setting is a U.S. ship in the Pacific Ocean during World War II. Read the lines of speech and stage directions carefully. Then answer the questions that follow.

DOC: What is it you want to be—a hero or something?

ROBERTS *(Shocked):* Hero! . . . Look, Doc, the war's way out there! I'm here. I don't want to be here—I want to be out there. I'm sick and tired of being a lousy spectator. I just happen to believe in this thing. I've got to feel I'm *good* enough to be in it—to *participate!* . . .

PULVER *(Offstage):* Doug! Doc! *(Entering.)* Listen to the radio. . . . Turn it up!

(ROBERTS *reaches over and turns up the radio. The excited voice of an announcer can be heard.*)

ANNOUNCER: . . . this broadcast to bring you a special news flash! The war is over in Europe! THE WAR IS OVER IN EUROPE! (ROBERTS *grasps* DOC's *arm in excitement*) Germany has surrendered unconditionally to the Allied Armies. The surrender was signed in a schoolhouse in the city of Rheims. . . .

1. Name the characters in this play.
   _____
   _____

2. How does Roberts say his first line of speech?
   _____

3. What does Roberts want?
   _____
   _____

4. Why does Pulver tell Roberts and Doc to turn up the radio?
   _____
   _____

Lesson 10 Reading Drama / 205

5. What does Roberts do when he hears the radio announcement?

6. If you were watching this play, who would be on stage at the beginning of this part?

Writing to Improve Your Reading

You learned how to summarize on pages 167–168. A summary can help you be sure you've understood what you've read. Read the drama below. Then write a summary of it. Don't use speech or stage directions in your summary. Instead, describe the main events in a paragraph.

Reading on Your Own

The following reading is part of a script. It's from a play called The Little Foxes. *In the play, Horace and Regina are married and are very rich. Horace tells Regina he's going to write a new will. In his new will, he's going to leave her only $88,000. That's only a small part of their fortune. Read the lines of speech and stage directions carefully. This will help you enjoy the drama.*

The Little Foxes

HORACE: . . . I am going to make a new will, Regina, leaving you eighty-eight thousand dollars in Union Pacific bonds. The rest will go to Zan. . . .

REGINA: You hate me very much.

HORACE: No.

REGINA: Oh, I think you do. *(Puts her head back, sighs.)* Well, we haven't been very good together. Anyway, I don't hate you either. I have only contempt for you. I've always had.

HORACE: From the very first?

REGINA: I think so.

HORACE: I was in love with *you*. But why did *you* marry *me*?

REGINA: I was lonely when I was young.

HORACE: *You* were lonely?

REGINA: Not the way people usually mean. Lonely for all the things I wasn't going to get. Everybody in this house was so busy and there was so little place for what I wanted. I wanted the world. Then, and then— *(Smiles.)* Papa died and left the money to Ben and Oscar.

HORACE: And you married me?

REGINA: Yes, I thought— But I was wrong. You were a small-town clerk then. You haven't changed.

HORACE *(Nods, smiles):* And that wasn't what you wanted.

REGINA: No. No, it wasn't what I wanted. *(Pauses, leans back, pleasantly.)* It took me a little while to find out I had made a mistake. As for you—I don't know. It was almost as if I couldn't stand the kind of man you were— *(Smiles; softly.)* I used to lie there at night, praying you wouldn't come near—

HORACE: Really? It was as bad as that?

REGINA *(Nods):* Remember when I went to Doctor Sloan and I told you he said there was something the matter with me and that you shouldn't touch me any more?

HORACE: I remember.

REGINA: But you believed it. I couldn't understand that. I couldn't understand that anybody could be such a soft fool. That was when I began to despise you.

HORACE *(Puts his hand to his throat, looks at the bottle of medicine on table):* Why didn't you leave me?

REGINA: I told you I married you for something. It turned out it was only for this. *(Carefully.)* This wasn't what I wanted, but it was something. I never thought about it much but if I had (HORACE *puts his hand to his throat.*) I'd have known that you would die before I would. But I couldn't have known that you would get heart trouble so early and so bad. I'm lucky, Horace. I've always been lucky. (HORACE *turns slowly to the medicine.*) I'll be lucky again.

(HORACE *looks at her. Then he puts his hand to his throat. Because he cannot reach the bottle he moves the chair closer. He reaches for the medicine, takes out the cork, picks up the spoon. The bottle slips and smashes on the table. He draws in his breath, gasps.)*

HORACE: Please. Tell Addie— The other bottle is upstairs. (REGINA *has not moved. She does not move now. He stares at her. Then, suddenly as if he understood, he raises his voice. It is a panic-stricken whisper, too small to be heard outside the room.)* Addie! Addie! Come—

> (Stops as he hears the softness of his voice. He makes a sudden, furious spring from the chair to the stairs, taking the first few steps as if he were a desperate runner. On the fourth step he slips, gasps, grasps the rail, makes a great effort to reach the landing. When he reaches the landing, he is on his knees. His knees give way, he falls on the landing, out of view. REGINA has not turned during his climb up the stairs.)

Thinking About What You've Read

1. Number the following events in the order in which they happen.
   _____ Regina tells Horace about her visit to Doctor Sloan.
   _____ Horace tells Regina he's going to make a new will.
   _____ Regina tells Horace she married him because she was lonely.
   _____ Horace tries to climb the stairs.
   _____ Horace drops the medicine bottle.

2. What is happening to Horace near the end?
   _____

3. How do Horace and Regina feel about each other?
   _____

4. Circle all the words that help describe the character of Regina.

   bright   cold-hearted   pretty   loving
   lying   greedy   pleasant   humble

5. Read the last stage direction again. What conclusion can you draw about the reason for Regina's behavior?
   _____
   _____

6. Did you write a summary of the drama? If not, you may want to write one now on your own paper.

A Test-Taking Tip

On many multiple-choice tests, you will have to choose your answer from among five options. The GED Test, for example, always gives five choices.

Do five options look like a lot to you? They do to many people! But there are ways to make these questions easier to manage.

Try to answer the question for yourself *before* you read the possible answers. Then match your idea to the five choices. Pick the one that is most similar.

Sometimes you can see quite easily that three of the answers are wrong. Cross them out. Then you can focus on the two options that remain.

Practice your test-taking skills on the question below. It refers to the play you just read.

GED Warm-up

Regina began to despise Horace when he
(1) believed he should not touch her
(2) became ill and needed attention
(3) decided to leave her very little money
(4) called for Addie instead of Regina
(5) remained a small-town clerk

① ② ③ ④ ⑤

Working with Words

Words like *I, he, she,* and *it* are pronouns. A pronoun stands for another, more specific word. For example, in the line "I am going to make a new will," the pronoun *I* stands for the name *Horace*.

Writers try to be clear when they use pronouns. They want you to know the word each pronoun stands for. But when people speak, they may use pronouns in an unclear way. A writer of plays wants the lines of speech to sound like the way people *speak,* not the way they write. So when you read drama, take extra care in matching pronouns to names.

As you read, try to understand what each pronoun stands for. The context of the pronoun will help you.

You can practice with the lines below. Read each line of speech. Find it in the play, **The Little Foxes,** if you need to. Then circle the words the underlined pronoun stands for.

1. "Well, we haven't been very good together."

    Regina and Horace   Regina and Zan

2. "Remember when I went to Doctor Sloan and I told you he said there was something the matter with me. . . ."

    Horace   Doctor Sloan

3. "But you believed it. I couldn't understand that."

    the doctor's story   Regina's lie

▲ Looking Back

In this lesson you learned to read the lines of speech and stage directions of a drama. You read parts of several plays, including a long selection about an unhappy couple. Finally, you practiced working with pronouns. Use this last skill whenever you read.

The Active Reader

Using the Powers of Your Imagination

Picture It

Dramas are meant to be *seen*. For that reason, visualizing can really help you understand a drama. Visualizing is creating a picture in your mind. *See* the characters talk to each other just as they would do on stage. See them talk just as people would do in real life. Picture the setting and the action as well.

Dramas are also meant to be *heard*. So *hear* the lines of speech you read. Sound out the words in your head just the way the characters would say them.

When you read a script, do these three things:

1. Read the lines of speech and stage directions carefully.
2. Picture the characters, the action, and the setting.
3. Hear the characters speaking their lines in your head.

Use the powers of your imagination. Then you'll not only understand drama, you'll also *enjoy* it.

Here's an Example

Go back to page 205 and read the script about Mr. Roberts. Look at the pictures on the page. They help show the characters and action in that play.

You can see the same kinds of pictures in your mind. You can also hear Roberts say, "Hero!" in a shocked voice. You can hear Pulver shout, "Listen to the radio!" And you can hear the excited announcer say the war is over. Try it.

Working It Out

Go back to page 204 and read the play about Miss Preen.

1. Write a short paragraph describing *all* the action in the play. If you'd like, draw pictures to show what is happening. Use a separate sheet of paper.

Answer the following questions in a few words.

2. How would Miss Preen's face look as she shouts, "Put me down!"?

3. How would the gentleman sound as he says, "I love you madly—madly!"?

Part B
Lesson 11

Reading Poetry

> *In this lesson you will*
> - learn tips for reading poetry
> - write your own poems
> - work with figures of speech

Skills for Reading: Understanding Poetry

Picture It

Look at the scene in this picture.

A good piece of writing would *tell* you about this scene. It would describe the sights and sounds. But a good *poem* would help you *experience* the scene. You would "see" the view and "hear" the sounds. You would feel as if you were part of the scene. Such experience is what poetry is all about.

If you want to experience a poem, you have to understand it. These steps can help you understand a poem.

1. Read the title.
2. Read the poem all the way through carefully. Read the poem aloud or "hear" the words in your head. In a poem, the sound of the words is just as important as their meaning.

Some poems rhyme; others don't. Some poems have one rhythm; others have rhythms that change. In some poems you need to pause at the end of each line; in others you may need to keep reading from one line to the next. You can hear these differences when you read poems aloud.

3. Read the poem a second time.
4. Ask yourself this question: What thought is the poet sharing with me?
5. Ask yourself this question: How does the poem make me feel?

Here's an Example

Here's part of a poem that a woman wrote. She wrote about a scene like the one in Picture It. Use the five steps to help you experience the view. This will help you understand the poem.

>Water Picture
>
>In the pond in the park
>all things are doubled:
>Long buildings hang and
>wriggle gently. Chimneys
>are bent legs bouncing
>on clouds below. A flag
>wags like a fishhook
>down there in the sky.

The poet looked at the scene in a different way than most people would. She shared that way in her poem. She also shared a feeling of fun and delight.

Poems don't just deal with sights and sounds. Poets also share their thoughts and feelings about life.

Follow the steps for understanding poetry as you read this poem. The poet is sharing a thought about famous people.

>Soup
>
>I saw a famous man eating soup.
>I say he was lifting a fat broth
>Into his mouth with a spoon.
>His name was in the newspapers that day
>Spelled out in tall black headlines
>And thousands of people were talking
>   about him.
>
>When I saw him,
>He sat bending his head over a plate
>Putting soup in his mouth with a spoon.

The poet is describing a famous man. Yet what is the man doing? Something we *all* do—he's eating soup. The poet is sharing this thought: Famous people are not really different from the rest of us. Did the poem make you think about this idea?

Working It Out

Read this poem. Be sure to follow the five steps on page 211.

>Seagulls
>
>Between the under and the upper blue
>All day the seagulls climb and swerve and soar,
>Arc intersecting arc, curve over curve.
>
>And you may watch them weaving a long time
>And never see their pattern twice the same
>And never see their pattern once imperfect.
>
>Take any moment they are in the air—
>If you could change them, if you had the power
>How would you place them other than they are?
>
>What we have labored all our lives to have
>And failed, these birds effortlessly achieve;
>Freedom that flows in form and still is free.

1. What scene is the poet sharing with you?

   _____

2. Read the first two lines again. Picture seagulls flying. What would be blue in the picture in your mind? Now complete these sentences:

   The "upper blue" that the seagulls fly under is the _____.

   The "under blue" that the seagulls fly above is the _____.

3. Fill in the blanks to tell the thought the poet is sharing:

   _____ succeed where people fail. They move in harmony with each other, yet each seagull is still _____ .

Writing to Improve Your Reading

You have ideas and feelings of your own. Writing your own poems can help you express those ideas and feelings. It can also help you understand other people's poems.

If you'd like to write a poem now, go ahead. Write about anything you want. Make it short or long. Make it funny or serious. Make it rhyme or not rhyme. If you want to wait until you've read the poems in Reading on Your Own, that's fine too.

Do you want to write a poem, yet don't know how? Here's a little help. Write one of these words on a sheet of paper: *Love* or *Hate.* What picture comes to your mind? Write about that picture. Write about the *things* you see in the picture. *Don't* use the word *love* or *hate* in your poem.

Reading on Your Own

Here are some poems for you to read and enjoy. After each poem, answer the questions about it.

A Time to Talk
When a friend calls to me from the road
And slows his horse to a meaning walk,
I don't stand still and look around
On all the hills I haven't hoed,
And shout from where I am, "What is it?"
No, not as there is a time to talk.
I thrust my hoe in the mellow ground,
Blade-end up and five feet tall,
And plod: I go up to the stone wall
For a friendly visit.

1. What is the speaker in the poem doing when the friend first called? (Clues are in lines 3–4 and line 7.)

   _____

2. What does the speaker do after the friend calls? (Clues are in lines 7 and 9–10.)

   _____

3. What is the poet telling you about visiting with friends? (A clue is in the title.)

   _____

African Dance

The low beating of the tom-toms,
   The slow beating of the tom-toms,
   Low . . . slow
   Slow . . . low—
Stirs your blood.

        Dance!
A night-veiled girl
   Whirls softly into a
   Circle of light.
Whirls softly . . . slowly,
Like a wisp of smoke around the fire—
   And the tom-toms beat,
   And the tom-toms beat,
And the low beating of the tom-toms
   Stirs your blood.

4. What does the poem make you hear in the first part of the poem?
   _____

5. What does the poet help you see in the second part of the poem?
   _____

6. What is the poet telling you about an African dance in this poem?
   _____

7. How does this poem make you feel?
   _____

The Fly

The Lord in His wisdom made the fly
And then forgot to tell us why.

8. What is the poet telling you about flies in this poem?
   _____
   _____

9. How does this poem make you feel?
   _____

Waking from a Nap on the Beach

Sounds like big
rashers of bacon frying.
I look up from where I'm lying
expecting to see stripes

red and white. My eyes drop shut,
stunned by the sun.
Now the foam is flame, the long
troughs charcoal, but

still it chuckles and sizzles, it
burns and burns, it never gets done.
The sea is
fat.

10. What experience is the poet sharing with you?
    _____
    _____

11. What does the sea sound like to the poet?
    _____

12. Why does the poet say the sea "never gets done"?
    _____
    _____

Broken Sky

The sky of gray is eaten in six places,
Rag holes stand out.
It is an army blanket and the sleeper
   slept too near the fire.

13. What scene is the poet sharing with you? (Clues are in the title and first line.)

_____
_____

Home Thoughts

The sea rocks have a green moss.
The pine rocks have red berries.
I have memories of you.

....

Speak to me of how you miss me.
Tell me the hours go long and slow.

Speak to me of the drag on your heart,
The iron drag of the long days.

I know hours empty as a beggar's tin cup
　　on a rainy day,
　　empty as a soldier's sleeve with an
　　arm lost.

Speak to me . . .

14. Whom is the poet referring to as "you"?

_____
_____

15. What does the poet want the person to do?

_____
_____

16. What feeling is the poet sharing?

_____
_____

A Test-Taking Tip

Sometimes poets twist words around. They put them in unusual order. They may leave out some words. A test question may ask you to restate such a line. If so, put the words into their usual order. Put in words you think are missing. You may even want to write your new sentence down. This will help you understand the meaning of the line. Then you can restate it in your own words, and match your restatement with one of the answer choices.

GED Warm-up

In the poem "Home Thoughts," what does the poet mean by saying, "I know hours empty"?

(1) The poet does not own anything.
(2) The poet has nothing to do all day.
(3) The poet is lonely without a loved one.
(4) The poet cannot sleep at night.
(5) Time moves by quickly.

① ② ③ ④ ⑤

Working with Words

Poets use words to show how different things are alike in some way. This kind of comparison is called a figure of speech.

For example, look back at the poem *African Dance.* Read the phrase "night-veiled girl." The poet is comparing night to a veil. Each one can hide things from view.

Another figure of speech occurs later in the same poem: the girl whirls "like a wisp of smoke." This figure of speech is easier to understand. The poet *directly* states that one thing (the girl) is "like" another (the wisp of smoke).

Remember: Figures of speech compare two *different* things. Sometimes they use a word such as "like" or "as." Now see if you can answer these questions. Circle the letter of your answer.

Read again *Waking from a Nap on the Beach.*

1. What is the sound of the sea compared to?
   A. bacon frying
   B. an alarm that wakes the poet

2. What is the foam on the waves compared to?
   A. the bright sun   B. a flame for cooking

Read again *Broken Sky.*

3. The broken sky is compared to a partly eaten food, a rag with holes, and
   A. an army blanket with burn holes
   B. a sleeper near a fire

Read again *Home Thoughts.*

4. The poet's empty hours are compared to a wounded soldier's empty sleeve and
   A. rocks covered with moss
   B. an empty beggar's cup

▲ Looking Back

In this lesson you read many different poems. You worked at understanding figures of speech. You may even have written some poetry of your own. If you haven't written a poem yet, perhaps you'd like to try writing one now.

The Active Reader

Reading Aloud

Getting Started

You know the *sounds* in a poem are just as important as the meaning of the words. The best way to hear the sounds is to read the poem aloud.

Here's an Example

Read the following poem aloud.

   Funny the Way Different Cars Start

Funny the way
Different cars start.
Some with a chunk and a jerk,
Some with a cough and a puff of smoke
Out of the back,
Some with only a little click—with hardly
   any noise.

Funny the way
Different cars run.
Some rattle and bang,
Some whirrr,
Some knock and knock.
Some purr
And hummmmm
Smoothly on with hardly any noise.

Did you hear the hard sound of the letter *k* in words like *chunk* and *jerk* and *knock*? What about the smooth sound of *purr* and *hummmmm*? All these different sounds help you *hear* how different cars sound.

Working It Out

Read this poem aloud. Hear its sounds.

   Snowy Morning

Wake
gently this morning
to a different day.
Listen.

There is no bray
of buses,
no brake growls,
no siren howls and
no horns
blow.
There is only
the silence
of a city
hushed
by snow.

"Snowy Morning" by Lilian Moore. Reprinted by permission.

1. The letters "b" and "g" in phrases like "brake growls" help you hear the normal harsh city sounds. What *soft* sounds do you hear?

Measuring What You've Learned

This test has 5 selections from literature and 21 questions. It will help you see how much you've learned. Read each selection carefully. Then answer the questions about it. This test is not timed, so don't feel you have to hurry. When you've finished, you can check your answers on page 243.

Items 1–5 refer to the following passage.

I had just turned 12 when my father took me on our only trip to Maine to go camping. We drove from first light to late darkness before we reached Baxter State Park. For a week we fished and canoed and kept a lookout for black bear and moose and deer. We talked more than we ever had before or perhaps ever did again. Mostly, though, what I remember about that week was the mountain. Katahdin.

. . . I'd never seen a mountain like this. There were no foothills to mute its staggering presence; 5,267 feet high, it bored into a boy's imagination. Each day I asked my father if we could climb, and each day he said to wait. Instead he led me to ponds and waterfalls and twisting forest trails that climbed lesser peaks. He read to me about the river drivers who long before there was a park rode thundering logs down these waters. He also read from Thoreau's account of climbing Katahdin. But I didn't want Thoreau. I wanted the mountain. I know now he was saving the mountain until last, as much for himself, I think, as for me.

We climbed Katahdin only once. A long, hot haul in mid-July. I wish I knew whether I walked the Knife Edge, where a sheer drop of 2,000 feet awaits the careless and the foolish. . . . Watching my own little boy, not yet three, leap from a tree limb onto a pile of leaves, I like to imagine I did.

I lived a long time in Maine, and now live in New Hampshire. Baxter is not close, a good six-hour drive, but nearly every year I manage to spend at least a few nights sleeping under its pines.

1. What is the main idea of this passage?
   (1) The writer had just turned twelve when his father took him to Maine.
   (2) The father kept putting off climbing the mountain called Katahdin.
   (3) Katahdin is an impressive mountain in the state of Maine.
   (4) Baxter State Park and Katahdin made a lasting impression on the writer.
   (5) The writer drives six hours every year to visit Baxter State Park.

2. The main thing the writer remembers about his boyhood trip to Maine is
   (1) looking for animals
   (2) the sight of Katahdin
   (3) listening to his father read stories
   (4) the long talks with his father
   (5) the waterfalls and forest trails
   ① ② ③ ④ ⑤

3. The writer used the first three paragraphs to describe a camping trip when he was twelve. What does he use the fourth paragraph to do?
   (1) reveal how that trip affects him today
   (2) persuade other people to take their children to Maine
   (3) summarize the events of his trip
   (4) describe what happened on their return from Maine
   (5) list the reasons he especially liked the trip
   ① ② ③ ④ ⑤

4. The mountain had a strong effect on the writer because
   (1) his father could not climb it
   (2) there were so many different animals on it
   (3) no one had ever climbed it
   (4) he had lived on flat land all his life
   (5) its height towered over the flat land around it
   ① ② ③ ④ ⑤

5. What does the word "good" mean as it is used in the phrase "a good six-hour drive"?
   (1) moral
   (2) right
   (3) full
   (4) skillful
   (5) healthful
   ① ② ③ ④ ⑤

Items 6–9 refer to the passage below.

"I want work, Miss Lady."

"Work?"

"Yes, ma'am. Anything."

Lady Jones smiled. "What can you do?"

"I can't do anything, but I would learn it for you if you have a little extra."

"Extra?"

"Food. My ma'am, she doesn't feel good."

"Oh, baby," said Mrs. Jones. "Oh, baby."

Denver looked up at her. She did not know it then, but it was the word "baby," said softly and with such kindness, that inaugurated her life in the world as a woman. . . . Lady Jones gave her some rice, four eggs and some tea. Denver said she couldn't be away from home long because of her mother's condition. Could she do chores in the morning? Lady Jones told her that no one, not herself, not anyone she knew, could pay anybody anything for work they did themselves.

"But if you all need to eat until your mother is well, all you have to do is say so." She mentioned her church's committee invented so nobody had to go hungry. That agitated her guest who said, "No, no," as though asking for help from strangers was worse than hunger. Lady Jones said goodbye to her and asked her to come back anytime. "Anytime at all."

Two days later Denver stood on the porch and noticed something lying on the tree stump at the edge of the yard. She went to look and found a sack of white beans. Another time a plate of cold rabbit meat. One morning a basket of eggs sat there.

6. What kind of person does Lady Jones seem to be?
   (1) snobbish
   (2) helpless
   (3) lively
   (4) stubborn
   (5) caring
   ① ② ③ ④ ⑤

7. Which of these details helps you see that the story takes place in a poor, rural community?
   (1) Lady Jones's treatment of Denver
   (2) the rabbit meat and basket of eggs
   (3) the condition of Denver's mother
   (4) Denver's request for work
   (5) the porch and tree stump in the yard
   ① ② ③ ④ ⑤

8. How is Denver's problem at least partly solved?
   (1) Lady Jones and her church committee bring food to Denver's yard.
   (2) Denver is given work doing chores two days later.
   (3) Denver's mother becomes well enough to work.
   (4) Denver leaves home and is able to get food for herself.
   (5) Denver begins to steal food for her mother and her.
   ① ② ③ ④ ⑤

9. Read this line from the story: "Lady Jones said goodbye to her and asked her to come back anytime. 'Anytime at all.'"

   The writer repeats the word "anytime" in Lady Jones's goodbye to show that she
   (1) was afraid Denver hadn't heard her
   (2) did not really mean what she was saying
   (3) wanted to stress to Denver that she was welcome
   (4) did not want Denver to leave
   (5) was not certain that Denver was telling the truth
   ① ② ③ ④ ⑤

Items 10–13 refer to the following piece of commentary.

The "Honeymooners Hidden Episodes" is a series of videos. They are now on sale for home viewing. The two shows on each tape were never really hidden. But they are not very well known either. The shows are *not* from the old half-hour series you see on your late-night TV screen. Rather they are comedy sketches from Jackie Gleason's hour-long show in the 1950s. This variety show ran on television before the actual "Honeymooners."

The pace is slower than in the tight, controlled, half-hour shows. But for those who worry that the loud-mouthed, lovable Ralph Kramden may not quite ring true, don't fret. Jackie Gleason's blue-collar hero is here in all his glory.

Also, the Jackie Gleason show was seen live rather than filmed or taped. This creates a sense of energy and excitement that only a live show can give. It also means that priceless mistakes are there for your viewing pleasure—including Jackie turning his back to the camera in order to zip his open fly.

These tapes are for those who want to see television during its live "Golden Age." And for those who enjoy the comic greatness of Jackie Gleason, the "Honeymooners Hidden Episodes" does not disappoint.

10. What is the *main* point the writer is trying to make?
   (1) Episodes of the "Honeymooners" that are slightly different but still good are on home videos.
   (2) Many people do not know that the "Honeymooners" was first seen on an hour-long show.
   (3) The "Honeymooners" is constantly being seen on late-night TV.
   (4) Jackie Gleason had an hour-long variety show on TV in the 1950s.
   (5) Fans love the character of Ralph Kramden even though he has a big mouth.
   ① ② ③ ④ ⑤

11. What is one reason the writer feels fans will be interested in the videos?
   (1) The character of Ralph Kramden is the same.
   (2) Fans are getting tired of watching the reruns.
   (3) There are fewer mistakes on the home videos.
   (4) The film quality of the old variety show was good.
   (5) The comedy is paced even more quickly.
   ① ② ③ ④ ⑤

12. How does the writer seem to feel about the "Honeymooners" videos?
   (1) disapproving
   (2) sad
   (3) respectful
   (4) enthusiastic
   (5) objective
   ① ② ③ ④ ⑤

13. What does the word "ring" mean as it is used in the phrase "may not quite ring true"?
   (1) a circle
   (2) a piece of jewelry
   (3) appear to be
   (4) sound a bell
   (5) telephone
   ① ② ③ ④ ⑤

Items 14–17 refer to the following selection from a play.

ALICE. Would you like a cold drink?

TONY. Wonderful.

ALICE *(pausing to switch on the light).* I'll see what's in the ice-box. Want to come along?

TONY. I'd follow you to the ends of the earth.

ALICE. Oh, just the kitchen is enough. *(They go out. A pause, a ripple of gay laughter from the kitchen, then they return.* ALICE *is carrying a couple of glasses,* TONY *brings two bottles of ginger ale and an opener)* . . .

TONY *(pouring . . .).* Now if you'll please be seated, I'd like to offer a toast.

ALICE *(settling herself).* We are seated.

TONY. Miss Sycamore— *(he raises his glass on high)* —to you.

ALICE. Thank you, Mr. Kirby. *(Lifting her own glass)* To you. *(They both drink)*

TONY *(happily).* I wouldn't trade one minute of this evening for—all the rice in China.

ALICE. Really?

TONY. Cross my heart. . . .

ALICE. Is it very late?

TONY *(looks at his watch).* Very. *(*ALICE *gives a little nod. Time doesn't matter)* I don't want to go.

ALICE. I don't want you to.

TONY. All right, I won't. *(Silence again)* . . . *(Another pause; their eyes meet. And at this moment,* PENNY *is heard from the stairway)*

PENNY. Is that you, Alice? What time is it? *(She comes into the room, wrapped in a bathrobe)* Oh! *(In sudden embarrassment)* Excuse me, Mr. Kirby. I had no idea—that is, I— (She senses the situation) —I didn't mean to interrupt anything.

TONY. Not at all, Mrs. Sycamore.

ALICE *(quietly).* No, Mother.

14. What is Tony's mood in this scene?
    (1) nervous and worried
    (2) lighthearted and gay
    (3) angry at Alice
    (4) tired and ready to leave
    (5) sad and upset
    ① ② ③ ④ ⑤

15. What has Penny walked in on?
    (1) a couple breaking up
    (2) her neighbors having a party
    (3) her daughter fixing dinner
    (4) her daughter on a date
    (5) her son having a drink
    ① ② ③ ④ ⑤

16. Where are Tony and Alice?
    (1) at work
    (2) at Tony's home
    (3) at Alice's home
    (4) at a restaurant
    (5) in a park
    ① ② ③ ④ ⑤

17. How do Tony and Alice feel about each other?
    (1) They're falling in love.
    (2) Tony loves Alice but she doesn't love him.
    (3) Alice loves Tony but he doesn't love her.
    (4) They don't care about each other.
    (5) They're angry at each other.
    ① ② ③ ④ ⑤

Items 18–21 refer to the following poem.

Wires

The widest prairies have electric fences,
For though old cattle know they must not stray,
Young steers are always scenting purer water
Not here but anywhere. Beyond the wires

Leads them to blunder up against the wires
Whose muscle-shredding violence gives no quarter.
Young steers become old cattle from that day,
Electric limits to their wildest senses.

18. How do young steers act on the prairie?
    (1) They fight with older cattle.
    (2) They fight with other young cattle.
    (3) They stand quietly in ponds of water.
    (4) They are always grazing on the grass.
    (5) They try to get past the electric wire fences.
    ① ② ③ ④ ⑤

19. What eventually happens to young steers?
    (1) They become electrically shocked and die.
    (2) The wire fences hurt them, so they no longer try to stray.
    (3) Cowhands tie them with wires and brand them.
    (4) They seriously hurt themselves by fighting each other.
    (5) They grow older and are allowed outside the fenced prairie.
    ① ② ③ ④ ⑤

20. What is the poet trying to say about young creatures in general?
    (1) They tend to be violent and eager to fight.
    (2) They are satisfied with their lives.
    (3) They think they will never grow old.
    (4) They must not be fenced in.
    (5) They have not yet learned the limit to their freedom.
    ① ② ③ ④ ⑤

21. What does the word "quarter" mean as it is used in the phrase "gives no quarter"?
    (1) mercy
    (2) twenty-five cents
    (3) an area of a city
    (4) one-fourth
    (5) a period of time
    ① ② ③ ④ ⑤

You can check your answers on page 242.

Your Results

Here's a table like the one for Measuring What You Know. It shows you three things: (1) the test questions, (2) the main skill each question tests, and (3) the lesson that teaches that skill.

Question	Skill	Lesson
1	Main idea	2
2	Supporting detail	2
3	Seeing patterns	3
4	Cause and effect	4
5	Understanding vocabulary	3, 8, 9
6	Character	7
7	Setting	7
8	Plot, conflict, outcome	8
9	Author's craft	9
10	Main idea	2
11	Supporting detail	2
12	Tone	5
13	Understanding vocabulary	3, 8, 9
14	Character in drama	10
15–17	Plot in drama	10
18–20	Understanding poetry	11
21	Understanding vocabulary	3, 8, 9

Which skills did you do well on? Which skills do you still need to practice? You can use the table to plan which lessons to review. Good luck in your GED studies and on the GED Test!

Part A
Answers

Measuring What You Know
pages 2–4

1. The author's main point is that computers affect us in nearly everything we do. Your answer should include that idea.

2. The final paragraph mentions two different ways in which computers affect our health. First, they keep records for doctors. This helps doctors spot trouble when it occurs. Also, computers help scientists learn about diseases.

3. The article is written in a serious manner. Facts and figures are given. The information helps us understand how our own lives may be changed by computers. The author does *not* seem to want to entertain us. So you can see that the main purpose is to inform.

4. *Track* can have many meanings. It can refer to a place where a race is run, the mark of a person's shoe or animal foot, or it can mean "to follow and be aware of." In the context of this paragraph, the last meaning makes the best sense.

5. The article describes ways in which the two bikes are different. One has wheels of different sizes; the other has wheels the same size. One has hard, thin tires; the other has soft air-filled tires. One is harder to ride; the other is safer.

6. In the fifth paragraph, the words *on the other hand* let you know that the writer is going to make a contrast. The paragraph before tells how the older bikes were unsafe. The fifth paragraph tells how today's bikes are different—they are safer because their wheels stay on the road better and the ride is softer and smoother.

7. *Jar* can mean a container, say for jelly or a liquid. But it can also have a very different meaning—to jump or shake roughly. In this context, the second meaning is more appropriate.

8. Choice A is a better summary. It gives all of the important information. It gives the details in order. It does not mention any information that is *not* given in the original.

9. Conclusion B can be drawn from the article. Since the game was a hit and other schools wanted to try it, you can conclude that these schools also need an indoor team sport.

10. Winters were cold and snowy, so the young men could not play baseball or football. Yet they missed playing a team sport.

11. The first baskets had sides and bottom. Once the ball was tossed in, the players had to use a ladder to get it. Then the baskets were changed. They were made so the ball could just drop through to the players below.

12. B. The article does not actually say why Naismith made up teams of nine each. It seems likely that he wanted to allow all his players to be in the game. He could do just that by splitting them into two equal teams of nine each.

Part A / Lesson 1

Working It Out
page 8

1. Tom and his son Andrew

2. B. Tom and Andrew's care helped save the bird. This idea tells the main point of the information in the paragraph. Statement A is only a detail, a small piece of information.

3. C

Thinking About What You've Read
page 10

1. Helen Keller and Anne Sullivan

2. A. Annie helped Helen understand words by working hard and patiently. This is the author's main point.

3. by spelling words with hand signals. Both the article and the side note help explain how Annie taught language to Helen.

4. *water.* This answer is in the next-to-last paragraph.

5. Sample answer: Yes, because Helen's parents became upset when Annie tried to correct her.

GED Warm-up
page 11

(2) The dining room seemed like a battlefield during mealtimes. All the details in the paragraph give you this idea. Statement (1) is just one of those details.

Working with Words
page 11

1. roundabout
2. outdoors
3. battlefield
4. anything

Part A / Lesson 2

Working It Out
page 15

1. Don. Every sentence tells something about Don.

2. His apartment was robbed. The first sentence tells you this.

3. Sample answer: Don put a lock on his door, engraved his name on things, and got the neighbors together to watch one another's apartments.

4. Sample answer: After Don was robbed, he took action to protect himself from burglars.

**Thinking About
What You've Read**
page 18

1. relaxing *or* ways to relax

2. B. Each paragraph talks about a way to relax your body and mind.

3. A. Clear your mind.
   B. Think of pleasant images.
This sums up the information in the seventh and eighth paragraphs.

4. Tense each muscle for a short time. Then relax it. Work up your body, from toes to head. This information is in the last paragraph.

5. Answers will vary. Be sure to give a reason for your answer.

GED Warm-up
page 18

(2) How to Relax. This title gives a clue that the main idea of the article is this: "There are different ways to learn to relax."

Working with Words
page 19

1. c 2. g 3. f 4. b 5. d
6. a 7. e

8. faster. *In a hurry* is a clue to choose *fast*. *Than* is a clue to use the *-er* ending.

9. hardest. *Difficult* is a clue.

10. heavier. *A 5-lb. bag* is a clue to choose *heavy*. You're comparing two things, so you use the *-er* ending.

11. busier. *A lot to do* is a clue to choose *busy*. You're comparing two people, so you use the *-er* ending.

12. healthier. *Healthy* and *healthiest* would also fit. The best choice is *healthier* because the sentence implies a comparison between two states.

13. richest. *Money* is a clue to choose *rich*. The best ending is *-est* because the meaning that fits is "the one with the most money."

**The Active Reader
Working It Out**
page 21

1. Sample prediction: Hubie Kern will tell how TV fights are made to look real.

2. Sample prediction: John Forster may tell the story about how he got a "very sore mouth."

Part A / Lesson 3

Working It Out
page 24

1. Gloria is learning to test the hearing of babies and children. This main point is stated in the first sentence.

2. Sample answer: She'll spend time watching babies and children with normal hearing. This detail helps explain *how* Gloria is learning to test hearing.

3. Someday, Gloria will work in a hospital. This detail does *not* explain how Gloria is learning to test hearing.

**Thinking About
What You've Read**
pages 25–26

1. Sample answer: A group called the mad housers build huts for the homeless in Atlanta. This statement sums up the main point of all the supporting details. It isn't stated in a sentence, though. You need to figure it out yourself from all the details.

2. A. This detail helps explain *how* the mad housers build huts for the homeless.

3. A. This detail helps explain *what kind of* huts the mad housers build for the homeless.

4. lumber, windows, and cinderblocks. This answer is given in the fourth paragraph.

5. They are large enough to stand in and sleep in. They have windows and shelves. They keep out the wind and rain. You can find this answer in the third paragraph.

6. the idea that many city officials must care about the home-

less too. If they didn't care at all, they would tear down all the huts. They would never "look the other way."

GED Warm-up
page 26

(2) learn what a good hut would be like. The second paragraph explains what Mike asked the homeless and how he used their answers.

Working with Words
page 27

1. supporting 2. borrowed

3. loving 4. trained

The Active Reader
Working It Out
page 29

Be sure you're grouping words as you read. Some groups will have only two words; others will have three or four.

Part A / Lesson 4

Working It Out
page 32

1. yes. The dates "1,000 years ago" and "in the past 500 years" are given. The place name "Iceland" within "Icelander" is given. And facts such as "most are made of gold and silver" are given.

2. no. The author isn't trying to persuade you at all.

3. no. The author isn't trying to entertain you.

4. to inform you about wedding rings. The author is giving information—facts and ideas—about the history of wedding rings.

Thinking About What You've Read
page 34

1. B. The author uses numbers that show only how more people are staying single. These numbers are facts. The author is mainly informing you with these facts.

2. A. The author is trying to amuse you with the stories of three brides. She's not trying to persuade you to do anything.

3. Several answers are given in the third paragraph: Some people are spending more time on their education or jobs before they begin a family. Others have decided to be career people.

4. Sample answer: perhaps because people like to talk about themselves, especially at an important point in their lives.

GED Warm-up
page 35

(2) to inform you of one reason there are fewer weddings. The fact that some divorced people decide not to remarry helps explain why there are fewer weddings. The author doesn't say if she believes the people are wrong.

Working with Words
page 35

1. statue = sculpture

2. career = vocation

3. story = anecdote

4. continue = persist

5. fancy = intricate

Part A / Lesson 5

Working It Out
pages 39–40

1. They name the kind of work the people's ancestors did. This main idea is given in the first sentence.

2. different last names from three different languages. The third sentence lists English names, and the fourth and sixth sentences give examples from German and French.

3. "Other English names." This beginning to the third sentence clues you to the list of names that follows.

Thinking About What You've Read
page 42

1. ways to learn about your family's past. Each paragraph after the first tells at least one way to do this.

2. talk to his older relatives. This answer is listed in the second paragraph.

3. joining a club or visiting a special library. These answers are listed in the fifth paragraph.

4. births, deaths, marriages, and land ownership. Combine the information in the second and third sentences of the fourth paragraph for this answer.

5. Sample answer: I'm interested in learning about my family's past because it would be fun to learn who my ancestors were. It would also give me a sense of belonging and of being part of history. And it would be wonderful to give a written family history to my children.

GED Warm-up
page 43

(2) to inform you on how to learn about your family's past. If the author had wanted to persuade you to learn about your roots, she would have listed *reasons* for doing so, not *ways* to do so.

Working with Words
page 43

1. countless 2. government
3. relationships 4. ownership

The Active Reader
page 45

2. *for enjoyment* of the story

3. *for information* on what happened

4. *to find out the author's opinions and beliefs* about the topic of the editorial

5. *to find out the author's opinions and beliefs* (could also be *for information*)

6. *to find out how to do something* (make a certain dish)

7. *for enjoyment* of the story

8. *for information* about the product

9. *for enjoyment* of the story

10. *to find out how to do something* (run a VCR)

Sample questions:

11. Why does the prison system need to be reformed?

12. How can I make a salad out of summer fruits?

13. Why did the President veto the gun-control bill?

14. What are the advantages of renting?

15. What new features do the fall cars have?

16. What foods should I eat to stay healthy?

Part A / Lesson 6

Working It Out
pages 47–48

1. joined the Air Force. The word *then* in the third sentence is a clue.

2. when he realized he couldn't go far without completing his education.

3. work hard for years. The word *after* in the second paragraph helps you see this order.

Thinking About What You've Read
page 50

1. He became a private investigator. Beginning with the sixth paragraph, the rest of the article gives you this answer.

2. Clue words you could list include *six years, That's when, after, then,* and *soon.*

3. 1, 2, 4, 3, 6, 5. Your time line could help you with this answer.

4. Sample answer: Armes definitely likes excitement and adventure. As a teenager, he tried to play with dynamite. As an adult, he wanted to be a movie star. He also went into an exciting business—private investigating.

GED Warm-up
page 51

(2) The fifth paragraph gives you this answer. Armes changed his name when a movie director advised him to.

Working with Words
page 51

Date also refers to a fruit.

1. leading actor
2. college diploma
3. problem to solve
4. manage
5. get on
6. committee
7. block of wood
8. perform music with
9. compete against

The Active Reader
page 53

1. medium speed. You're reading for enjoyment, so a medium speed will help you catch the main events.

2. skimming speed. You just want to know one piece of information—a percent—so skimming is best.

3. slow speed. You want to understand a number of details, so a slow speed is best.

Part A / Lesson 7

Working It Out
page 56

1. B and C.

2. Because the maple sap flows in early spring, that is when the process begins.

3. 5, 2, 1, 4, 3

Thinking About What You've Read
page 58

1. because it would be impossible to take off the wheel (which is part of the third set of steps) if the car is still resting on it (raising the car is part of the second set)

2. B and D. The third picture shows what each tool is like. The others help you see how the steps fit together.

3. for their own safety and the safety of the person changing the tire, since the extra weight may make the jack fail. You can infer this answer from information in the first set of steps.

4. Check to be sure it has enough air. This answer is given in the second set of steps.

5. Sample answer: Only if you read all the steps can you have a clear idea of what the process involves. Reading all the steps also allows you to know the tools you will need beforehand.

GED Warm-up
page 59

(2) This answer is given in the second set of steps.

Working with Words
page 59

Sample answers:

1. to turn in a circle
2. to move with care
3. a small hole
4. a method of personal transportation

The Active Reader
Working It Out
page 61

1. the clock ringing, the tape recorder playing music, the boss saying "Get up!"

2. Your drawing should include the bed, the alarm clock, and the mechanical foot. You might show the bed raised up at a slant.

3. the fumes from cars and buses; the hot dog stand. These details give off smells.

4. the cars and buses; church bells. These details make sounds.

5. the cars and buses; the red and yellow hot dog stand; people. These details can be seen.

6. the heat of the summer day. This detail can be felt; it makes you feel hot.

Part A / Lesson 8

Picture It
page 63

Sample answers:

Meats, fish, and nuts—tuna

Grains—wheat

Fruits and vegetables—pears, squash

Dairy products—cottage cheese

Working It Out
page 64

1. Elaine's job duties. The third sentence points out how many categories of job duties you should look for.

2. *categories* in the first paragraph; *group* in the fourth paragraph

3. managing the clerks, handling money matters, and controlling the stock. These three categories are listed in the first paragraph. Then each is discussed in its own paragraph.

Thinking About
What You've Read
page 66

1. sales; repair; programming; operating

2. computer operator

3. He had difficulty speaking English.

4. d. Some jobs involve operating.
 b. Part-time

5. Sample answers: painting, landscaping, musician, bookkeeping

GED Warm-up
page 67

(2) He drew a picture of what he did. This answer is given in the tenth paragraph: "He took a pencil and paper. He drew a stick figure...." If you chose (1) or (3), you chose words that are repeated from the article. But those do not answer the question.

Working with Words
page 67

1. to see beforehand
2. to trust wrongly
3. not honest
4. before the war
5. not to please
6. to lead wrongly
7. to heat beforehand
8. before the age of going to school
9. to fail to agree
10. lack of respect
11. to pass from sight

The Active Reader
Working It Out
pages 68–69

1. As time went on, another bank took over the bank Bill worked for.

2. Bill lost his job.

3. Bill decided to open a business.

4. Bill has a good business selling car parts.

5. Vanessa's bike was stolen.

6. The police reported that Vanessa's bike was stolen.

7. Vanessa's friend had borrowed her bike for a time.

Sample restatements:

8. The weather forecast said we'd have a big wind storm.

9. Huge hailstones hit our house very hard.

10. We stayed indoors because of the rain.

11. The rain kept up all evening.

Part A / Lesson 9

Working It Out
page 71

1. They both taste good. They cost the same. They have the same number of slices. These points of comparison are in the second paragraph.

2. Golden Loaf has ingredients that do not sound natural; Baker's does. This point of contrast is in the third paragraph.

Thinking About What You've Read
page 74

1. A. The end of the third paragraph gives you this point of comparison.

2. B. The fifth paragraph talks about the different amounts of interest (from 12% to 21%).

3. A. Paragraph 4 gives you this information. Bank cards can be used in many places. Travel and entertainment cards can be used in fewer places. And retail cards can be used at only one kind of store or gas station.

4. Sample answers: Some charge more interest than others. Some allow family members to share cards. Some can be used in more places.

5. Sample answer: Yes, because having a credit card makes it too easy to spend money. You buy things you don't really need.

GED Warm-up
page 74

(3) Travel cards are given by travel companies; bank cards are given by banks. This difference is given in the fourth paragraph.

Working with Words
page 75

1. *Option* means "choice." The context clue "that choice" is in the second sentence.

2. *Unsolicited* means "not asked for." This context clue is in the first sentence. Also, the word *such* helps you connect the word *unsolicited* with "a card you did not ask for."

3. *Liable* means "responsible." This context clue is a definition set off by commas.

4. *Transaction* means "a money deal between people." This context clue is an example. "A purchase or other transaction" tells you a purchase is an example of a transaction. A purchase is a deal in which money is given from one person to another.

The Active Reader Working It Out
page 77

Sample summary: Three different kinds of aid are available to adult students. A grant is money that does not have to be paid back, while a student loan is money that does. A work-study program gives money for work and school. To receive one of these kinds of aid, a person must be a good student and meet certain requirements.

Part A / Lesson 10

Working It Out
page 80

1. B. Edison thought the Kinetoscope would be good for teaching. He made only a few movies for fun. This suggests he did not think movies would be popular entertainment. Otherwise, he would have made a lot of entertaining movies.

2. Yes. The author writes, "Sadly for us, it has been lost over the years." The word *sadly* suggests the author wishes Edison's horror film could be seen today.

3. B. This fact suggests that many people were going to see movies.

Thinking About What You've Read
pages 82–83

1. jazz. The first sentence in the last paragraph points out that Ray played jazz when the teacher left the room. That means he played jazz when he wasn't being told to play classical. He must have preferred jazz if he played it whenever he had the chance.

2. the café of Wylie Pittman

and the Florida State School for the Blind. The seventh paragraph and the next-to-last paragraph name these two places.

3. A. Ray's mother meant that even though he could not see, he could still use his mind to learn how to take care of himself.

4. Sample summary: Ray Charles had to overcome a hard childhood. He became blind when he was seven, partly because his family was too poor to pay for proper medical care. Yet with strong support from his mother, Ray learned to care for himself and to play music, especially jazz.

5. Sample answer: Even though Ray Charles was blind, his desire to learn, especially music, helped him be a success.

GED Warm-up
page 83

(1) be able to take care of himself. Aretha's reason is given in the fifth paragraph.

Working with Words
page 83

Here are the correct words in **bold** and the context that helps you choose the words.

1. put a few **drops** into his eyes
2. bright **lights** were
3. sight in both his **eyes**
4. been told by **doctors** (there is no word *a*, so you know the answer isn't "a doctor")
5. learned to do many **things**

The Active Reader
Working It Out
page 85

Sample questions:
1. What causes nightmares? Why do people have nightmares?
2. Why do we sometimes have the same dream again and again? How many dreams do most people have each night?

Part A / Lesson 11

Working It Out
page 87

1. A. Only one other skier had won all three events, so you can conclude it must be a difficult thing to do.

2. A. You can conclude he was determined because he didn't let illness or injury stop him. You can conclude he was daring because he loved speed and "racing down snowy slopes."

Thinking About What You've Read
page 90

1. B. Tommy picked his gloves and shoes because they looked fancy. Yet they made it difficult for him to drive.

2. His gloves shrank, so he couldn't move his hands freely. His shoes hurt. The steering wheel became sticky.

3. It "gave out," or broke. You find this out in the fourth paragraph.

4. Howdy Wilcox. This answer is given in the seventh paragraph.

5. Yes. Sample answer: Tommy quickly realized he was having trouble and found ways to solve his problems. He was a fast driver, for he made up the time that Howdy Wilcox had lost. And he won the race twice.

6. Sample answer: How will you prepare for a race *next* time?

GED Warm-up
page 91

(1) told Howdy Wilcox to drive the car. The first three sentences of the seventh paragraph help you with this answer.

Working with Words
page 91

1. decked: dressed or decorated
2. kid: soft leather from a young goat
3. adhesive: sticking to something
4. ooze: flow slowly
5. pierced: cut sharply
6. riveted: fastened by a short metal bolt

The Active Reader
Working It Out
page 93

A. Laura thought her boss wanted her to put *two* pencils in each office. He really wanted her to put *number 2* pencils in each office. The phrase *number 2* tells how hard the lead is.

B. 1. It is about a bus driver's job.

2. Its purpose is to inform people about how to apply for the job of bus driver.

3. Al misread the line about "uniform caps" in the first paragraph.

4. Sample words you might have listed:
benefits: rewards given to a worker in addition to the regular salary
references: letters from people that recommend you for a job

Part A / Lesson 12

Working It Out
page 95

1. His bike was stolen. No clue words are used, but look at the first paragraph and the first sentence of the second paragraph. They help you *infer* the cause of the boy's anger.

2. He felt the boy would feel better if he could work off his anger with exercise. See the last two sentences of the second paragraph for this answer.

3. His career as a boxer began. The last paragraph helps you with this answer.

Thinking About What You've Read
page 98

1. The change allowed Ms. Hunter to try painting and to find out she was good at it. The fifth paragraph helps you with this cause-and-effect relationship.

2. Clementine had to work to earn money for the family. You'll find this reason, or cause, in the third paragraph.

3. She did not have any special art training. She painted scenes of people from her own memories. Information in two places helps you answer this question. The first paragraph describes what a folk artist is. The fifth paragraph shows how Ms. Hunter matches that description.

4. Clementine lost her sight as she became older. This cause-and-effect relationship is in the last paragraph.

5. Sample answer: I like the way picture shows different activities going on at the same time. I also like the details of the punch table and wedding cake.

GED Warm-up
page 99

(3) In the fourth paragraph, the author says that machines began to take over part of the work of the people.

Working with Words
page 99

1. folk artists. Notice that both *they* and the term *folk artists* refer to more than one person. That's a clue to this answer.

2. Ms. Hunter. You can tell that *her* refers to Ms. Hunter because no other woman has been mentioned in the sentence.

3. artists. One clue is that *their* and *artists* both refer to more than one person. Also, no other group of workers has been mentioned.

4. pickers. The sentence order is a clue. *Pickers* is the first word in the first sentence. *They,* the first word in the second sentence, refers to the same people.

The Active Reader Working It Out
page 101

The first group should include *traffic jam* and *driver cuts in.* They relate to each other because they are kinds of traffic problems you might meet on the road.

The second group should have the words *gauges, radiator,* and *tire.* They relate to each other because they are car parts that might cause mechanical problems.

Part A / Lesson 13

Working It Out
page 104

1. A. Jogging rapidly once a week does not apply this advice: "Then do it for at least twenty minutes every day or so." You could also write, "It's better *not* to exercise heavily all at once."

2. A. Iris would be applying this advice: "Choose one that works your whole body." You could also write, "With an exercise such as walking. . . ."

Thinking About What You've Read
page 106

1. Brushing your hair is a good way to take care of it without buying many products. This idea is in the first paragraph.

2. A. The author says there's no really good way to cure baldness. She does *not* claim that brushing makes your hair curly. But she does explain how it makes your hair look clean and healthy.

3. because a steady stream of hot air can dry out your hair and skin. The last paragraph under the heading "Washing" explains this cause-and-effect relationship.

4. C. Under "Washing," the author says there's no rule that works for everyone. You should wash your hair when you see it's becoming dirty.

5. A. Under "Hair loss," the author says it's natural to lose a few hairs each time you wash or brush.

6. The article does not discuss hair dyes. You might say that you'd like to know how dyes affect your hair. Any other

unanswered question would do.

GED Warm-up
page 107

(3) A woman buys plain detergent shampoo. The second paragraph under "Washing" says the best shampoo is usually the simplest—the kind without beer, strawberries, or other foods. It's the detergent that cleans the hair.

Working with Words
page 107

1. The idiom *open your eyes* means "to make aware of something surprising and important."

2. The idiom *go broke* means "to lose all your money."

3. The idiom *down in the dumps* means "sad" or "depressed."

4. Sample answers: "raining cats and dogs," "don't lose your head"

The Active Reader
page 108

No, the person didn't follow all the directions. Question 2 is not answered. The directions say, "Be sure you answer every question. You will not have points taken off for wrong answers."

Part A / Lesson 14

Working It Out
page 111

1. fact; looking at an encyclopedia. An encyclopedia would tell when Montana became a state. The article says Ms. Rankin was born in 1880. You could compare the two dates to prove the statement.

2. opinion. You can't prove this statement. The words "most important" are a clue. They show a personal judgment.

Thinking About What You've Read
page 113

1. A. "You used to be a good man" is an opinion because it states a personal judgment. The word "good" is a clue. The first wife's idea of good might be different from other people's judgments.

2. Sample answers: Since the Cherokees had a written language, they may have had records to prove it was true. History books and encyclopedias would also be good ways to prove the statement.

3. Sequoyah's first wife. She threw his work into the fire, said he had gone "crazy" over it, called him worthless, and told him to get out. These actions help show you her opinion.

4. Sally, Sequoyah's second wife. She learned the symbols, called them a "great thing," and told Sequoyah to show his work to the Cherokee council.

5. Sample answer: Letters sent between the separated people could have shared information about traditions. So too could records of ceremonies, births, and deaths.

GED Warm-up
page 113

(2) The question asks you for a reason you can *not* conclude. Sequoyah had no way of knowing the Cherokee leaders would reward him with money. So that could not be a reason for his hard work.

Working with Words
page 114

1. a. a weapon used to shoot an arrow
   b. bend from the waist

2. a. a special task
   b. cast onto something else

3. a. to get meaning from written words
   b. to have gotten meaning from written words (This is the past form of the word *read* in the first sentence. It rhymes with "bed.")

The Active Reader Working It Out
page 116

A. Sample notes:
drunk drivers injure about 500,000 each year
kill about 24,000
You probably would *not* take notes on the first paragraph. It's just an introduction. The ideas there are not important enough to take notes on them.

B. Sample notes:
problems caused by drunk drivers cost money—
car repairs, insurance costs, medical bills, property damage, lost work hours
ideas for solving problems—
changing attitudes, stronger laws, helping young people say no, keeping drunk driver off road

Part A / Lesson 15

Working It Out
page 119

1. The second article. It tells the events from Hyde's point of view only. It uses words that make you feel sorry for Hyde. The first article tells only the facts of the story.

2. Any three of these words and phrases are good answers: "lives alone," "relatives are dead," "no one to care for him," "nothing to brighten his life," "lonely, dirty jail cell," "tears in his eyes," "no one to post bond," and "no one to help a lonely old man." You probably feel sorry for Hyde when you read these words.

Thinking About What You've Read
page 121

1. He's against burning. He tells only the bad side of burning. He also uses biased words.

2. Sample answers: "an idea to solve the problem is even worse," "toxic," "dangerous," "poisonous," "harmful," "cancer," "poisoned," and "worse problems." These words show disapproval.

3. **A.** Opinion **B.** Fact **C.** Fact **D.** Opinion
Statement **B** could be proved by studying current dumps. Statement **C** could be proved in a laboratory. Statements **A** and **D** are judgments. The words "bad" and "worse" are clues.

4. Chemicals from garbage or ash in a dump can move down through the ground. They get into the ground water. This cause-and-effect relationship is explained in the second paragraph.

5. Sample questions: What else could be done to solve the garbage problem? Where is the proof that substances in them smoke and ash are dangerous? Can these substances be filtered from the smoke? Can the ash be put somewhere else?

GED Warm-up
page 122

(1) He would probably be for recycling. The author is very much against burning. He seems interested in the environment. You can apply that idea. Recycling helps the environment. So the author would probably like the idea.

Working with Words
page 122

1. dump—landfill
2. garbage—waste
3. stink—smell
4. get rich—make money
5. are being buried in—have too much of

The Active Reader Working It Out
page 123

1. people having to leave an office building. The first sentence tells you what happened. So does the headline.

2. Monday afternoon at the office building at 27 North Front Street in Hume, Ohio. The first sentence tells when and where the event happened.

3. Two cleaners meant to unplug a drain were mixed. The third sentence explains how the event happened.

Part A / Lesson 16

The Active Reader
page 130

1. encyclopedia, atlas, or almanac. You could look in the M (for Maine) volume of an encyclopedia. In an atlas, look up a map of the state of Maine.

2. encyclopedia. In the H (for heart) volume of an encyclopedia, you would find an overview of the heart.

3. A road atlas of the United States would show major roads and highways.

4. Spanish-English dictionary.

5. a book of quotations. You could look under *love* for a list of famous sayings.

6. A dictionary would tell you the meaning of the word. It would also tell you how to pronounce it.

7. a current almanac. An encyclopedia would tell you what causes an eclipse, but probably not *when* an eclipse would happen next.

Measuring What You've Learned
pages 131–135

1. **(B)** You might think **(A)** is the answer because that idea is mentioned in the first paragraph. But that is not the main idea of the *whole* article. You can rule out choice **(C)** because it is not even mentioned in the article. Only choice **(B)** tells the main idea of the whole article.

2. **(C)** The author mentions that scary movies make lots of money, in order to support the main idea that we all like scary stories. Scary movies make money because lots of people are willing to pay to see them.

3. **(A)** The comment about children liking to tell ghost stories is a supporting detail. It supports the main idea that we all like to be scared a little bit by a movie or books.

4. **(C)** Investors are people who want to make money. From the context, you can tell that the

word *successful* means "money-making" here.

5. (C) The author doesn't use persuasive language, so you can rule out choice B. The author doesn't give any facts or figures that inform you, so you can rule out answer A. However, the article does seem light and entertaining. It entertains us by making a comment about human nature. So **(C)** is the best answer.

6. (A) The article tells what people used before money, then when early coins were used, and finally how paper money came into use. It traces the ways in which money has changed over the years. We can understand how our own ideas about money gradually developed.

7. (C) The article says that coins came into use about 2,500 years ago, but paper money was not used until 1,300 years ago. That means coins were used more than a thousand years before paper money.

8. (A) Summary **(A)** does not give all the important information. Summary **(B)** lists the most important facts in order.

9. (A) Sentence **(A)** gives the important ideas from the article that are missing in Summary **(A)**.

10. (A) A context clue to the meaning of *compensation* is given right in the sentence. The sentence says soldiers were given their compensation, or *pay*, in the form of playing cards. The word *pay* is a synonym for *compensation* in this context.

11. (C) Answer **A** can be ruled out. The article says that we enjoy relaxing in a hot tub, but it does not say that it leads to good health. Answer **(B)** can be ruled out because the article discusses personal cleanliness, not housekeeping. Answer **(C)** is the best. The article gives details that help us see how our ideas about bathing have changed over the centuries.

12. (B) Queen Elizabeth the First had over an inch of makeup on her face when she died. If she had washed her face often, the layers of makeup would not have built up to that point.

13. (C) The Puritans felt they should have their bodies covered at all times to avoid sin. They avoided bathing so they would not have to take off their clothes.

14. (C) Normal activities such as horseback riding or working would have made people dusty and dirty. Body oil and bacteria can cause odors. Because the dirt and odors were not removed by bathing, people covered them with perfumes and powders.

15. (A) Puritans felt that people should not show their bodies. They approved of being covered up. Today's bathing suits and beach wear—often leaving much of the body uncovered—would probably offend them.

16. (A) Gandhi felt that the power of the mind was greater than the power of violence. Answer **(A)** applies that idea. Both **(B)** and **(C)** suggest using violence.

17. (B) Gandhi would not want to jail shop owners, because he did not like to use force. Answers **(A)** and **(C)** are actions Gandhi would support. They are similar to Gandhi's ideas of making cloth and salt instead of buying them from England.

18. (C) A context clue helps you find the answer to this question. The article says that Gandhi "fasted. He did not eat."

19. (B) A statement of fact can be proved true by checking with a reliable book or a person who knows about the subject. Statement **(B)** could be checked in an encyclopedia. The other statements, however, are based on personal feelings or beliefs and cannot be proved.

20. (C) Statement **(C)** uses the words *terrific, great,* and *good* to make you want to join the club. In other words, it uses biased language to make you want to join the club.

21. (A) The letter mentions only the benefits of joining the club. It does not point out possible drawbacks. For instance, learning Esperanto might take quite a bit of time. And you might not find many people outside the club who could use Esperanto with you.

22. (A) The author invites people to join and points out the many ways in which the club can benefit its members. It uses words with appealing connotations to make you feel good about the club. All these things help you see that the author is trying to persuade people to join the club.

23. (C) You can use both context clues and word structure clues to discover the meaning of *international*. The second paragraph gives a context clue. It says that Esperanto was invented so that people of all countries, or nations, could speak together. If you know that the word part *inter* means "between," you can use word structure clues to see that *international* means "between nations."

Part B
Answers

Measuring What You Know
pages 138–140

1. (2) The first choice is an idea you might get from the last paragraph. The third choice is an idea from the first paragraph. But the *main* idea of the *entire* passage has to include both those ideas, *plus* the horrible murder described in the second paragraph. Choice (2) does that.

2. (1) The first paragraph tells you the writer "did not often get angry" and tried not to react to all he saw. Another way to say those ideas is that he keeps his emotions under control.

3. (2) The first paragraph tells you in one instance the author got angry. The second paragraph goes back in time to describe the murder that made him angry. The last paragraph goes ahead in time to explain what happened in the murder case. So the author told the story of Evers's death to explain his anger.

4. (2) The author tells you "both trials resulted in hung juries." A hung jury is one that cannot decide. The person is then set free. So legally de la Beckwith had to be considered innocent.

5. (3) The words around "tried"—"arrested," "for the murder," and "trials"—help you understand its meaning in this case.

6. (1) The words "he was sick to death of waiting, and tongue-out thirsty to begin" help you answer this question.

7. (3) This statement is made by the P.A. announcer. An announcer telling of a change in batters is a clue that the setting is a baseball game.

8. (3) The last two sentences give the answer to this question. The "straining, ripping sound" noted earlier is the cover tearing away from the ball.

9. (3) Imagine a "noise like a twenty-one gun salute" cracking the sky. Such a noise would produce tension and drama, wouldn't it? The noise is a thunderclap that occurs at the instant Roy hits the ball.

10. (2) In the first part of the poem, the poet is describing a lecture by an astronomer. The second part explains how he "wander'd off" by himself into the night and looked at the stars.

11. (3) The poet is helping you feel two things: the boredom of listening to a talk about stars and the wonder of looking at the stars yourself.

12. (1) The poet is describing a quiet, thoughtful time of looking at stars in the night sky. For that reason, you probably felt quiet and thoughtful yourself.

13. (1) The words around "figures"—"ranged in columns," "to add, divide"—help you see that in this case figures are numbers related to stars.

Part B / Lesson 1

Working It Out
page 144

1. to persuade. The author gives an argument in favor of working one's way up on the job. This argument is intended to persuade the reader.

2. to inform. The paragraph gives information about the game of basketball.

3. to entertain. The idea of a child turning six only after he or she gets off the trolley is amusing.

Part B / Lesson 2

Working It Out
page 147

1. Charley, a dog. Every sentence is about Charley.

2. The fourth sentence gives the main idea.

3. He shakes himself and his collar loudly. He gets a sneezing fit. He sits beside the bed and stares. All three details give examples of how Charley wakes up the author.

Thinking About What You've Read
pages 149–150

1. beach living. The author describes what it's like to live by the beach.

2. Beach living teaches the author that a person doesn't really need very many clothes. This fact is stated in the first paragraph of the passage.

3. B. Option B gives the most important idea about the topic. Options A and C are details in the passage but are not the main idea.

4. A and C. Options B and D do not support the main idea of the passage.

5. Make sure you clearly explain why you can get along without each of the two things you list.

GED Warm-up
page 150

(1) In the first paragraph, the author says about clothes: "Of course, one needs less in the sun."

Working with Words
page 150

1. One
2. some
3. bare
4. here
5. see

The Active Reader
Working It Out
pages 151–152

Sample purpose: to learn about the author's thoughts on personal letters

1. If you did not meet your purpose, you might want to reread the passage.

2. Sample answer: I learned the author's thoughts about personal letters.

3. Sample answer: I learned about the advantages personal letters have over telephone calls.

Part B / Lesson 3

Working It Out
page 155

1. comparison and contrast. The passage compares the skills and contrasts the personalities of Babe Ruth and Hank Aaron.

2. listing. The passage lists reasons why it was hard to get information about Germans lost in World War II.

3. time order. The passage describes the order of events as the Eagle landed on the moon.

Thinking About
What You've Read
pages 157–158

1. She still had strong teeth. She walked a long way, carrying a heavy load.

2. her hands, feet, and face. The answer is in the first paragraph.

3. manager, producer, and leading lady. The answer is in the second paragraph.

4. A. The author lists examples of her strength, beauty, and activities.

5. Sample answers: by remaining interested in hobbies, by keeping as physically active as possible, by not dwelling on the past.

GED Warm-up
page 159

(3) The theater is described as "one of her great passions."

Working with Words
page 159

1. remove
2. remained
3. lessened
4. village

The Active Reader
Working It Out
page 160

1. skimming. You are reading to find a particular fact.

2. reading for details. You are reading to understand the ideas the writer presents.

3. previewing. Your purpose is to get a general idea of what the article is about.

4. rereading. Your purpose is to understand ideas better.

Part B / Lesson 4

Working It Out
page 162

1. It was the first foreign war in which U.S. combat forces failed to achieve their goals. This is stated in the second and third sentences of the paragraph.

2. deep psychological problems. This is stated in the fifth sentence of the paragraph.

3. Both Congress and the public became more willing to challenge the President on U.S. military and foreign policy. This is stated in the last sentence of the paragraph.

Thinking About
What You've Read
pages 165–166

1. Red was a large bully. He could stop any boy and have his

lieutenants take the boy's money. If the boy resisted, he would get a real beating. Also, Red carried brass knuckles. These facts are stated in the eighth and ninth paragraphs of the passage.

2. first to third; second to first; third to second. Red's blow to the author's head caused him to be knocked out. The author spent three weeks learning jujitsu because he wanted to conquer his fear of Red. When the author squeezed Red's wrist, he caused the brass knuckles to drop from Red's fingers.

3. There is no need to fear the strong, and if he wished to be a poet, he must not only write poems but know how to stand up for them. These facts are stated in the last two paragraphs of the passage.

4. Be sure you have clearly described how you conquered your fear.

GED Warm-up
page 166

(4) You know that Red was quite angry because he hit the author in the head and knocked him out after hearing about the poem.

Working with Words
page 166

1. The simile is "like lightning." The two unlike things being compared are Red's hand and lightning. Both are very fast.

2. The simile is "like a bull." The two unlike things being compared are Red and a bull. They swing their heads from side to side in a similar way.

The Active Reader
Working It Out
page 168

1. B. The other sentences contain ideas that are not important enough to be included in a summary.

2. A. The other sentences contain ideas that are important enough to include in a summary.

3. The wording of your summary may vary somewhat from the following example. It should, however, contain all the ideas in this summary. Sample summary: A personal letter is special for several reasons. First, it is something you can keep, unlike a phone call. Second, you can say things in a letter that you might not say in person. Third, you can say things without interruption.

Part B / Lesson 5

Working It Out
page 171

1. "Problem," "mystery... takes second billing," "weakly solved," "countless characters" help show the writer disapproves of the book.

2. probably disapproving, a little frustrated, stern, displeased. That's how a person's face would look if she were saying such disapproving things.

3. disapproving. Putting the answers to the first two questions together helps you infer the tone.

Thinking About
What You've Read
page 173

1. "Rock around the Clock" was released, the skiffle group became popular, and Elvis appeared on the scene. The beginnings of the second, third, and fourth paragraphs are clues to this answer.

2. because almost anyone could play it. This answer is given in both the third and the last paragraph: "Anyone could have a go."

3. He was deeply affected and excited by Elvis. This answer is given in the last sentence of the fifth paragraph.

4. enthusiastic, admiring, excited. The author talks of the excitement of rock 'n' roll, of the "kids'" reaction to it, and of its lead singer, Elvis. He sounds enthusiastic about the first two and admiring of Presley himself.

5. "Heartbreak Hotel" was popular in 14 countries. This statement supports the idea that Presley was exciting. If he weren't, people in 14 different countries would not have bought his record.

GED Warm-up
page 174

(1) scornful. The last two sentences of the first paragraph make several bad points about pop music up to the mid-1950s: "remote," "no connection with real life," "very show-businessy," and "lovely suits with lovely smiles who sang lovely ballads." The author is making fun of the music with that last comment.

Working with Words
page 174

1. number one, the best-selling record. A record that is "top" must be first, or number one.

2. slow love songs. "Singing" and "slushy" are context clues for the term *ballad*.

The Active Reader
Working It Out
page 176

1. B. The student would know how to compare the worth of the art with other artists' work.

2. A. The veteran's background would help him judge if the book was accurate, or true to life.

3. B. The musician would know about pop *before* the Beatles arrived, so he would be better able to judge their impact.

4. A. Someone who enjoys poetry would most likely have read many poems and perhaps even studied poetry. Knowledge of poetry would be more important than knowledge of the poet.

5. B. A TV critic knows about television in general and reviews shows with an open mind.

6. A. An instructor would know about skills because he or she teaches them. A fan may like to watch but would not necessarily know the skills needed to dance.

Part B / Lesson 6

Working It Out
page 179

1. A and C. The people and events in the passage are not real.

2. fictional. You know it is fictional because it contains characters, a setting, and a plot. It also contains an exact conversation between people.

Part B / Lesson 7

Working It Out
page 181

1. ten o'clock at night in the parking lot of a supermarket. The first two sentences tell you this.

2. so that her car won't be hit by another car. You know this because she says she has parked by the exit ever since her car was rammed. The exit must seem safer to her because there are fewer cars there.

3. nervous, perhaps afraid. You can guess her mood from two facts: the parking lot is deserted, and the narrator says her car looks "a mile away."

Thinking About What You've Read
page 184

1. an old, green, faded coat; and old, torn gloves. The author describes the old man's clothing in the second paragraph of the story.

2. that he's poor. It is likely that his clothes are old and torn because he doesn't have money to buy new ones.

3. You should have underlined the last three sentences of the first paragraph.

4. proud, honest, polite, dignified. You know the old man was not greedy, because he refused the extra money offered for his land. You know that he was not dishonest, because he would not even take money that was rightfully his.

5. Answers will vary. Possible answer: Don Anselmo was a person who valued his honor more highly than money. He had given his word to sell at a particular price, and he felt it was important to keep his word.

GED Warm-up
page 185

(3) You know they were fair because they offered to pay the old man for the additional land. It was reasonable for them to want the children to stay off their property.

Working with Words
page 185

1. B. The suffix *-or* means "a person or thing that does something."

2. A. The prefix *re-* means "again."

3. A. The suffix *-ion* means "the act or process of doing something."

4. B. The suffix *-able* means "able to be." The prefix *-in* means "not."

The Active Reader
Working It Out
page 186

You should have circled the picture on the bottom. This picture shows a nearly empty parking lot.

Part B / Lesson 8

Working It Out
page 188

1. B. This is stated in the story.

2. C. This is stated in the story.

3. A. Don Anselmo says that the trees belong to the children of the village. He didn't sell them because they are not his.

4. B. This is stated in the story.

5. A. The conflict is among the new owners, Don Anselmo, and the children of the village.

Thinking About What You've Read
pages 191–192

1. He thought the dog had jumped out the window and had fallen to the pavement below. This is stated in the story.

2. C. George asks himself whether he has to admit the truth to Professor Werner.

3. C. George faces a struggle with himself over whether to do what is right.

4. A. This is stated in the story.

5. Sample answer: Yes. Telling the truth was the right thing to do, even if it meant not getting the job.

GED Warm-up
page 192

(1) Professor Werner's last statement helps you see that the dog likes to show off by jumping out the window onto the balcony.

Working with Words
page 192

1. the study of ancient life and culture. The comma after *archaeology* gives you a clue that an explanation of the word will follow.

2. great size. The comma after *enormity* and the clue word *or* tell you that *enormity* means "great size."

3. a voyage made for a special purpose. The comma after *expedition* gives you a clue that an explanation of the word will follow.

The Active Reader Working It Out
page 194

1. Sample answer: Yes. The secret agent seems honest and sincere. He says that he also is searching for freedom. He tells Janos to be careful and wishes him good luck.

2. Sample answers: Janos will arrive in America safely. Janos will be caught and sent to prison. Janos will decide to stay in his own country.

Part B / Lesson 9

Working It Out
pages 196–197

1. The narrator is one of the characters. He uses the word *I* in telling the story.

2. C. You probably felt tense because the two men are arguing about how to approach the problem.

Thinking About What You've Read
page 200

1. It isn't until the end that you learn Mr. Parsons is *also* blind. The narrator had told you only that the beggar was blind.

2. B. When Mr. Parsons reveals who he is, Markwardt is shocked and angry. You probably felt tense when Markwardt began to scream "fiendishly."

3. They were both in an accident in a factory. Chemicals exploded, and many people were killed or blinded. Markwardt tells this story. He mentions "Westbury" to Parsons, and Parsons says "Ah, yes. The chemical explosion. . . ."

4. Mr. Parsons works in the insurance industry. Markwardt sells cigarette lighters on the street, but he is also a beggar. He wants people to give him money because he is blind.

5. Markwardt switches the roles of the two men. He says he was trampled by another man. Actually it was Markwardt who trampled Parsons.

6. He says that he struggled beneath handicaps. He says his pity for blind creatures is "foolish."

GED Warm-up
page 201

(4) He told the story "with the bitter and studied drama of a story often told, and told for money." This means Markwardt often told his story so that people would feel sorry for him and give him money.

Working with Words
page 201

1. rude. The clue phrase *on the other hand* tells you that *polite* is an antonym for *boorish*. So *boorish* means "rude."

2. ragged. The clue word *not* tells you that *well-dressed* is an antonym for *shabby*. So, *shabby* means "ragged."

The Active Reader Working It Out
page 202

1. walking through a wood. The paragraph refers to a wood and says that Winnie was "walking timidly under the interlacing branches."

Part B / Lesson 10

Working It Out
pages 205–206

1. Doc, Roberts, Pulver, and a radio announcer. These names are in capital letters on the left.

2. in a shocked voice. The first stage direction tells you this.

3. to fight in the war. Roberts's first lines of speech tell you this: "The war's way out there.... I want to be out there."

4. because the radio is announcing the war is over

5. grasps Doc's arm in excitement. You can find this answer in the stage direction in the middle of the announcer's speech.

6. Doc and Roberts. Pulver enters from offstage as he first speaks. The announcer is only heard, not seen on stage.

Thinking About What You've Read
page 208

1. 3, 1, 2, 5, 4

2. He is becoming seriously ill. Regina has mentioned Horace has "heart trouble." You can infer he may be having a heart attack.

3. They don't love each other at all. Regina says she despises Horace. *Despises* means "hates."

4. cold-hearted, lying, greedy. She's cold-hearted because she doesn't help Horace. She admits she lied to Horace. And she wants more money from Horace. She married him only when her father died and did not leave her any money.

5. You can conclude that she wants him to die, especially before he has a chance to change his will. She doesn't help Horace. She doesn't even look at him.

GED Warm-up
page 209

(1) believed he should not touch her. This answer is found in the lines of Regina's speech that begins, "But you believed it."

Working with Words
page 209

1. Regina and Horace

2. Doctor Sloan

3. Regina's lie

The Active Reader Working It Out
page 210

1. Sample answer: *Miss Preen goes to the door and opens it. A man comes through the door. He picks her up and carries her into the room. He kisses her as she tries to get away from him.* The stage directions tell you most of the action in the play. You can guess the rest from what the characters say.

2. Sample answers: upset, alarmed, angry. To answer this question, *picture* Miss Preen shouting, "Put me down!"

3. Sample answer: romantic, excited, passionate. To answer this question, *hear* the gentleman saying, "I love you madly."

Part B / Lesson 11

Working It Out
page 212

1. the sight of seagulls flying at the beach. The title and first part of the poem help you see the scene.

2. sky; sea. The blue sky is above the birds; the blue sea is below them. The picture in your mind could help you with these answers.

3. Seagulls; free (*or* one *or* an individual). The title and the last line help you understand this complete thought.

Reading on Your Own
pages 213–215

1. hoeing in his fields. Clues are "hills I haven't hoed" and "I thrust my hoe."

2. stops working and goes to talk. Clues are "I thrust my hoe" and "I go up to the stone wall/For a friendly visit."

3. Taking time to talk with a friend is just as important as work.

4. tom-toms beating. Did the first four lines help you hear the drums?

5. a girl dancing. Did lines 7–11 help you see the girl dance in the night?

6. Sample answer: The sight and sound of an African dance moves you inside. The line "Stirs your blood" means "moves you inside."

7. You probably felt aroused and quietly excited by the beat of the drums, the night, and the dancing girl.

8. No one knows why such a pest as the fly exists. *Or* No one can figure out why God would make such a pest as the fly.

9. You probably felt amused. You may even have smiled or laughed.

10. the sound of the waves you hear when you wake from a nap on the beach. The title is a clue to this answer.

11. like bacon frying. The first two lines help you with this answer.

12. because the sea never stops sounding like bacon frying. You know that the waves of the sea never stop moving onto the beach. That's why their sound never stops.

13. the sight of a cloudy sky with a few breaks in the clouds. Picturing the scene in your mind would help you answer this question.

14. his loved one back home. The title and the third line help you understand who "you" is.

15. tell him how much she misses him. Line 4 gives you this answer.

16. his loneliness, emptiness, sadness. You may even have felt sad or lonely as you read this poem. The poet's lonely thoughts create such a feeling.

GED Warm-up
page 215

(3) He is lonely without his loved one. His hours are "empty" because his loved one is not there to fill them.

Working with Words
page 216

1. A   2. B   3. A   4. B

The Active Reader Working It Out
page 217

1. the sound of "s": "silence," "city," and "snow"

Measuring What You've Learned
pages 218–223

1. (4) Each paragraph helps you see how the park and mountain impressed the writer. This is the main idea of the entire passage. The other four choices are details that help support this main idea.

2. (2) This answer is given in the first paragraph when the author writes, "Mostly, though, what I remember about that week was the mountain. Katahdin."

3. (1) The action in the first three paragraphs takes place in the past, when the writer was twelve. The last paragraph explains how the trip impressed the writer so much that even "today" he manages to camp at the same park for a few days every year.

4. (5) Look at the first two sentences of the second paragraph, and you'll find this answer. There were no foothills around the mountain. The flatness of the land helped stress the height of the mountain.

5. (3) Only this choice defines "good" *as it is used in the passage.* To see how, put the word into the phrase: "a full six-hour drive."

6. (5) Lady Jones calls Denver "baby" in a soft and kind way, asks her to visit anytime, and gives her food. These are the actions of a caring person.

7. (2) People who live in a poor, rural community would be likely to hunt rabbits for food. They might also raise chickens for eggs and put the eggs in baskets rather than buy them in cartons at a store. The other options could happen in many kinds of places.

8. (1) Denver's problem is that she needs food. Food begins to appear in Denver's yard two days after she's told her problem to Lady Jones. This fact suggests that Lady Jones and her church committee to aid the hungry are placing food there.

9. (3) As you read "anytime" twice, don't you get the feeling that Lady Jones is urging Denver to come back?

10. (1) Look at what each paragraph tells you. The first paragraph talks about episodes on home videos. The second paragraph tells what's different and what's the same. The third and fourth paragraphs talk about the good points of the videos. All these ideas are expressed in option (1).

11. (1) The last two sentences of the second paragraph help you with this answer.

12. (4) Words such as "energy and excitement," "viewing pleasure," and "comic genius" show the writer's enthusiasm for the videos.

13. (3) All the choices are meanings of "ring," but only "appear to be" fits with the phrase: "may not quite appear to be true."

14. (2) Tony is described as speaking "happily." He makes a toast. He says he doesn't want to go. There is laughter from the kitchen.

15. (4) Alice calls Penny "mother," so you know Alice is Penny's daughter. Alice and Tony have been out, and it's late. From the conversation you can guess they were on a date.

16. (3) Alice offers Tony a drink. Later, Alice's mother walks in. You can tell they must be at Alice's home.

17. (1) Tony says he'd follow Alice anywhere. He says he wouldn't trade their evening for anything. Each of them toasts the other. Neither one wants Tony to go, even though it's late.

18. (5) The first line of the second part of the poem tells you what young steers do: they "blunder up against the wires." They make the mistake of trying to get past the wires.

19. (2) The second part of the poem tells you the young steers are hurt by the fences (the words "muscle-shredding violence" tell you this). In other words, the wires tear into the flesh of the young steers. The third line tells you the young steers then become "old cattle." In other words, they no longer try to stray past the fences, just as the truly old cattle do not.

20. (5) In the poem, young steers discover they cannot go just anywhere they please. Can you see how this limit on freedom also applies to young *people* and other young animals?

21. (1) One meaning of "quarter" is "mercy." And this is the only meaning that fits in the context of the poem. The wires show no mercy; they cut into the young steers.

Answer Key

Part A

Measuring What You Know
pages 2–4

1. Computers affect our lives in many ways.

2. Possible answers: Keeping doctors' records; helping find new ways to cure illness.

3. inform

4. record information or follow and be aware of

5. different

6. With today's bikes, it is easier to keep the wheels on the road; today's air-filled tires make the ride softer and smoother.

7. bump hard

8. A gives all the important ideas. It does not mention any ideas that are *not* in the article. B, in contrast, does not explain an important idea: how today's bikes are safer to ride.

9. B

10. The young men wanted an indoor team sport because the cold weather made it hard to play outside.

11. The baskets were changed—the new ones had a hole in the bottom so the ball would drop through. As a result, the players did not have to climb a ladder to get the ball out of the basket.

12. B

Part A

Measuring What You've Learned
pages 131–135

1. B	9. A	17. B
2. C	10. A	18. C
3. A	11. C	19. B
4. C	12. B	20. C
5. C	13. C	21. A
6. A	14. C	22. A
7. C	15. A	23. C
8. A	16. A	

Part B

Measuring What You Know
pages 138–140

1. (2)	6. (1)	11. (3)
2. (1)	7. (3)	12. (1)
3. (2)	8. (3)	13. (1)
4. (2)	9. (3)	
5. (3)	10. (2)	

Part B

Measuring What You've Learned
pages 218–223

1. (4)	8. (1)	15. (4)
2. (2)	9. (3)	16. (3)
3. (1)	10. (1)	17. (1)
4. (5)	11. (1)	18. (5)
5. (3)	12. (4)	19. (2)
6. (5)	13. (3)	20. (5)
7. (2)	14. (2)	21. (1)

Especially for You

You can enjoy yourself and practice your reading skills with these books. They are especially good reading for adults and older teens who are working to improve their basic reading skills.

If you can't find these books in your public library, ask a librarian to help you find other Adult Basic Reading books.

Nonfiction

Arnold, Caroline. *The Winter Olympics.* New York: Franklin Watts, 1983.
Skiing, hockey, and other events of the Winter Olympics are described.

Clark, Thomas. *People and Their Religions: Part I, Judaism and Christianity; Part II, Islam, Hinduism, Buddhism.* New York: Cambridge, 1983.
This book gives a general background on the major world religions.

Coughlin, Merle T. *Your Body in Health and Sickness.* Glenview, Illinois: Scott, Foresman and Co., 1982.
Diagrams and short, clear chapters explain how your body works. Major health problems are discussed.

Davidson, Margaret. *I Have a Dream, The Story of Martin Luther King, Jr.* New York: Scholastic, 1986.
Martin Luther King, Jr., knew that segregation and prejudice were wrong. His weapons against them were words and ideas, faith in God, education and nonviolent resistance.

Dolan, Edward F., Jr. *Great Moments in the Indy 500.* New York: Franklin Watts, 1982.
Thrills and humor on the race track make up these true stories.

Eichhorn, Dennis P. *Cosby.* Seattle: Turman Publishing Co., 1986.
This story of Bill Cosby's life includes his work on TV's "Cosby Show."

Harries, Joan. *They Triumphed Over Their Handicaps.* New York: Franklin Watts, 1981.
The author tells the stories of six physically disabled adults.

Prager, Arthur and Emily. *World War II Resistance Stories.* New York: Dell, 1979.
This book tells five exciting stories about people who lived in occupied countries during World War II. These people risked their lives to fight the Nazis and Japanese.

Simonsen, Peggy. *Getting and Keeping a Job.* Glenview, Illinois: Scott, Foresman and Co., 1982.
You'll learn how to prepare for a successful career.

Wulffson, Dan L. *Incredible True Adventures.* New York: Dodd, Mead & Co., 1986.
These are amazing stories of survival.

Fiction

Goodman, Burton, ed. *Spotlight on Literature, Vols. 1–8.* New York: Random House School Division, 1988.
This delightful literature series has short stories, essays, and poems. It's especially useful for those beginning study toward the GED Test.

Hallman, Ruth. *Panic Five.* New York: Dodd, Mead & Co., 1986.
Can Jeff stay safe during a hurricane?

Jackson, Anita. *ZB 4.* (Specter Series) Belmont, California: Fearon, 1979.
A chilling and suspenseful tale. A spy changes bodies for each new case. But it takes a toll on him.

Kenna, Gail Wilson. *Along the Gold Rush Trail.* Syracuse, New York: New Readers Press, 1982.
Adventures of the California Gold Rush are told.

Knudson, Rozanne R. *Speed.* New York: E. P. Dutton, 1983.
A high school track star tries to deal with sadness.

Malin, Amita. *Carlotta's House.* Glenview, Illinois: Scott, Foresman and Co., 1982.
Susan moves into her grandmother's house. But can she leave an unhappy past behind?

Otfinoski, Steven. *The Verlaine Crossing.* Belmont, California: Fearon, 1977.
In this thriller, Roger tries to keep himself safe from spies.

Reed, Fran. *A Dream with Storms.* Syracuse, New York: New Readers Press, 1979.
Rosa hopes for something better for her life.

Robinson, Kathleen, ed. *The Diary of Anne Frank and Other Plays About Courage.* New York: Scholastic, 1986.
Five plays, one based on a true story, about decision making and courage.

Steinbeck, John. *The Pearl.* New York: Bantam Books, 1987.
Kino and Juana find a pearl of great worth. The pearl changes their lives in ways they never expected.

Poetry

Dunning, Stephen, and others. *Reflections on a Gift of Watermelon Pickle.* Glenview, Illinois: Scott, Foresman and Co., 1966.
This book is a collection of unusually imaginative poems.

Index

-able, 185
Answer sheet, 108
Antonyms, 201
Applying ideas, 102–6
Autobiography, 143

Bias, 117–21
Biography, 142
Brainstorming, 37

Cause and effect, 94–98, 161–66
Characters
  conflict and, 187
  in drama, 203–4
  in fiction, 177, 178, 180–84
  visualizing, 186
Classifying, 62–66
Clue words
  for bias, 118
  for cause and effect, 95, 161
  classifying and, 63
  for comparisons and contrasts, 70–71, 154
  for figures of speech, 166, 216
  for lists, 39
  steps in a process and, 55
  time order and, 47, 51
Commentary, 169–73, 175
Comparing and contrasting, 70–74, 154, 155
Compound words, 11
Conclusions, drawing, 86–90
  about characters, 180, 181
Conflict, 187–92
Context clues, 75, 88, 91, 114, 150, 192
  antonyms, 201
  plurals, 83
  special terms and, 174
  synonyms, 159
Contrasting, 70–74, 154, 155
Craft, author's, 195–200

Definitions, 59, 75. *See also* Word meanings
Details
  reading for, 160
  summarizing and, 76–77, 80, 167
  supporting, 7, 22–26, 145–150
  word meanings and, 75
Dictionary, 59, 91, 130
Directions, reading, 108
dis-, 67
Drama, 203–8, 209, 210

-ed, 26–27
Encyclopedia, 130
-er, 19, 185
Essay, 143
-est, 19
Eye movements, 28–29

Facts, 109–13
Fiction, 177–79
Figure of speech, 166, 215–16

Ideas. *See* Applying ideas; Main idea; Restating
Idiom, 107
im-, 185
in-, 185
Inferring, 78–83. *See also* Conclusions, drawing
-ing, 26–27
-ion, 185

Journals
  reading, 143
  writing, 40, 88

-less, 43
Library, 129–30
Lists
  making, 37, 104, 171
  reading, 38–42, 154, 155

Magazines, 56, 130, 142
Main idea, 6–10, 93, 145–50. *See also* Details, supporting
  summarizing and, 76, 80, 167
  unstated, 14–18
Margin notes, 16, 111, 162, 163, 197
-ment, 43
Microfilm, 130
Mind, 36–37. *See also* Visualizing
mis-, 67

Narrator, 195–96
Newspapers, 123, 130, 142
Nonfiction, 142–44, 178–79
Note-taking, 115–16, 119, 155–56
  See also Margin notes

Opinions, authors, 109–13, 175–76
-or, 185
Outline, 64, 146, 147

Paragraph, 7
Patterns, 38–39, 153–58, 159
Plays. *See* Drama
Plot
  in drama, 203–4
  in fiction, 177, 178, 187–92
Plurals, 83
Poetry, 211–16, 217
Point of view, 195–96
pre-, 67
Predictions, 20–21, 24, 193–94. *See also* Previewing
Prefixes, 67, 91, 185
Previewing, 84, 95–96, 115, 160. *See also* Predictions
Pronouns, 99, 209
Pronunciation
  of names, 111
  of words, 114, 150
Purpose, author's, 30–34, 39, 143–44
Purpose, reader's, 44–45, 151–52
  reading rate and, 52–53, 160

Qualifications, author's, 175–76

re-, 185
Reading, equipment for, 12–13
Reading rate, 52–53, 160
Reading skills, survey of, 2–5, 131–36, 138–41, 218–24
Reference books, 130
Rereading, 160
Restating, 8, 26, 68–69
  poetry, 215
Root words, 43, 67

Script, 203–4, 210
Self-checking, 92–93, 202
Self-questioning, 84–85
Setting
  in drama, 203–4
  in fiction, 177, 178, 180–84
  visualizing, 186
-ship, 43
Skimming, 52, 160
Special terms, 174
Speech, in drama, 204–8, 209, 210
Speed, of reading. *See* Reading rate
Stage directions, 204–8, 209
Steps in a process, 54–58
Subheadings, 84, 178
Suffixes, 43, 91, 185. *See also* Word endings
Summarizing, 76–77, 80, 167–68, 206
Synonyms, 35, 75, 159, 174, 201

Tables, 95–96
Test taking, 11, 18, 26, 35, 67, 74, 98–99, 108, 113, 122, 159, 174, 209, 215
Time line, 47, 48, 188
Time order, 46–50, 154–55
  plot and, 188
Titles, 18, 20, 30, 84
Tone, author's, 169–74
Topic, 7, 8, 14, 30, 37, 145, 146

un-, 185
Underlining, 32, 72

Verbs, 26
Visualizing, 60–61, 186
  drama, 204, 210
  fiction, 186
Vocabulary. *See* Word meanings

Word endings, 19, 26–27. *See also* Suffixes
Word groups, 28–29
Word history, 59
Word maps, 100–101
Word meanings, 51, 88, 91, 150. *See also* Context
  compounds, 11
  prefixes, 67, 91, 185
  suffixes, 43, 91, 185
  synonyms, 35, 159